P9-APU-807

Norway and the United States, 1905–1955

Wayne S. Cole

Norway
AND THE
United States

1905–1955

Two Democracies in Peace and War

Iowa State University Press / Ames

ROBERT MANNING
STROZIER LIBRARY

MAR 6 1990

Tallahassee, Florida

E
183.8
N8
C65
1989

Also by Wayne S. Cole

America First: The Battle Against Intervention, 1940–1941 (*1953*)

Senator Gerald P. Nye and American Foreign Relations (*1962*)

An Interpretive History of American Foreign Relations
(*1968, 1974*)

Charles A. Lindbergh and the Battle Against American
Intervention in World War II (*1974*)

Roosevelt and the Isolationists, 1932–45 (*1983*)

WAYNE S. COLE is a professor of history at the University of Maryland in College Park.

©1989 Iowa State University Press, Ames, Iowa 50010
All rights reserved

Manufactured in the United States of America

No part of this book may be reproduced in any form or by any electronic or mechanical means, including information storage and retrieval systems, without written permission from the publisher, except for brief passages quoted in a review.

First edition, 1989

Libray of Congress Cataloging-in-Publication Data

Cole, Wayne S.
    Norway and the United States, 1905–1955: two democracies in peace and war / Wayne S. Cole. – 1st ed.
        p. cm.
    Bibliography: p.
    Includes index.
    ISBN 0–8138–0321–7
    1. United States – Foreign relations – Norway. 2. Norway – Foreign relations – United States. 3. Norway – Foreign relations – 1905–1955. 4. United States – Foreign relations – 20th century. I. Title.
E183.8.N6C65 1989
32.730481 – dc19

FLORIDA STATE
UNIVERSITY LIBRARIES

SEP 4 1992

TALLAHASSEE, FLORIDA

To Our
Norwegian Ancestors

Contents

Preface

NORWAY is one of the larger countries in Europe. With its magnificent fjords, towering mountains, and awesome glaciers, its scenic beauty is rarely equaled. Though most of its area is unsuitable for agriculture, and though its rocky terrain includes surprisingly little mineral wealth, in the twentieth century the sturdy Norwegian people have managed to achieve one of the highest standards of living in the world. Though bound to Denmark for hundreds of years and to Sweden for nearly a century, Norway's constitution of 1814 is one of the most enduring in the world. Under that constitution the Norwegian people have combined democracy, freedom, civil rights, stability and order, and social welfare as successfully as any people on earth.

In foreign affairs the Norwegians are very nearly unique. Their merchant ships and seamen sail the seven seas and serve ports on every continent. Except only Ireland, no country contributed so large a percentage of its sons and daughters to the peopling of North America in the nineteenth and early twentieth centuries as Norway. Most striking, however, has been the relative absence of war and violence in modern Norwegian history. Norwegians accomplished their separation from Sweden peacefully. Norway long and tenaciously adhered to policies of neutrality and non-involvement in European wars. Its brief role in the Napoleonic wars was a product of its attachment to Denmark; Hitler's Nazi Germany brought war to Norway in 1940 entirely without provocation from the Norwegians. Despite their Viking heritage, modern Norwegians do not rank the military arts high in their scale of values. Their peaceful history may be due partly to the persistence and artful skill with which they prevail through diplomacy. Modern Norway has sustained an impressively peaceful history.

Nonetheless, American diplomatic historians have largely ignored Norway. Most written history tends to be elitist, focusing on the high and the mighty. That pattern has extended into the study of international affairs. Books on foreign affairs tend to focus either on the large, powerful states or on the troublesome, warlike states, or on both. Peaceful, orderly, democratic states such as Norway tend to be overlooked. Newspapers focus on the bad news, not on the good. In international affairs Norway generally has been quiet good news, and it deserves more attention than scholars have given it. This little volume is designed to introduce readers to the fascinating good news of diplomatic relations between the United States and Norway.

This study traces United States relations with Norway from 1905 (when Norway separated from Sweden) through World War I, World War II, and the early cold war to 1955 – the first half-century of relations between those two democracies. The two world wars and the cold war serve as the three pillars for the story. In World War I both the United States and Norway were neutrals until the United States declared war in 1917; Norway continued as a neutral. Both were brought into World War II by Axis attacks – the German invasion of Norway in 1940 and the Japanese attack on Pearl Harbor in 1941. The Yalta and United Nations approaches foundered for both countries after World War II, and both played constructively cooperative roles in NATO in the cold war era. This book is a study of the processes by which two democracies with well-established traditions of neutrality and noninvolvement in European wars turned away from those traditional policies toward multilateral collective security roles in world affairs.

This study is based on four years of research in all available United States government records in the Washington, D.C. area and on the best Norwegian scholarly accounts. Among the outstanding scholars whose publications, based on research in Norwegian documents, have been particularly helpful to me are Geir Lundestad, Helge Ø. Pharo, Olav Riste, Ingrid Semmingsen, Sigmund Skard, Magne Skodvin, and Nils Ørvik. Of comparable value is the dissertation by an American scholar, Doris H. Linder. I have also done research in the Library of Congress, the Franklin D. Roosevelt Library, the Herbert Hoover Library, the Norwegian-American Historical Association Archives, the Minnesota State Historical Society Library, and the State Historical Society of Wisconsin Library. I have traveled widely in Norway and have consulted scholars and government officials there.

This study makes no attempt to be exhaustive or definitive. It is designed as a brief overview and introduction to a fascinating and much neglected aspect of the history of American foreign relations. Norwegian scholars have made valuable contributions to this field. My hope is that this book may encourage other American scholars to explore this rich and absorbing subject.

I am indebted to many librarians and archivists for their generous professional assistance. Most important has been David A. Langbart. He went far beyond the call of duty in sharing with me his knowledge of diplomatic and military archival materials relevant for this subject both in the National Archives in Washington, D.C., and in the Washington National Records Center in Suitland, Maryland. I am deeply grateful to him. Dale C. Mayer and the technical staff at Herbert Hoover Library identified and made available to me relevant items from the Hoover papers. My friend and colleague at the University of Maryland, Keith W. Olson, generously shared his knowledge and interest in Scandinavia with me. I am especially indebted to Helge Ø. Pharo of the Historisk Institutt at the University of Oslo for carefully reading my manuscript and giving me the benefit of his knowledge of Norway and of Norwegian international history. His suggestions substantially improved the quality and accuracy of this volume; it might have been further improved if I had accepted more of his guidance. Mrs. Solveig Morgenstierne Padilla, daughter of the late Ambassador Wilhelm Morgenstierne, and Robert D. Stuart, Jr., United States ambassador to Norway, generously made photographs available for use in illustrating this book. A sabbatical leave from the University of Maryland in 1986 and a travel grant from its General Research Board facilitated my research.

My wife, Virginia Rae Cole, has been a source of support for each of my research projects. On this one, however, she has provided even more support than ever. She fully shares my fascination

with Norway, its people, its culture, and its history. I am deeply
grateful for her support, her encouragement, and her shared enthusiasm for the subject. Like millions of other Americans, she and
I trace our roots to Norway. To those Norwegian ancestors I grate-
fully dedicate this book.

Norway and the United States, 1905–1955

1

Tranquil Beginnings

IT was a comfortable day in early June, a pleasant change from the short, bone-chilling days of Norway's long winter. The slender, greying old man with his bushy mustache and loose-fitting suit was a familiar figure as he walked from his home to his office at Stortings Gade 14 in Christiania, Norway's lovely capital city of 230,000 people. His office was in the business section of the city, not far from the ships that plied that busy harbor carrying products and emigrants requiring his services as United States consul general.

As he walked that morning, he greeted friends and acquaintances in fluent Norwegian, revealing his Norwegian birth (in the Lofoten Islands much further north, in 1844) and his education in Bergen on the west coast of Norway. More than forty years earlier, as Lars Broderick, he had joined thousands of other Norwegians in emigrating to America. He had arrived just in time to serve in the Union navy on the Mississippi River during the final year of the Civil War. After the war he had worked as a seaman on Great Lakes ships, moved west to Iowa, and finally settled in Granite Falls, Minnesota. Under the name Henry Bordewich he had been a loan agent for a Chicago bank, had been elected to seven terms as county auditor for Yellow Medicine County, had served as local postmaster for four years, and with his wife had reared a family of five children. He spoke English with a Norwegian accent, and poor health had brought him back to Norway in 1896. The old man and his wife had little time (or inclination) for social life, but that did not prevent him from performing his consular duties ably and responsibly. It was not an exciting life, but it suited the temperament of that modest, quiet, undemonstrative old man. He was content.[1]

This particular day, however, was to be something out of the ordinary. It was to mark the beginning of formal diplomatic relations between Norway, his native land, and the United States, his adopted land, whose government and people he served. On that day, June 8, 1905, Henry Bordewich, as United States consul general in Norway's capital city, received the first formal communication from the independent government of Norway after its separation from Sweden. Sofus Arctander of the Norwegian Ministry for Foreign Affairs asked Bordewich to inform the United States government of the contents of three documents that he provided. Those documents, in effect, described the political impasse that had, on June 7, ended the dual monarchy that had bound Norway to Sweden for nearly a century.[2]

Norway had not been a fully sovereign monarchy since the fourteenth century. During nearly four and a half centuries it had been bound to Denmark. The Napoleonic wars at the beginning of the nineteenth century found Denmark (and Norway) aligned with Napoleon against coalitions led by Great Britain (and including Sweden). The tides of war compelled Denmark to yield Norway to Sweden in 1814. Though Norway drafted and adopted its own enlightened constitution on May 17, 1814, it was bound to Sweden in a dual monarchy. And in that relationship Sweden played much the larger role in controlling foreign affairs.

In the course of the nineteenth century, growing nationalism and democracy made Norwegians increasingly restive in the relationship. Specifically, the Norwegians pressed for the establishment of an independent Norwegian consular service. At least as early as March 1903 the United States minister to Sweden, William W. Thomas, Jr., had reported to Secretary of State John Hay on the issue and on its seriousness for Norway and Sweden.[3]

A succession of complicated political and constitutional maneuvers, in which the Swedish government and King Oscar II opposed the Norwegian insistence on an independent Norwegian consular service, resulted in a complete deadlock. On June 7, 1905, the Norwegian Storting (parliament), under the skilled political leadership of Christian Michelsen, proclaimed the dual monarchy at an end. The processes of separating from Sweden and establishing a new Norwegian monarchy evolved through succeeding months.[4] But the Norwegian government immediately initiated steps to open formal diplomatic relations with foreign governments, including the United States. The United States did not have diplomatic representation in Norway, and Norway had none in America except jointly with Sweden. So Henry Bordewich, as the ranking American consular official in Norway, was to be the channel through whom the Norwegian government initiated its official dealings with the United States government.[5]

Bordewich acknowledged receipt of the communication and documents and promptly forwarded translations of them both to the new United States minister to Sweden, Charles H. Graves, and to Assistant Secretary of State Francis B. Loomis in Washington, D.C. Graves concluded that the course to be pursued was "too important a question to be decided except by the authority of the State Department at Washington." On specific instructions from President Theodore Roosevelt, Graves kept Washington fully informed on developments in relations between Sweden and Norway. The United States government under Roosevelt and Secretary of State Elihu Root carefully took no action until after Sweden's King Oscar II in October sadly announced the dissolution of the union between the two Scandinavian countries.[6]

Only at the end of October, after both Norway and Sweden had formally acknowledged and agreed to the dissolution of the union, did Secretary of State Root agree to receive Christian Hauge as Norwegian chargé d'affaires ad interim in Washington. Subsequently Hauge was promoted to be minister plenipotentiary from Norway to the United States. After his death near the end of 1907 the Norwegian government named Ove Gude to be minister to the United States. Roosevelt and Root directed Graves to represent the United States as envoy extraordinary and minister plenipotentiary to Norway apart from his continuing responsibilities as minister to Sweden. The American consul general (Bordewich), consuls, and consular agents were recognized by the Norwegian government and continued to function as before. In June 1906 President Roosevelt appointed Herbert H. D. Peirce to be United States minister to Norway, the first diplomat assigned exclusively to represent the United States in that country.[7]

NORWAY is a beautiful land of contrasts and surprises. It is one of the larger European states. With an area of some 125,000 square miles, it is larger than Italy or than Great Britain and Ireland combined. It is slightly larger than all the New England states in America, plus New York and New Jersey. Its elongated shape extends through more than thirteen degrees of latitude—some 1,100 miles from its northernmost to its southernmost points. A Norwegian in Kristiansand in the extreme south of Norway is about as far from his compatriots in Hammerfest in the north as he is from Moscow or Rome. The easternmost point in the north is as far east as Cairo. Norway's coastline measures some 1,650 miles, but if one stretched its total coastline, including islands, fjords, and inlets, it would extend halfway around the world.

Much of the large area of Norway, however, is less than hospitable. One third of the country lies north of the Arctic Circle. Save only Reykjavik and Helsinki, no other national capital is located closer to one of the poles than is Oslo (Christiania) in southern Norway. It is in the same general latitude as Alaska, northern Labrador, and Siberia. Much of the country is high mountainous plateau, rocky, or forested. That terrain is less rich in commercially usable minerals than one might suppose. The mainland of Norway has no commercial quantities of coal and not much iron. Only about 3 percent of Norway's total area is suitable for farming. Its rugged terrain provides spectacular scenery, but until tourists began to discover that natural beauty, it did little to pay the bills for either the people of Norway or their government.

Nonetheless, the Gulf Stream, the seas, water power, and a hardy people combined to make Norway more prosperous and appealing than its northern location and mountainous terrain might have led one to imagine. That was before the discovery and development of offshore oil resources in the last third of the twentieth century greatly enhanced Norway's wealth and prosperity. The currents of the Gulf Stream give Norway a more temperate climate than one would expect at its latitudes. Its long coastline, fjords, and natural harbors turned Norsemen to the seas for fishing and shipping—both of which have been major sources of income and livelihood for Norwegians over the centuries. Its water power potential has been developed steadily in the twentieth century, providing hydroelectric power for homes and industries.

And then there are the people. Norway has a smaller population than most European countries. It had some 2.3 million people in 1905, and its population did not reach 3 million until World War II and 4 million until 1975. It is the least densely populated country in continental Europe. The greatest concentrations of people are in the southern half of the country, especially along the coasts. Except Laplanders (Sami) in the far north (and a few more recent immigrants), the Norwegians are a strikingly homogeneous people ethnically and racially. The Norwegian language officially is in two forms, Bokmål and Nynorsk, each comprehensible to all Norwegians—and to most other Scandinavians. Broadly Germanic, Norwegian has many similarities to both German and English. Nearly all Norwegians are members of the state Evangelical Lutheran Church.

Norwegians can be dour and stolid. They are honest, slow to anger, and slow to act. But in their struggles to cope with a harsh nature on land and on the seas, Norwegians have developed a dogged and stubborn persistence that is not easily blunted. Historically Norwegian society and economy have not been characterized by extremes of wealth and power. Though there are class differences, Norway in the twentieth century has a more nearly egalitarian society (and more egalitarian values) than most European states. Norwegians prize their independence and liberty, and they have learned to make democracy work.

The industrial revolution spread to Norway in the middle of the nineteenth century, but it developed slowly. Given Norway's limited population and resources, its economy continued to rely heavily on the resources available to it in the first half of the twentieth century—farming, forestry, fishing, shipping, and trade.

Norwegians were and are proud of their constitution, which was adopted in 1814. Influenced by the examples of both the

United States Constitution and British parliamentary practices, the Norwegian constitution served as the vehicle for evolving democracy and representative government through the course of the nineteenth and twentieth centuries. It was characteristically Norwegian that in 1905 both the decision to separate from Sweden and the decision to invite Prince Carl of Denmark to become King Haakon VII of Norway were submitted to a vote of the people (both were approved by overwhelming margins).[8]

NORWAY and the United States in many respects provide a study in contrasts. The United States is a huge country with an area some thirty times greater than that of Norway. The population of the United States in 1905 was more than thirty-five times that of Norway; by 1989 its population was more than fifty-five times that of Norway. The United States has incomparably greater natural resources, industrial capacity, wealth, and power than Norway. In the twentieth century the United States has been a leading world power, whereas Norway is weak and has comparatively little impact on world politics.

There are other contrasts as well. The heterogeneous and pluralistic American society contrasts with the homogeneous Norwegian population. Norway has had a Labor (democratic socialist) government much of the past half-century, whereas in the United States socialism is politically weak and the major political parties emphasize private enterprise.

Those and other differences, however, should not obscure important fundamental similarities and shared interests and values. Both Norway and the United States are part of Western Civilization. Both countries are largely Christian in their religious affiliations. During much of their history both Norway and the United States had substantial rural societies, and in the twentieth century both have become increasingly urbanized. Both have well-established constitutions that provide for effective representative government. Both enjoy political democracy with universal suffrage. Both protect civil rights, political freedoms, and religious tolerance. Despite its socialist governments, most productive property in Norway is in private hands; the Labor governments have not pressed nationalization. Similarly, despite its free-enterprise system, the United States has enacted and implemented sweeping social-welfare programs not unlike those in Norway.

There are also parallels in foreign affairs. Through much of their earlier histories, partly reflecting their geographic remoteness and their rural societies, both Norway and the United States developed traditions of neutrality and noninvolvement in European wars. Both countries face the seas; both border the North Atlantic. Both have large merchant marines and long traditions in international trade and commerce. In the twentieth century both countries gradually and reluctantly turned away from their traditional policies of neutrality and noninvolvement. Both became increasingly committed to multilateral and collective security arrangements, including the United Nations and NATO. Both have maintained close ties with Great Britain in world affairs. The similarities between the two countries are, indeed, more fundamental than their differences.

THOUGH formal diplomatic relations between the United States and Norway opened in 1905, those were by no means the earliest contacts between the two peoples. Diplomats from the royal government in Stockholm represented and bound Norwegians as well as Swedes in their dealings with the United States (as they did, for example, in the Treaty of Commerce and Navigation of 1827). The dual monarchy maintained consular offices in the United States, and the United States had consular agents in both Sweden and Norway. At various times in the nineteenth century the United States appointed consular agents in five Norwegian coastal cities: Bergen, Kristiansand, Christiania, Stavanger, and Trondheim. The earliest of them were in Kristiansand and Bergen in 1809. In each city the consular agent was a Norwegian national, usually a businessman who performed his consular duties on a part-time basis and who charged fees for his services. None of them found the duties particularly burdensome. Few American ships touched Norwegian ports in the nineteenth century, and though trade developed, it was only a small part of the foreign commerce of either country.[9]

Far more important were two related forms of nineteenth-century contact: emigration and the American image. Individual Norwegians found their way to the Dutch colony of New Amsterdam (later New York) in the seventeenth century. A few others were in English colonies in America and even fought (on both sides) in the Wars of the American Revolution. Norwegian merchant ships stopped at colonial American ports.[10]

The real beginnings of Norwegian emigration, however, date from 1825 when the tiny sloop *Restauration* (one quarter the tonnage of the *Mayflower*) carried fifty-two Norwegians from Stavanger in southwest Norway to New York. They were the first in what became a growing flood of emigrants from Norway. Those who came wrote letters back to family and friends in Norway telling of their experiences in the New World. Some wrote of discouragement, disappointment, and failure. Some returned to Norway. And life was never easy for those who remained in America. But for most the New World provided opportunities they could describe attractively or hopefully in letters from America. Those letters, and often the money that accompanied them, drew more emigrants to the United States. Altogether more than six hundred thousand Norwegians emigrated to America during the eighty years before the United States and Norway established formal diplomatic relations in 1905. The peak year was 1882, when 28,668 migrated. A larger percentage of the native population emigrated to the United States from Norway than from any other country except Ireland. At the present time there are nearly as many people of Norwegian descent living in the United States as there are in Norway.[11]

In Norway (and elsewhere) those who remained in Europe looked on the United States with dreams of a better life or with disdain and scorn – according to their values and interests. In contests between different conceptions of the nature of man, the good life, and political systems, one could point to America as the hope of mankind or as an ominous portent of the evils that could befall the unwary. The images of America could be, and often were, wildly distorted and subjective. It was easy to seize on what one wanted to find in viewing the incredible adventure across the seas. As they viewed and interpreted developments in the United States,

Norwegians (like other Europeans) were influenced in their ideals, in their politics, and often in their personal plans by their images of the glories or disasters the great experiment in America seemed to represent.[12]

That emigration and those images did not end in 1905. They continued in constantly changing forms during the course of the twentieth century. From 1905 onward, however, those and other developments evolved within a framework that included formal diplomatic relations between the governments of the United States and Norway.

ONE may think of international diplomacy in terms of affairs of state, realpolitik, intrigue, secrecy, and statecraft affecting war and peace, life and death. So it was—and is. That was the way it was especially during World War I, World War II, and the cold war.

But much of the work of United States ministers to Norway (and of diplomats to other states as well) involved routine record keeping, housekeeping, and ceremonial matters of no great importance beyond establishing and maintaining an attractive and dignified official American presence in Christiania, the capital city. That was particularly true during the first decade of United States diplomatic relations with Norway and in the years between the two world wars. The early American ministers spent much time locating appropriate facilities in which to house the legation, the minister, and his staff. They had to get suitable furnishings and see to it that the legation and its grounds were properly maintained. They recruited and supervised staff for the legation—down to and including maids, cooks, janitors, gardeners, and messengers. They had to meet the right people, entertain graciously at dinners and receptions, and serve as dignified, affable, intelligent, and responsible American representatives at social and ceremonial gatherings. And they had to persuade officials in Washington to provide them with sufficient personnel, facilities, supplies, and money to enable them to discharge their responsibilities properly and effectively.

American diplomats had to listen, learn, and report accurately to the Department of State about goings-on in the capital and in the country. If they neglected that reporting function, or if they did it poorly, they could leave Washington officials ill informed on matters that could affect decision making. Much of what diplomats learned and reported was routine or trivial, rumor or hearsay. Diplomatic intelligence gathering and reporting could be as casual as a sentence or paragraph in a hurried despatch, as mundane as researching and writing a school term paper, or as scholarly and erudite as a graduate seminar paper or thesis. It could be time-consuming, and it was essential.

Charles H. Graves of Minnesota was United States minister to Sweden for eight and one-half years from 1905 through 1913. For nine months of that time, from November 14, 1905, to August 6, 1906, he served separately as United States minister to the independent government of Norway "until other arrangements may be made."[13] Graves maintained his residence in Stockholm, but in December he made an official trip to Christiania. There the tall, slender, thirty-three-year-old King Haakon VII formally received him as United States minister to Norway. On instructions from Washington, Graves extended to the king America's "cordial congratulations with wishes for his welfare and the prosperity of Norway, with earnest desire to promote best relations between Norway and the United States." President Roosevelt also wired his congratulations to the new king, and the two heads of state later exchanged cordial letters.[14]

Graves's most exciting responsibility, however, was as special ambassador to represent the United States at the formal coronation of the young king and queen in the medieval cathedral at Trondheim on June 22, 1906. Accompanied by military and naval assistants, he reported that "high honor was paid to the United States of America in the position accorded to the Embassy at the Coronation and in all the attendant receptions." Graves and his wife were luncheon guests of the Prince and Princess of Wales on their yacht to meet King Haakon and Queen Maud (a granddaughter of Great Britain's Queen Victoria and a daughter of Britain's King Edward VII). He was pleased that at the elaborate coronation he was assigned a privileged place near the ceremonies along with princes and princesses attending from Great Britain, Germany, Russia, and Denmark. The American diplomat later drew $393.54

from authorized funds to cover his expenses while attending the coronation.[15]

On August 6, 1906, Herbert H. D. Peirce arrived in Christiania and assumed his duties as the first United States minister assigned exclusively to Norway. He was accompanied by M. Marshall Langhorne, secretary of the soon-to-be-established legation, and by Consul General Bordewich, who had traveled to Sweden to escort the new minister to Christiania. Peirce served for nearly five years until 1911. Born in Cambridge, Massachusetts, in 1849, the son of one Harvard professor and the brother of another, Peirce had studied both at Harvard and at the Royal School of Mines in London. He was a classmate and friend of Henry Cabot Lodge. A successful engineer for some years, he began his career in government service in 1894. As secretary to the American legation (later embassy) in Russia for more than seven years, and as third assistant secretary of state in Washington for nearly five years, Peirce had had more prior experience in foreign affairs than most who became ministers to Norway. A Democrat, he had won his initial appointment to the foreign service from the Democratic administration of President Grover Cleveland. His next three appointments, however, came at the hands of Republican presidents on the basis of merit. He spoke French fluently and knew some German and Russian (but no Norwegian). With a stocky build, grey hair parted in the middle, and a grey mustache, and wearing a stiff collar, Peirce had a dignified and distinguished appearance and style appropriate to the position he filled. His initial salary as minister to Norway was seventy-five hundred dollars a year, considerably less than his expenses. Like most American chiefs of mission at that time, Peirce had to draw on his own financial resources to supplement his salary as minister. Though in comfortable circumstances, he was not a rich man.[16] The minister's professional staff consisted of one secretary of the legation (initially Langhorne at an annual salary of two thousand dollars) and one clerk.[17]

On August 8 the Norwegian foreign minister, Jörgen Lövland, received America's new minister cordially. The two expressed their mutual hope for continued friendly relations between Norway and the United States. A few days later, escorted by a master of ceremonies and conducted to the palace in a royal carriage, Peirce was received by King Haakon with military honors. The young king, in the presence of the foreign minister, warmly welcomed the minister. He expressed the hope that Norwegian-American relations would continue to be marked by a spirit of cordial amity and that they would become even closer with the progress of time. Peirce spoke highly of the character of Norwegians who had emigrated to the United States, and the king expressed his gratification at the kindness with which those Norwegians had been treated there. That sort of ritual and language was standard in diplomatic ceremonies, but there was no reason to doubt the sincerity of the warm wishes for friendly and close relations between the two countries.[18]

The United States had no legation in Christiania when Peirce arrived in 1906, so the new minister arranged temporary quarters in two furnished rooms in Victoria Hotel, where he was staying. He rented a Remington typewriter, which the secretary of the legation used for his earliest despatches to Washington. But notes to the Norwegian foreign ministry and other correspondence at first had to be handwritten.[19]

Christiania and other Norwegian cities had chronic housing shortages, but fortunately Peirce was soon able to rent a suitable house at 17 Kronprinsensgade. Beautifully situated on a spacious lot in the heart of the city, it was near the foreign ministry and a five minute walk to the royal palace. It had only candles, lamps, and gas for lighting, but Peirce arranged to have electric lights installed before he took possession. It had no central heating or furnace and was heated by stoves in the various rooms. In 1909 Peirce was able to rent the owner's house on the same lot, providing separate facilities for the minister's residence and the legation offices. Not until 1911 did the city construct a sewage system in that part of Christiania, which made possible the installation of "water closets." That rented property served as the minister's residence and the legation for eighteen years until 1924, when the United States government finally purchased a building in which to house the legation.[20]

Peirce (as well as other foreign service officers who served in Norway) found the climate and weather difficult to cope with. He complained that "the months of November and December are very dark and gloomy the sun being above the horizon but a few hours each day," and "fog and cloudiness" often made it impossible to see the sun even then. He explained to his superiors in Washington that "autumn rains also make it very damp and conducive to coughs," from which he suffered. He worried that it all might "have a grave effect" upon his health. He never really grew accustomed to the weather there. In his third winter he wrote that the "winter climate of Christiania with its long period of darkness and its smoky fogs" was "extremely trying." He recommended avoiding "either the setting in of winter or its breaking up," which he contended "tax the constitution considerably." He advised that "in winter, after the Court season has commenced—usually about the end of January, and during the summer months of July and August and in September it is important that so far as possible the Legation staff should be here." It is a bit difficult to determine for certain whether his analysis of the needs of legation responsibilities were controlling or whether his reactions to the weather were foremost in his thinking as he drafted that guidance in a despatch to Washington on a day in February.[21] Norwegian diplomats did not like the heat and humidity of Washington summers any better than Peirce liked the Norwegian climate. Like him, they regularly fled to more comfortable climes when the weather of the capital was at its worst.

Peirce and his tiny staff did not, however, permit either the weather or the "housekeeping" chores to prevent them from conducting their official duties responsibly. The colorful "Rough Rider" Theodore Roosevelt was the focal point for the most exciting episode during Peirce's tour of duty in Norway. Roosevelt had named him to his post in the Department of State in 1901, and Peirce's official duties made him an observer at Roosevelt's mediation of the Treaty of Portsmouth between Japan and Russia in 1905. For that successful diplomatic accomplishment Roosevelt was awarded the Nobel Peace Prize in 1906. Though Alfred Nobel was Swedish, his will provided that the persons awarded the prize for peace should be chosen by a committee elected by the Norwegian Storting, and the prize was to be awarded in Christiania. Roosevelt's presidential duties initially prevented him from accepting the award in person, but after he left the White House in 1909 he went on an African safari. He returned to America by way of a triumphal tour of major European capitals. Everywhere he was treated with extravagant and enthusiastic hospitality.

From May 4 to May 6, 1910, in the course of his travels, he went to Christiania to deliver belatedly the address he should have delivered on the occasion of being awarded the Nobel Prize. He traveled as a private citizen with his wife, two children, and a small entourage. But he was treated as only royalty might expect to be treated. King Haakon, Queen Maud, and a host of other dignitaries met his train, and he was a guest at the royal palace during his stay in Norway. Minister Peirce gave a luncheon in his honor attended by the king, the queen, the prime minister, the foreign minister, and other leading government and diplomatic officials. Two hundred people attended a dinner given in Roosevelt's honor by the royal family, and four hundred attended another banquet in his honor. Roosevelt even agreed to a half-hour sitting at the palace for Norway's famed sculptor, Gustav Vigeland. The former president delivered his address to the Nobel committee in the National Theater, the largest auditorium available, and it was filled to overflowing by persons eager to hear him. The University of Christiania awarded Roosevelt an honorary degree, only the third it had ever conferred. Everywhere he went in the city he was greeted by enthusiastic crowds in streets decorated with American and Norwegian flags.

After it was all over, Peirce reported to Secretary of State Philander C. Knox that the demonstrations "exceeded anything" he had ever witnessed in Norway. He thought they indicated "the warmth of feeling for our country on the part of the Norwegian people." It might have been at least as accurate to have credited the enthusiasm to the appeal of the colorful personality on whom it focused. But the whole episode was consistent with, and conducive to, good relations between the two countries and their people. In 1912 the Nobel Peace Prize went to Elihu Root, who had been Roosevelt's able secretary of state, the second American to be so honored. Root deserved the honor, but that quiet, low-key statesman never aroused the enthusiasm that Norwegians (and Americans) accorded to Roosevelt.[22]

Less spectacular, but at least as important, were treaties between the United States and Norway. The United States, Sweden, and Norway separately agreed that treaties concluded before the two Scandinavian countries separated in 1905 would continue to be binding insofar as the treaty provisions related to the individual countries. Most important in that regard was the Treaty of Commerce and Navigation concluded between the United States and the dual monarchy on July 4, 1827. Sweden, Norway, and the United States all agreed that that treaty should continue to be binding on each of them separately even after the two Scandinavian countries were no longer in the dual monarchy. The same was true for the Convention and Protocol between the United States, Sweden, and Norway on Naturalization signed on May 26, 1869, and a treaty for the extradition of criminals concluded between the United States and Norway on June 7, 1893.[23]

During the decade following the initiation of diplomatic relations between Norway and the United States in 1905 the two countries concluded additional treaties with each other, including in 1908 a five-year arbitration convention. It was extended by additional five-year periods in 1913, 1918, and 1923.[24] In 1914 Norway and the United States negotiated and approved the Treaty for the Advancement of General Peace, one of the so-called "cooling-off" treaties urged by President Woodrow Wilson's Secretary of State William Jennings Bryan.[25] Those treaties were products of earnest efforts by many all over the world to develop peaceful ways to resolve international disputes without recourse to war. The United States and Norway entered into the agreements in good faith. In actual practice, however, the Bryan treaty was never invoked in relations between the two countries.

And then there was a treaty that was not signed. It concerned Spitsbergen, an Arctic archipelago northwest of Norway. The severe climate made the islands almost uninhabitable. They contained coal deposits, but only of inferior quality. No country claimed sovereignty over the islands, but there was enough interest and activity there to encourage deliberations that might regularize their status. In 1907 Foreign Minister Lövland of Norway communicated with the governments of Great Britain, Russia, Germany, France, and others to see if they might be able to reach some kind of agreement that would protect the interests of their nationals without endangering Spitsbergen's status as a *terra nullius*, or no-man's-land. He asked if the United States would like to be included in such deliberations. (American businesses did have mining interests there.) But initially the Department of State responded that "in view of the well known policy of the United States of non-interference in matters purely European" there was little likelihood that the Senate would approve any agreement growing out of such multilateral negotiations.[26]

American businessmen interested in coal-mining operations at Spitsbergen, however, made clear their concern about the matter. Consequently in 1908 the State Department reversed itself and indicated that it would welcome an invitation from Norway to participate in such negotiations, always with the proviso that "the Government of the United States could not be a party to any arrangement involving responsibility for the administration of the islands." When the Norwegian foreign minister responded that he would have to clear it with the other invited governments first, when he challenged an American assertion that there was an "apparent preponderance of actual American interests in the islands," and when he contended that "Norwegian interests are preponderant in these islands and their vicinity," Peirce got his dander up. He was prepared to do battle for American interests there, and made that quite clear in rather undiplomatic language.[27]

Actually none of the other governments objected to having the United States participate in the negotiations about Spitsbergen. Early in 1912 representatives of Norway, Sweden, and Russia drafted a tentative convention to be used as a basis for negotiations at a full conference later. When serious negotiations got underway in Christiania in 1914, the United States was well represented by its minister to Norway at that time, Albert G. Schmedeman, and others. (One of the diplomats appointed to represent the United States in the negotiations suffered a nervous breakdown just after deliberations began and had to be replaced.) The Americans successfully persuaded the other diplomats to accept most of the amendments they proposed to the agreement. At that juncture, however, the Russian delegates received instructions from the czarist government not to sign any agreement and to return to Saint Petersburg immediately. As a result the conference adjourned, and the governments reached no agreement. The issue dragged on until the Versailles Conference after World War I when an acceptable agreement finally was concluded concerning the Spitsbergen Islands.[28]

A large part of the time and energy of American diplomats and consuls in Norway focused on economic matters relating to trade and, to a lesser extent, investment. The United States was not the leading foreign state in Norway's economy; Great Britain was, followed by Germany. American diplomatic and consular personnel tried to help Americans who showed an interest in doing business in Norway. They advised them on ways to make their business efforts more effective. For example, they pointed out that the American insistence on cash transactions, and the failure to extend credit comparable to that regularly extended by businessmen from England and Germany, seriously handicapped American businesses in Norway. They also pointed out that when American businesses sent catalogues printed in English they were, at that time, wasting their money. They encouraged American businesses to send agents or representatives to Norway.

Before World War I, however, American businessmen for the most part were not interested in Norway. Similarly, American bankers and financiers were not pounding on Norway's economic doors. At the same time, Norwegian laws imposed strict limitations and regulations on foreign businesses in their country. Perhaps American businessmen thought the Norwegian market was too small to be worth their efforts. In any event America's diplomats and consuls were more energetic in trying to promote American business and trade in Norway than American businessmen and bankers were. And those government efforts were less successful in Norway before World War I than one might have expected in that "Age of Imperialism."[29]

American diplomats and consuls spent much time and energy processing the continued flood of emigrants from Norway to the United States. In those years, unlike in the nineteenth century, there were organized efforts in Norway to discourage that flow of talent and muscle to America. But those efforts had comparatively little success during the decade before World War I.[30]

On May 17, 1914, Norway celebrated the centennial of its independence from Denmark and of the adoption of its constitution. That special day was the centerpiece for a four-month exposition focusing on the achievements and progress made by the Norwegian people during that century. Three states in America that had large Norwegian-American populations—North Dakota, Minnesota, and Wisconsin—had exhibits at the exposition. Thousands of Norwegian-Americans made the pilgrimage to Norway to participate in the festivities. President Woodrow Wilson sent a warm message of greeting to King Haakon on the occasion. North Dakota presented a gift to the Norwegian people in the form of a statue of Abraham Lincoln, which was unveiled on July 4 by the governor of the state. The whole jubilee was a gala occasion for the Norwegians—just at the moment that the clouds of war were darkening the skies over Europe. They celebrated their centennial in an atmosphere that underscored, in small but significant ways, Norwegian-American kinship, accord, and community of interests.[31]

THE TOURS of Norway's first two ministers to the United States were cut short prematurely by death. Christian Hauge died in 1907, and his successor, Ove Gude, died in the United States in 1910. The Norwegian government then named Helmer H. Bryn to be its minister to the United States. Bryn proved to have a much longer stay in that position. The first of two Norwegian ministers to the United States who served unusually long tours, Bryn was minister from 1910 through four presidential administrations to 1927. Born in 1865, he was a career foreign service officer and had had diplomatic assignments in Stockholm, Paris, Copenhagen, and the Hague before taking up his duties in the United States.[32]

America's first resident minister to Norway, Herbert Peirce, regularly went on leave from his post in Christiania each winter from October to January. In the summer of 1910 he suffered a severe multiple fracture of his right arm in an automobile accident (he was not the driver). Though he received excellent medical care in Norway, he requested a leave of absence so he might consult a surgeon in the United States. Consequently again from October until February he was on leave, and in April 1911 he resigned his position as minister to Norway. President William Howard Taft accepted his resignation with warm thanks for "the able manner" in which he had transacted the affairs of his mission. He left his post at the end of May, and in June King Haakon VII conferred upon him the Grand Cross of the Order of St. Olav.[33]

Having depleted his financial resources in government service overseas, Peirce sought various positions in the Department of State or the foreign service. The better assignments eluded him, but with political support from Senator Henry Cabot Lodge and others, he won appointment as counsel for the United States in the American and British Pecuniary Claims Arbitration. In 1915 the Wilson administration appointed him a temporary special agent assigned to the American embassy in Russia with responsibility for assisting the ambassador "in matters relating to the present political disturbances in Europe." His assignment there ended in 1916. He died in Portland, Maine, on December 5, 1916, at the age of sixty-seven. Except for his difficulties in coping with Norway's weather, and unpaid bills he left behind him, Herbert H. D. Peirce served ably and responsibly in helping establish diplomatic relations between the United States and Norway on a sound and amicable basis.[34]

In 1911 President Taft appointed Laurits S. Swenson to be Peirce's successor as United States minister to Norway. Like Norway's Bryn at the same time in the United States, Swenson eventually was to have a long tour as minister. He served only two years before the Democratic Wilson administration replaced him in 1913. But when the Republicans regained control of the White House in 1921, President Warren G. Harding appointed him to again be America's chief of mission in Christiania. He served through that decade of the 1920s until replaced by President Herbert Hoover in 1930. His total service of a dozen years as minister to Norway was longer than that of any other person who has filled that position.

Born in Minnesota in 1865, the son of Norwegian immigrants, Swenson was educated at Luther College in Iowa and at Johns Hopkins University in Baltimore. For a time he was head of Luther Academy in Albert Lea, Minnesota, but he was a politically active banker in Minneapolis when he first won appointment to a diplomatic post. Though a Republican political appointee, Swenson, like Peirce, had had more prior diplomatic experience than most persons who were appointed minister to Norway. He was United States minister to Denmark from 1897 until 1905 and minister to Switzerland in 1910-11, before moving on to head the legation in Christiania.[35]

Henry Bordewich continued to serve faithfully as United States consul general in Norway as others came and went. But the years caught up with him eventually. He died of Bright's disease on March 19, 1912, in Christiania at the age of sixty-eight, still serving as consul general. They lowered the flag to half-mast at the courthouse in Granite Falls, Minnesota, the day of his funeral. He was cremated, and his widow returned his ashes with her to Minnesota where their children continued to live. Charles Adams Holder replaced Bordewich as American consul general for Norway. He performed ably, as did others who followed after him in that post. But none surpassed old Henry Bordewich in devotion to his duties there the last fifteen years of his life.[36]

ALL OF THAT went on in a peaceful, almost bucolic setting that seemed worlds away from the violence and bloodletting of modern warfare. Norwegians were proud of their tradition of neutrality and noninvolvement in Europe's wars. They were determined to adhere to that tradition in the future. It was even sanctioned and reinforced by a multilateral agreement between the kingdoms of Great Britain, France, Sweden, and Norway in 1855 guaranteeing the integrity of the Scandinavian peninsula. In 1907 that agreement was abrogated and replaced by a similar treaty concluded by Norway, Great Britain, France, Germany, and Russia guaranteeing the independence and territorial integrity of Norway. The new multilateral treaty won unanimous approval in the Storting.[37]

Some were uneasy about the frequent visits of German naval vessels in Norwegian waters. But Kaiser William II of Germany was popular in Norway, and Norwegians welcomed German tourists. The ships of other navies also visited Norwegian ports, including in 1911 a practice squadron of the United States Navy, composed of the battleships *Iowa*, *Massachusetts*, and *Indiana*, along with supporting vessels. Those naval visits were seen as friendly gestures and were accompanied by elaborate courtesies, dinners, and ceremonies.[38]

As a young man King Haakon had trained as an officer in the Danish navy, and he encouraged stepping up Norway's naval preparations. There was never any thought, however, that Norway would or could build a dreadnought fleet capable of engaging an enemy on the high seas. Its limited naval preparations were designed to guard its neutrality in the sheltered waters of Norway's fjords and rocky coast.[39]

When World War I erupted in Europe in the summer of 1914, both Norway and the United States proclaimed their neutrality. Both countries had well-established traditions of neutrality and noninvolvement in European wars. Their leaders and people determined to guard their neutrality and to stay out of the bloody conflagration raging in Europe.

2

Neutrals and the Great War

ON June 28, 1914, Serbian nationalists assassinated the Austrian Archduke Francis Ferdinand at Sarajevo, Bosnia, in southeastern Europe. That was the spark in the tinder of European nationalism and alliance systems that set off the train of events that led to World War I. Austria-Hungary declared war on Serbia on July 28; Germany declared war on Russia on August 1, and on France on August 3; the next day Kaiser William's Germany initiated its Schlieffen war plan by sending its military forces smashing into neutral Belgium; Great Britain declared war on Germany on August 5; Japan and Italy entered the war on the side of Britain and France; and most of the rest of Europe and much of the world were drawn into that terrible conflagration before the fighting ended more than four years later on November 11, 1918. The war spread death and destruction on land, sea, and air. It defeated Germany, destroyed the Austro-Hungarian dual monarchy, led to revolutions that ended the czarist regime and put the Bolsheviks in control of Russia, eroded the power of France and Great Britain, took the lives of nine million soldiers and millions more civilians, ruined the lives of countless others, destroyed hundreds of billions of dollars worth of property, and severely strained the world economy. Europe and the world were never the same again.

The governments of both Norway and the United States

promptly proclaimed their neutrality at the beginning of World War I. Those proclamations expressed the honest and earnest determination of nearly all people in both countries. They were consistent with well-established traditions of neutrality and noninvolvement in European wars. Both Norway and the United States had large fleets of merchant ships trading all over the world, and Americans commanded huge quantities of investment and loan capital; there were many in both countries who profited from the war. Their leaders and most of their people, however, determined to give no just cause to any belligerent to draw them into the hostilities.

Geography provided some insulation from the fighting. Norway, on the northern fringe of Europe, was separated from the battlefields by the Netherlands and Denmark, by the Baltic and North seas, and by Sweden. The United States was three thousand miles away in North America, on the western shores of the North Atlantic. Though both had close relations with Great Britain, neither was allied with any of the belligerents on either side. The United States had a powerful navy, but neither Norway nor the United States was militarily prepared to fight a major war on land or in the air. Norwegians realized that they were incapable of defending themselves successfully against a determined major military assailant.

At the same time, however, if Norway conducted itself with impartial neutrality in accord with international law, it was reasonable to believe that it could avoid giving any belligerent cause for attacking it and drawing it into the war. America's large population, productive economy, and military potential could make it an invaluable ally on either side in the war. But its distant location and its determined noninterventionist tradition encouraged widespread hope in the United States that it, too, could stay out of the conflagration. The leaders and people of both countries believed that neutrality and noninvolvement were in their separate national interests and that they were realistic national goals for their governments in the course of World War I.

Norway succeeded in its determined efforts to remain uninvolved—but just barely. The United States failed in its comparable efforts – but only after severe provocation and heated debate, and with mixed feelings. Though Norway would have welcomed a more positive leadership role by the United States on behalf of countries committed to neutrality and noninvolvement, each of the two governments shaped its course largely independently of the other. Once the United States became a belligerent in April 1917, it was little more solicitous of Norwegian neutrality than the Allies or Central Powers had been earlier.[1]

PRESIDENT WOODROW WILSON led the United States and directed its foreign policy throughout World War I. Born and reared in Virginia, Wilson earned a doctorate in history and political science at Johns Hopkins University. He had a successful career as a history professor and university president before he won election as governor of New Jersey in 1910. Acclaimed as a progressive, Wilson won election to the presidency on the Democratic ticket in 1912 and was reelected in 1916. Idealistic, devoutly religious, a moving orator, and a talented political leader, he has been identified with progressive reforms at home and with internationalism in foreign affairs. When World War I erupted in 1914, however, President Wilson proclaimed American neutrality and called on Americans to "be impartial in thought as well as in action." Though ultimately he failed in his efforts to keep the United States out of the war, he tried earnestly and honestly to preserve American neutrality and noninvolvement.[2]

Wilson's first secretary of state was William Jennings Bryan of Nebraska. Though he had traveled widely, Bryan had had no experience in the conduct of American foreign affairs when he became secretary of state in 1913. He had been defeated three times as the Democratic party candidate for the presidency, but he still commanded a substantial following as leader of the western agrarian progressives within the party. It was his political standing in the party, not his knowledge of foreign affairs, or his skills as a diplomat, that won for him the top position in Wilson's cabinet. Consistent with his western progressive background, Bryan was firmly committed to noninvolvement by the United States in foreign wars. In the middle of 1915, he resigned from the cabinet when he thought Wilson's protests against the sinking of the *Lusitania* by a German submarine were so severe that they endangered American neutrality and risked involving the United States in the war.[3]

In 1915 President Wilson appointed Robert Lansing of New York to succeed Bryan as secretary of state. Prosperous, conservative, and aristocratic, he was a successful attorney and an authority on international law and arbitration. Alert to the role of power in international politics, Lansing did not share Bryan's (or Wilson's) noninterventionist priorities. Wilson had little confidence in him, however, and kept control of foreign affairs firmly in his own hands.[4]

Under President Wilson the United States minister to Norway from 1913 to 1921 was Albert G. Schmedeman of Madison, Wisconsin. His mother was of Norwegian descent, but he had had no previous diplomatic experience or training. His was strictly a political appointment. But even his political credentials were not particularly impressive when he became minister—though later he won election to three terms as mayor of Madison and to one term as Democratic governor of Wisconsin from 1933 to 1935.[5]

Norway's prime minister during World War I was Gunnar Knudsen, a prosperous shipowner and manufacturer. He had been active in politics for many years and was a talented leader of the Liberal party. He took much interest in domestic social welfare programs. Knudsen was concerned with foreign commerce and shipping, as well as with domestic industry. Sympathetic with Great Britain, he also admired American institutions and wanted good relations with both of those western democracies.[6]

Norway's foreign minister under Knudsen from 1913 to 1920 was Nils C. Ihlen, an engineer and manufacturer. He had had no prior diplomatic experience and was not Knudsen's first choice for the position. But Ihlen had received part of his education in Switzerland, spoke German and French (but not English), and had had international experience in the course of his engineering and business activities. Less colorful and energetic than Knudsen, his talents lay in day-by-day practical problem solving rather than in sweeping conceptions of policy. He shared Knudsen's friendly attitudes toward Britain and the United States.[7]

Helmer H. Byrn, a career foreign service officer, was Norway's minister to the United States during World War I (and from 1910 to 1927). He had had prior diplomatic experience in Stockholm, Paris, Copenhagen, and the Hague before moving on to his long tour of service in the United States.[8]

FROM the beginning of World War I in the summer of 1914 until April 6, 1917, Norway and the United States in their separate ways shared the advantages and difficulties of neutrality. The war was a life-and-death struggle for both the Allies and the Central Powers. Neither side was any more solicitous of the rights of neutrals than their war efforts, self-interests, national survival, and loosely defined international law required. Despite efforts to codify international law, there were substantial differences in interpretation. Belligerents favored broad definitions of belligerent rights and narrow definitions of neutral rights; neutrals, understandably, reversed those patterns. Total war and modern military technology (including submarines) raised questions that traditional laws of war had not adequately anticipated.

Belligerents on both sides determined to control, reduce, or block neutral trade with their enemies; neutrals wanted freedom to trade with both sides, subject to international law relating to contraband and blockade. Great Britain's powerful navy enabled it to control sea lanes in the Atlantic and the North Sea, and in March 1915 it initiated what amounted to a blockade of Germany. Germany, in turn, challenged British control of the seas with its submarines.

Both Norway and the United States had huge fleets of merchant ships and highly developed trade with countries on both sides of the war – particularly with Great Britain and, to a lesser extent, with Germany. Trade profits encouraged merchants from both Norway and the United States to continue and expand their trade with belligerents. Interruptions of trade patterns could have had damaging effects on the economies of both Norway and the United States – and on the war efforts of the belligerents. With its limited resources and productive capacity, Norway was particularly dependent on imports from abroad.

Britain's de facto blockade could not effectively stop Norway's direct trade with Germany by way of the North and Baltic seas. Thus the blockade did not affect all neutrals alike; it closed America's sea lanes to Germany but not Norway's. At the same time, however, Norway was heavily dependent on food from America and on coal and bunker supplies from England. Consequently Norway was much more vulnerable to economic pressure and more subject to effective controls by England than was the United States.

Both Great Britain and Germany only gradually developed and implemented their controls or interdiction of supply lines between neutrals and their enemies. Great Britain's controls were more effective, whereas Germany's were more violent, destructive, and sensational. For all practical purposes Britain stopped America's trade with Germany and its allies. Conceivably the United States might have used its tremendous economic might in retaliation to force Great Britain to desist. It did not do so. The United States lodged formal diplomatic protests but acquiesced in the British practices. As a result America's trade with Britain ballooned, but its trade with Germany virtually ceased.[9]

Norway's trade with Germany continued, but only insofar as Britain allowed it. Great Britain controlled Norwegian trade with Germany initially by laying mine fields in the North Sea, then by extending its blockade to include North Sea waters through which ships and products passed en route to Norwegian ports, by controlling much-needed coal supplies for Norway and essential bunker coal and oil for Norway's merchant ships in British harbors, and by "black lists" of Norwegians and Norwegian firms accused doing business with Germany.

Using those pressures, the British compelled Norwegian shipping companies and trade associations to accept agreements in which they made firm commitments not to allow any of the products they imported to be reexported directly or indirectly to Germany. Those were agreements between the British government and private Norwegian companies and business associations relating to products imported from abroad into Norway.[10]

In addition, in 1916 Great Britain forced the Norwegian government to ban or severely limit the sale, direct or indirect, of products produced within Norway to Germany or other Central Powers. Those agreements focused particularly on fish and fish products (Norway's most abundant exports) and on copper and pyrites. When Norway interpreted the copper agreement less rigidly than the British did, Britain stopped supplying coal to Norway. As a result Norway backed down and yielded to the British interpretation of the agreement. By the end of February 1917 the British government commanded decisive control over Norway's imports and exports. That control severely restricted Norway's trade with Germany even though the British navy was not in a position to block direct shipping lanes between Norway and Germany.[11]

Those developments inevitably caused irritation on all sides. The Norwegians negotiated stubbornly, but they had no practical alternatives but to submit to British controls. The United States might have retaliated economically against British practices but did not; Norway lacked the power to retaliate effectively even if it had wanted to do so.

The whole pattern of events provoked less hostility against Great Britain among Norwegians than one might have expected. There was a long tradition of friendly attitudes toward Britain in Norway. Norwegians understood Britain's need to control trade with its enemies in the course of that terrible war. They realistically faced the fact that as a weak state contending with a major world power, Norway had no practical alternative but to acquiesce. As did Americans at the same time, Norwegian shippers and traders prospered under the arrangements. In any event, the methods Germany used with its submarines were more destructive of life and property than anything the British did. The Norwegians adjusted to the British demands with impressive dignity and aplomb.

More shocking was German submarine warfare. Traditional international law did not clearly cover the use of that alarming new weapon under the seas. Those early craft were small and fragile, and initially Germany had very few of them. But they could strike with terrifying suddenness and deadliness. There were significant differences of opinion within the German government on the wisdom and likely effectiveness of submarine warfare.

The German government limited its initial use of the submarine to minimize its damaging effects on neutrals. In February 1915 and again one year later Germany announced limited submarine warfare in a zone around Great Britain and Ireland. In each case it was directed only against enemy merchant ships. Germany warned neutral ships to stay out of the zone to prevent unintentional incidents. Neutrals (including both Norway and the United States) protested against the German policy. German submarines did sink neutral ships, and nationals from neutral countries did die both on neutral ships and while traveling on belligerent merchant ships. The most spectacular and inflammatory incident was the sinking of a British liner, the *Lusitania*, off Ireland on May 7, 1915. Among the 1,198 who died were 128 Americans.

German submarines sank more Norwegian ships, however, than American. And more Norwegians died than Americans as a consequence of German submarine warfare in 1915 and 1916. Norway lost more ships and more lives to submarine activity than any other neutral and more than any belligerent except Great Britain and France.[12] Norway protested the German submarine warfare and sinkings, as did other neutrals. And on October 13, 1916, when Norwegian losses to German submarines were running at nearly one ship a day, the Norwegian government by royal decree closed its territorial waters to any use by German submarines.[13]

But it was the United States that commanded sufficient muscle to make a difference. Under President Wilson it warned that it would hold Germany to "strict accountability" for any loss of life and property due to submarine sinkings.[14]

Divided counsels in German leadership, along with neutral protests (particularly from the United States), led the German government to back off temporarily from its limited submarine warfare both in 1915 and in 1916. But on February 1, 1917, the German government began unrestricted submarine warfare in the zones surrounding Great Britain. In contrast to the earlier cycles, the unrestricted submarine warfare aimed at all ships in the war zones—belligerent and neutral, armed and unarmed. Germany initiated the action with the realization that it would draw the United States into the war but with the hope that it could crush the Allies before American involvement could become effective.[15]

As expected, unrestricted submarine warfare quickly led to

the sinking of neutral ships—including both Norwegian and American ships. Americans and Norwegians died on those ships. When protests by the United States, Norway, and other countries failed to reverse the German policy, the United States under President Wilson's leadership formally declared war on Germany on April 6, 1917.[16]

Norway protested the German policy, as it suffered increased loss of its ships and seamen to German submarines. But under Prime Minister Knudsen and Foreign Minister Ihlen, and with the support of the Norwegian people, Norway tenaciously clung to its policy of neutrality and noninvolvement in the European war.[17]

Throughout the months and years that the United States and Norway shared the trials and tribulations of neutrals, the two governments empathized with each other. They felt a certain community of interest in their separate efforts to preserve neutrality. Nonetheless, each government shaped its policies and actions largely independent of the other. Leaders of the three neutral Scandinavian countries—Norway, Sweden, and Denmark—consulted with each other during the war. Those consultations improved relations between the northern states and facilitated common planning. The three governments issued various joint statements and protests.[18] The United States, however, did not join with the Scandinavian countries in their deliberations or statements.[19] On occasion Norwegian leaders lauded the United States for its statements in defense of neutral rights; its efforts were seen as consistent with the interests of all.[20] But when Norway invited the United States to share in joint statements, it declined. Likewise, when the United States invited Norway to join with it in common action by all neutral countries in response to Germany's unrestricted submarine warfare, Foreign Minister Ihlen politely declined, noting Norway's exposed geographic position.[21]

Trade between the United States and Norway increased during the war, but that was a temporary development.[22] With European financial resources closed to it during the war, the Norwegian government in 1914 arranged a short-term loan from the National City Bank of New York—the first loan the Norwegian government had obtained in the United States.[23] That action did not mean, however, that New York was replacing London as the leading source for outside capital and credit in Norway.

The shared experience of neutrality in World War I from 1914 to 1917 drew Norway and the United States a bit closer to each other. But Great Britain continued to be the most important foreign state in Norway's economic and diplomatic concerns. Both Norway and the United States continued to guard their independent ways.

THE American declaration of war on Germany on April 6, 1917, was a source of excitement and discussion in Norway. Generally Norwegians sympathized with the United States in its action and saw it as joining the Allies in a just cause. Though realizing that serious differences and difficulties would arise, many in Norway hoped the United States might be more understanding of, and sympathetic with, the needs and interests of neutrals than the Allies and Central Powers had been earlier.[24]

The American decision for war, however, did not reduce the near-unanimous determination by Norwegians to stay out of the war. They feared that the shift of the United States from the role of a neutral to that of a belligerent would broaden and intensify German submarine assaults on already hard-pressed Norwegian merchant ships in the North Atlantic. Norway's heavy dependence on the United States for food supplies made that a particularly alarming concern. But no matter how ruthless the Germans might become in the conduct of their submarine warfare, Norway determined to stay out of the war at all costs.[25] Norway's losses of ships, cargoes, and seamen to assaults from German submarines did in fact grow alarmingly.[26]

Ironically, however, German submarines and torpedoes were not the primary cause of the stoppage of shipments of food and other supplies to Norway from America in 1917 and the early months of 1918. The United States took over where the British left off in controlling shipment of goods to neutrals that might fall into the hands of the enemy or might directly or indirectly help the war effort of the Central Powers.

Under authority of the Trading With the Enemy Act of 1917 President Wilson on July 9 prohibited all exports from the United

States except under license. The purpose of that action was to preserve supplies essential for the war effort and to prevent supplies from reaching the enemy either directly or through neutrals. The president's proclamation applied to exports to all countries, including Norway.[27]

Since the British had already worked out effective control in Norway through its agreements with shipping companies, trade associations, and the government, one might have thought further action by the United States unnecessary. Or one might have expected the United States to pursue a more sympathetic and less demanding course than the British. But that was not to be. The British contended that the controls provided by those earlier agreements were inadequate and that commodities produced in Norway and helpful to the German war effort were still being exported from Norway to Germany.

As one British memorandum phrased it, "all these exports should be stopped." It raised the question, "Why should Norway be permitted to import food-stuffs, metals, minerals, textiles, fertilizers, leather etc. from us when she is exporting food-stuffs, metals, minerals, and electro-chemical products to our enemies?" The agreements already concluded with Norway were helpful, but they also tied British hands. If the British were to denounce the agreements, "it would mean loss of control." The best solution, they contended, was for the United States to take over and build on the British control system. From the British perspective the United States was "in a position to exert pressure wherever necessary by the refusal of food-stuffs, metals, bunkering facilities, etc., without causing the Allies to lose any part of their valuable control."[28] That was essentially the course followed – with the British in the background stiffening the American positions throughout the negotiations.

Norwegian leaders were fully aware of their need for imports from America – particularly food – and of their vulnerability in that regard. Foreign Minister Ihlen, the Norwegian minister to the United States, and numerous businessmen and industrialists voiced their concerns to American officials. They earnestly hoped the United States government would "realize the position of Norway and not consider it necessary to restrict the exports" to the country.[29] Though designed to persuade Americans to show compassion, those appeals underscored Norway's vulnerability and, to that extent, almost invited American pressure. The British particularly were urging the Americans to capitalize on that very vulnerability.

With the American export embargo initiated, with the British pressing Americans to pursue a hard line with the Norwegians, with German submarines taking a heavy toll of Norwegian shipping, and with Norwegian leaders painfully aware of their dependence on imports from the United States, Norway made its move. In mid-July the Norwegian government sent one of its most able and distinguished citizens, Dr. Fridtjof Nansen, as minister plenipotentiary on special mission to the United States.

Justly famed for his arctic explorations, Nansen had served from 1906 to 1908 as Norwegian minister to Great Britain and later as a professor of marine zoology and oceanography at the University of Christiania. Politically he did not share the views of the Knudsen ministry, but he accepted the mission as a public duty. The five-man commission he led to the United States was composed largely of prominent Norwegian businessmen, shippers, and manufacturers. Secretary for the commission was Wilhelm T. von Munthe de Morgenstierne, a fast-rising young foreign service officer who later was to be Norway's longest-serving minister and ambassador to the United States. Nansen and his commission were directed to conduct negotiations with the United States to secure for Norway "the necessary importation of necessities, especially food," from the United States.[30]

President Wilson extended a warm welcome to the distinguished scientist and explorer. He said that the United States could "not fail to deeply sympathize with Norway in the crushing blows which have been inflicted upon her commerce and the lives of her subjects." The president received Nansen with the assurance that his mission would "receive the attentive consideration of the officials of this Government."[31] It was a cordial and encouraging beginning. But surely there must have been times in the course of the long, drawn-out negotiations when the explorer wished he were back in the raging blizzards of Greenland and the Arctic.

Though the British knew exactly what they wanted, Americans were divided on the course to be followed. The Norwegians, too, were slow and hesitant initially, partially because they were uncertain what positions the Americans would take. Serious negotiations between the Nansen commission and America's new War Trade Board under Vance C. McCormick did not get under way until November. Nominally they were bilateral negotiations between Norwegian and American representatives. But with the British and, to a lesser extent, the French in the background, the actual situation involved a commission representing a weak, vulnerable neutral government negotiating with representatives of three powerful belligerents. On the surface it seemed a grossly unequal contest.[32]

President Wilson had much sympathy for the Norwegians, and he took seriously America's traditional commitment to neutral rights. Though he did not personally conduct the negotiations, the Norwegians would have had greater difficulty without his influence. Vance C. McCormick at the head of America's War Trade Board eventually embraced positions not greatly different from the British.[33]

Though he did not personally participate in the negotiations, the United States minister to Norway, Albert Schmedeman, went through a significant transition. In July he advised the State Department that because Norway's shipping and attitudes were favorable toward the Allies, Norway should be treated differently than the other Scandinavian countries, Sweden and Denmark. He pointed out that Norwegian trade with Germany was "already as well controlled by the Allies as was possible before we came into the war." He worried that if the United States were "too severe" with Norway's imports from his country it might "react to the detriment of ourselves and the Allies." He recommended "regulating rather than restricting the imports" to Norway.[34]

Schmedeman consulted frequently with British and French diplomats in Norway, however, and developed close and cordial relations with them. By September he was completely won over to the position urged by the British. He advised the United States government to "prohibit all exports to Norway, unless an embargo be placed by Norway on the export of all goods constituting succor to the enemy." He was convinced that if Norway did stop all trade with the Central Powers, Germany would not retaliate by waging war against Norway. In any event, Schmedeman urged the hard line in dealing with Norway "even though the fear of [German] reprisals be justified."[35]

The British urged that the negotiations be shifted from Washington to Christiania. That would have moved them further from Wilson and the mixed American sentiments, to Europe where the British influence might be greater and where (though they did not say so) America's minister Schmedeman was fully persuaded of the wisdom of the British position. The United States never permitted the negotiations to move to Europe. But every American diplomatic initiative and every Norwegian response or counterproposal had to contend with the British input just barely behind the scenes.[36]

By February 1918 the Americans and Norwegians believed they had reached agreement and the accord could be signed. King Haakon, Prime Minister Knudsen, Foreign Minister Ihlen, and the Norwegian public were delighted with what they thought was a favorable conclusion to the negotiations. But the British promptly raised objections to the terms, and agreement was blocked.[37]

When Nansen set out on his mission to the United States, Norway had food supplies sufficient for several months. But as the negotiations dragged on, those supplies gradually were depleted. By December the Norwegian government was compelled to begin rationing certain foods. As food supplies fell lower, Norway's capacity to prevail in the negotiations further weakened. It was approaching the point where the Norwegians might have to choose between starvation or knuckling under in the negotiations. It had not yet reached that point, but with negotiations going on and on, all parties to the negotiations had to consider that eventuality in shaping their tactics and in calculating their timing.[38]

Not until April 30, 1918, did McCormick for the United States and Nansen for Norway affix their signatures to the final agreement (an executive agreement, not a treaty). It continued the absolute ban against Norwegian exports, either directly or indirectly, to the Central Powers of any products imported from the United States or the Allies. Norway was allowed to export no food products to the Central Powers except a maximum of forty-eight thousand tons of fish and fish products per year. The Norwegians were also allowed to ship some calcium carbide, calcium nitrate, and iron ore, but no pyrites or ores containing manganese. The agreement made it possible for the United States to take over negotiation of agreements with businesses and trade associations in Norway on imports. With those and other assurances, supplies were to go from America to Norway, including a wide range of foodstuffs. None of those imports was allowed to go directly or indirectly to Germany or the other Central Powers.[39]

The agreement was not nearly so harsh as the British (and United States Minister Schmedeman) would have preferred. Norwegians were much relieved and pleased by the outcome of the negotiations. That generally happy result was due to Nansen's patient, skillful, and tenacious negotiations and to the residue of American sympathies for neutrals in general and for Norway in particular. Concluded more than a year after the United States became a belligerent and only a little more than six months before the armistice ended the fighting in Europe, the agreement left many details to be worked out between the United States and Norway. But it provided a mutually satisfactory foundation from which to work in handling those details.

UNDER the terms of the Norwegian-American agreement concluded on April 30, 1918, representatives from the United States, Great Britain, France, and Italy worked out detailed arrangements in Norway controlling that neutral country's imports and exports during the rest of the war. The War Trade Board, established by presidential order in October 1917, was the administrative authority for that control so far as the United States was concerned.[40] Its representative in Norway, along with comparable representatives there from Great Britain, France, and Italy, formed the Inter-Allied Trade Committee which handled details in implementing those import and export controls.[41]

Norwegians still owned and operated that country's domestic economy. But Norway's economy was heavily dependent on foreign trade. And that foreign trade was subject to control by the Inter-Allied Trade Committee. It, in turn, was responsible to Lon-

don, Washington, Paris, and Rome. Those foreign belligerent governments were controlling exports and imports of a country that
nominally was both sovereign and neutral.

The War Trade Board representative in Norway, and America's representative on the Inter-Allied Trade Committee there, was
Alexander V. Dye. He proved to be an exceptionally able person.
Born and reared in the Middle West, he earned a doctorate in 1904
at the University of Leipzig in Germany. Before taking up his duties in Norway late in 1917, Dye had been successively a college
professor in Missouri, an American consul in Mexico, and an assistant general manager for Phelps Dodge Corporation in Arizona.
Dye was bright, quick, thorough, and efficient. Equally important,
he could work well under pressure and had the good judgment and
the necessary tact and skills to enable him to work effectively with
others who had different interests and responsibilities.[42]

Initially in 1917 Dye was a special assistant for the Department of State with specific responsibilities for Norway. He prepared thoroughly by means of briefings and careful study of relevant despatches and documents in Washington and London before
reaching Christiania in December 1917. In March 1918 the War
Trade Board appointed him as its representative in Norway. He
supplied reports and data to help the American negotiations with
Nansen. He was attached to the American legation in Christiania,
worked out of an office in the legation, and communicated through
the American minister to Norway, Albert Schmedeman. He was
not subject to Schmedeman's authority, however. To the credit of
both of them, they worked well together. Schmedeman provided
such help and support as he could, but he did not interfere with
Dye's duties.[43]

Though time-consuming and involving endless details, Dye's
dealings with Norwegian businessmen, trade associations, and the
government progressed smoothly and efficiently. The work built
on the earlier agreements Britain had concluded in Norway. Dye
also facilitated the organization of additional trade associations in
fields of business not covered by the British. In the thousands of
declarations obtained by Dye and his small staff the Norwegians
pledged not to allow imported goods to go to Germany or the
Central Powers directly or indirectly.[44]

More difficult and requiring more patience, persistence, firmness, and tact were Dye's dealings with British representatives in Norway. Months before Dye arrived the American consul general in Norway wrote that "the control of Norwegian trade with the United States is centralized at the British Legation in Christiania under the supervision of officials who are designated as commercial attachés."[45] When Dye reached Norway, he quickly learned that the British commercial attaché had "built up a very efficient organization of some twelve or fifteen men" and that they had in their files "detailed and indexed information relative to some thirty thousand firms and individuals doing business in Norway." Dye was glad the British had done so much so well, but he was not content to be just an adjunct to the continuing British system.[46]

The British were so accustomed to running matters that they inclined to continue doing so even after the Americans, French, and Italians were brought in as part of the Inter-Allied Trade Committee. They even wanted representatives of Norwegian trade associations to travel through submarine-infested waters to London to sign the new branch agreements rather than simply sign them in Norway. Dye successfully blocked that move.[47] As he phrased it in one letter, "They [the British] have done wonderfully good work here in Norway and we admire them tremendously for the efficient way in which they have handled it but we must very gently and sweetly but most firmly insist on either running our own business by ourselves or else running the whole business jointly, and we very much prefer of course the latter."[48] Actually the Inter-Allied Trade Committee largely handled Norwegian trade with the United States, and to some extent with France and Italy; Britain continued to control its own trade with Norway without participation by American or Allied representatives. By the time the war was over Dye was able to write in 1919 that "while we have had at times strong differences of opinion, we have never had any very serious friction, and we have kept a united front in our transactions with the Norwegian Government and people."[49]

In September 1918 Dye fell seriously ill and was hospitalized for Spanish influenza. Others took over his duties temporarily until he could resume them early in November, a few days before the armistice was signed.[50] After the fighting ended, Dye stayed on to phase out the controls and dismantle the organization. When Dye departed Norway in the summer of 1919, the American minister, Schmedeman, was able to write: "Doctor Dye's position has been an extremely difficult one, but with his wonderful tact, splendid power of organization and the diplomatic and capable manner in which he has handled all commercial matters, he has succeeded in gaining the friendship and confidence of practically every business man and shipowner he has come in contact with, notwithstanding the fact that he has often been compelled, in the interests of the United States, to have recourse to severe measures." It was a tribute to the skill with which he conducted his duties that in 1919 the Norwegian government awarded him the Order of Saint Olav.[51] While he served in Norway, Dye was paid an annual salary of thirty-four hundred dollars plus four dollars a day.[52]

AT the same time that Norway's exports and imports were being controlled firmly by the United States and the Allies, neutral Norway continued its carefully monitored trade with Germany on a reduced scale. In January 1917 Norway and Germany had signed a temporary commercial agreement, valid only from month to month. Norway did not renew it beyond February 1, 1918. With the conclusion of the Norwegian-American agreement at the end of April, the Norwegian foreign ministry and the German minister in Christiania worked out in detail the trade permitted under that new agreement. Trade between Norway and Germany continued in the commodities and quantities permitted under the Norwegian-American agreement.[53]

While that restricted trade went on, German submarines continued to take a heavy toll of Norwegian merchant ships and seamen on the high seas. By the time the fighting stopped near the end of 1918, Norway had lost more than eight hundred ships totalling in excess of 1.2 million tons—nearly one-fourth of the ships it had had before the war and nearly half of its prewar tonnage. More than eleven hundred Norwegian seamen died as a result, and many more were injured.[54] Those losses were suffered by a country that repeatedly proclaimed its neutrality and was never a belligerent in the war.

One special phase of German submarine warfare involved Norwegian territorial waters and successful United States and Allied diplomacy. The United States Navy had heavily mined North Sea waters off the Norwegian coast in 1918. German submarines consequently began using Norwegian territorial waters to evade those mines. That German action was in direct violation of Norwegian decrees barring submarines from its waters except in particular situations. Early in August 1918 the British minister in Christiania, Sir Mansfeldt de Cardonnel Findlay, demanded that Norway mine its outer channel south of Bergen to stop the use of those waters by German submarines. He told the Norwegian foreign minister that failure to take the action could be considered an unneutral act in favor of the Germans. The British minister invited American diplomatic assistance to win Norwegian compliance.[55]

Diplomatic responsibilities at the American legation in Christiania at that time were being handled temporarily by a young career foreign service officer, H. F. Arthur Schoenfeld, serving as chargé d'affaires.[56] He promptly won authority from the Department of State to urge the Norwegian government to take measures to stop use of its territorial waters by German submarines. Schoenfeld consulted closely with the British minister. In line with President Wilson's wishes, however, he conducted his negotiations independently of the British.[57]

When the Norwegians responded more slowly and more ambiguously than the British had hoped, the British threatened to mine the outer channel themselves if Norway did not do so. President Wilson objected to the harsh British approach,[58] so the United States carefully made certain it was not a party to those threats. Schoenfeld conducted his negotiations with the Norwegian foreign minister with the utmost friendliness, tact, and courtesy. He insisted, however, that failure of Norway to prevent passage of hostile submarines through its territorial waters would have the effect of providing safe refuge for those submarines as surely as if they had been lying at their German base in Kiel under the protection of the enemy's fortresses and minefields.[59]

Schoenfeld wanted to avoid press coverage and public discussion of the matter. He thought that "fear of the enemy still very largely controls all the decisions of this [Norwegian] Government," but that "with candid, skilful, and kindly handling of this matter, we may fairly expect success." As the negotiations continued, Schoenfeld concluded that "the course of events on the western front, as distinguished from the diplomatic representations made in Christiania, will probably determine the eventual action of the Norwegian Government."[60]

When Norway received no response from Germany to its inquiry on the matter, on September 28 Foreign Minister Ihlen informed Schoenfeld and other belligerent diplomats in Christiania that by October 7 Norway would mine appropriate places in its western territorial waters to put a stop to that submarine activity. Norwegian newspapers carried the announcement inconspicuously at a time when they were prominently headlining major articles on Allied military victories. Schoenfeld tactfully and graciously told Ihlen that America had felt confident that Norway would provide for that protection of the neutrality of its territorial waters. He assured Ihlen that Norway could count on continued respect by the United States Navy for the neutrality of those waters.[61]

Secretary of State Lansing cabled his cordial commendation to Schoenfeld for the "satisfactory manner" in which he had "conducted the negotiations leading to the decision of the Norwegian Government regarding the North Sea Barrage." The whole operation involved laying of hundreds of mines by the Norwegian navy in its own territorial waters.[62]

In a sense the diplomatic episode, like the trade restrictions at that same time, was a further invasion by the United States and the Allies of Norway's dwindling control of its own sovereignty. But it was also consistent with Norway's determined policies of neutrality and nonintervention in the war. In addition, Schoenfeld's tactful diplomacy helped to enable the Norwegians to maintain their own dignity while acceding to American (and British) wishes.

NORWEGIANS viewed the end of the fighting in 1918 and the peace negotiations in 1919 with mixed feelings. They placed their hopes for a secure and peaceful future with America's President Woodrow Wilson, his fourteen-point peace program, and the League of Nations, which he fathered. Unlike the United States, which ultimately turned its back on membership in the League, Norway sought and accepted membership. Despite divided views in both countries, neither the United States nor Norway after World War I turned away from its traditional policy of noninvolvement in European wars. But whereas the United States hoped to maintain that noninvolvement through its traditional unilateral foreign policy, Norway turned cautiously to the multilateral approach represented by the League of Nations.

Norwegians were pleased by the way President Wilson handled the German peace initiatives in October 1918, and they were relieved by the armistice on November 11. But for all its horrors and tragedies war had brought prosperity to many in Norway; they did not relish the economic dislocations likely to come with the end of the fighting. As in all countries, peace brought economic and political difficulties that were not at all welcome.[63]

President Wilson's peace program and his decision to come to Europe personally at the head of the American peace delegation pleased and encouraged Norwegians. The Norwegian government wanted to send delegates to the peace conference in France to represent its interests in negotiations relating to freedom of the seas, membership in the League of Nations, control of Spitsbergen, and compensation for loss of shipping and seamen during the war.[64] It eagerly responded to invitations to send delegations to the conference to participate.[65]

As the peace negotiations progressed, Norwegians viewed the emerging terms as too harsh but just. They conceded that the terms were less severe than they would have been if Germany had triumphed, but they were troubled that they failed to live up to Wilson's ideals as spelled out in his Fourteen Points. For that failure they generally blamed the European allies.[66] Despite the small number of Americans resident in Christiania, the legation managed to gather nearly fifty guests for a dinner celebrating the signing of the peace. It proved to be quite a successful occasion.[67]

Sentiment in Norway was cautiously hopeful about the League of Nations and about Norwegian membership in that new world organization. As the time of decision drew closer in the autumn of 1919, however, there was some thought that Norway's course might depend partly on what the United States did. When the United States Senate failed to approve the Versailles Treaty and membership in the League of Nations in November, the Norwegian government postponed its formal deliberations on the matter. Both Schmedeman and Nansen believed that Norway would not join if the United States ultimately rejected membership. Nansen feared that if neither the United States nor Germany joined, the League would become less an organ for peace than an organization against Germany.[68]

Norwegian leaders regretted the American decision not to join the League of Nations. But after careful deliberations, and after consulting leaders of the other Scandinavian governments, Foreign Minister Ihlen proposed that the Storting approve Norwegian membership in the League. After lively debate the Storting on March 4, 1920, approved Norwegian membership by a vote of 100 to 20. Sixteen of the eighteen Socialists in the Storting voted against membership, but the leader of the opposition was a Conservative and the editor, C. J. Hambro. Hambro thought the Versailles Treaty was unjust, and he urged Norway to follow the American lead in rejecting it. Most in the Storting disagreed, however, and on March 5 King Haakon signed the resolution making Norway a member of the League of Nations.[69] It remained a member throughout the League's troubled history, though in its final phases Norway rejected any collective security responsibilities.

There were other concerns involving United States relations with Norway in the immediate aftermath of World War I. Russia was torn by revolution and civil war in 1917. The revolution in March ousted the czar, and a second revolution in November brought Vladimir Lenin, Leon Trotsky, and the Bolsheviks to power. Both the United States and Norway recognized the provisional government that replaced the czar, but neither extended recognition to the Communist government in the fall. As American diplomats and consuls fled their posts, the American ambassador to Russia, David Francis, and Secretary of State Lansing asked the Norwegian government to look after American interests in those Russian cities and districts from which Americans had withdrawn or might withdraw. They promised that the United States would pay the expenses thus incurred.[70]

The Norwegian government responded helpfully and directed

its chargé d'affaires in Petrograd, Mikal A. Holmbo, to look after American interests. He did so as carefully as he could in the chaotic and violent circumstances then prevailing in a country swept by revolution, counterrevolution, and civil war.[71] The Norwegian government reimbursed him for his expenses with the expectation that the United States would cover the costs sooner or later. It proved to be later.

Year after year the Norwegians requested payment, and the American ministers in Norway dutifully forwarded those requests to the Department of State with their recommendations that they be paid—with no results. Holmbo fell seriously ill and died, and still the United States did not pay. Finally in 1925, a half-dozen years late, the United States paid the expenses Norway incurred for services rendered by Holmbo in Russia in 1918 and 1919. Even then it did not pay the interest that had accrued on its obligation.[72]

Norwegians and Americans cooperated in extending food relief in Russia and central Europe after the war. Specifically Norway provided quantities of cod-liver oil to assist those relief efforts, supplementing the millions of dollars provided by the United States. At the same time Dr. Fridtjof Nansen, who led those food relief efforts for Norway, also worked patiently and skillfully to obtain the release of Americans held in Russia. For his efforts and his accomplishments Dr. Nansen won the thanks of the American government and the 1922 Nobel Peace Prize.[73]

The peace conference after World War I also made possible the resolution of the long-festering controversy over Spitsbergen. In July 1919 it agreed to appoint a subcommission made up of representatives from Italy, France, Great Britain, and the United States to consider the claims of the different countries and to report on their findings. By that time American coal-mining interests in Spitsbergen had sold out to a Norwegian company. That transaction changed American attitudes and policies. Secretary of State Lansing favored assigning sovereignty over Spitsbergen to Norway; he pressed for that solution throughout. Neutral countries, including Norway, were invited to express their views on the matter. The subcommission reported in favor of Norwegian sovereignty over Spitsbergen. A treaty to that effect was signed in 1920 and won final ratification in 1925. Foreign Minister Ihlen expressed his sincere thanks to President Wilson and the other American delegates in Paris for their support in helping Norway gain possession of Spitsbergen.[74]

WORLD WAR I was a terrible tragedy. Many Americans and Norwegians died in the war. But Norway and the United States suffered much less than most in Europe. Many in both countries prospered because of the war. Both the United States and Norway successfully preserved their democratic institutions and political freedoms. Norway even managed to maintain its technical neutrality. Its traditions of neutrality and nonintervention, however, were severely strained; America's were temporarily broken when the United States entered the war in 1917. The American decision to reject membership in the League of Nations and Norway's conviction that its membership was a means to sustain its noninterventionist ways were evidences of the continued determination by people and leaders in both countries to stay out of European wars.

The Nobel committee of the Norwegian Storting awarded the 1919 Nobel Peace Prize to America's Woodrow Wilson.[75] Despite Wilson's heroic leadership on behalf of peace through a League of Nations, and despite Norway's decision to join the League, neither the United States nor Norway was yet prepared to turn away from traditional policies of neutrality and noninvolvement in European wars. More time, more changes, and more war were necessary before either country would acknowledge that developments at home and abroad in the twentieth century were making those traditional policies obsolete and impracticable.

3

Between the Wars

THE two decades that separated World War I from World War II—the 1920s and 1930s—were times of troubles. There were those, inspired by the leadership of Woodrow Wilson, who hoped that the Allied victory would "make the world safe for democracy." They looked to the League of Nations as the instrument through which men of good will could accomplish and preserve peace in the world. But a cruel reality fell far short of those dreams and ideals.

The tragedy of World War I proved to be a destructive tornado that left havoc in its wake. The United States rejected membership in the League of Nations. Broken in health, Wilson was a pathetic symbol of his shattered dreams until his death in 1924. Much of the world seethed in severe and continuing economic crises that led many in desperation to believe that authoritarian regimes were essential to accomplish stability, order, and prosperity. Lenin's totalitarian communism emerged triumphant from the ashes of war and revolution in Russia. In 1922 Benito Mussolini's Fascists gained power in Italy. Adolf Hitler's Nazis took over in Germany in 1933. Japan followed the lead of its militarists in the 1930s. Dozens of other countries fell under the control of military dictatorships and one-man rule. Both democracy and peace were under siege, and millions had empty stomachs.

Norway and the United States fared better than most. Both continued to make constitutional democracy work. They maintained friendly relations with each other; they handled the problems that inevitably arose between them through orderly diplomatic procedures. But sweetness and light did not prevail either within those two north Atlantic countries or in relations between them.

In the United States the conservative Republican administrations of Warren G. Harding and Calvin Coolidge rode the crest of domestic prosperity in the 1920s, though farmers did not share in that prosperity. A third and far more able conservative Republican, Herbert Hoover, hoped to make the presidency the capstone for his already highly successful career. But the stock market crash in the autumn of 1929 and the ensuing economic depression ruined his administration. The Great Depression left Americans floundering in economic hard times and put the Democrats, under the charismatic Franklin D. Roosevelt, in the White House in 1933. Roosevelt's New Deal brought hope, relief, and reforms but did not end the depression. Most in America did not experience real economic recovery until World War II provided a much more massive "pump-priming" stimulus to prosperity than had the New Deal.[1]

War had brought prosperity for many in neutral Norway; peace brought hard times and restiveness that lasted much of the decade following the war. Partial recovery came just in time to be shaken by the world depression triggered by America's stock market crash in 1929. The Great Depression of the 1930s arrived in Norway a bit later; it was slightly less severe there and ended sooner than in the United States.[2]

Neither the Liberal nor Conservative parties could win absolute majorities in the Storting; each had to patch together shaky coalitions to sustain short-lived ministries that alternated from one party to the other. Most prominent and politically effective among the leaders of those two parties was the Liberal, Johan Ludwig Mowinckel. During each of his three ministries (1924–26, 1928–31, and 1933–35) Mowinckel served as both prime minister and foreign minister. He had much interest in foreign affairs, was devoted to the League of Nations, and had a friendly attitude toward the United States. But he had to govern from a shrinking Liberal party base. It was not the opposition Conservative party, however, that chipped away at his political strength so much as it was the growth of the Labor party and the smaller Agrarian party.[3]

Like both the Liberal and Conservative parties, the Labor party had its beginnings in the nineteenth century. The Bolshevik revolution in Russia in 1917 had set off noisy radical activity in Norway. In succeeding years complicated political mergers and cleavages left the Communist party isolated and weak. The Labor party, benefiting from talented leadership and feeding on economic hard times, gradually gained strength and moderated its rhetoric and program. A ministry it formed in 1928 using radical rhetoric was premature and lasted only a fortnight. In 1935 the Labor party won control of the Norwegian government; it was to maintain control, under one prime minister or another, for nearly three decades. In 1935, however, it lacked an absolute majority in the Storting and had to depend on an uneasy accord with the Agrarian party. That political weakness, along with responsible leadership by Prime Minister Johan Nygaardsvold and Foreign Minister Halvdan Koht, moved that Labor government along more moderate paths both at home and abroad than the bourgeois parties had feared and the radicals had hoped.[4]

So far as relations with the United States were concerned, those various changes in government had little effect. In their separate ways each of the governments (under the Conservative, Liberal, Agrarian, and Labor parties) had a friendly attitude toward the United States. And each in its negotiations on problems in relations between the two countries was consistently civil, responsible, and persistent.

BETWEEN the wars four Americans served as minister to Norway, and three Norwegians served as minister to the United States. In the 1920s Laurits S. Swenson of Minneapolis returned to duty in Christiania, where he had served earlier under the Taft administration. Born in Minnesota and of Norwegian descent, Swenson spoke Norwegian fluently. He was well educated and had served as a Republican political appointee in diplomatic positions as early as 1897. His eldest daughter had died at sea while accompanying him to his post in Switzerland in 1910, and his wife had died in 1912 during his first tour of duty in Norway.[5]

Through his earlier diplomatic service in Denmark he had known King Haakon since the king had been young Prince Carl there. King Haakon and Swenson enjoyed playing bridge together. He was a frequent guest in the royal palace, and the king in turn was often the minister's informal guest for bridge in the legation. Swenson had excellent contacts in both official and business circles. He was active socially and entertained often and well.[6]

Swenson ran the legation with a sure hand. Though he always had a career foreign service officer as legation secretary, in important essentials Swenson's was a one-man show. As one foreign service inspection report phrased it, "The position of the minister is unassailable in Norway; he is well liked in all circles. He is a keen observer of men, a fair judge of human nature, and a very clever, canny politician. He is also a hospitable gentleman who is a very gracious host." He lacked the urbanity and sophistication that might have been called for in London or Paris, but he was extremely well informed and effective in Christiania.[7] (In 1925 Norway changed the name of its capital city from the Danish back to its ancient Norwegian name, Oslo.)[8] By 1928 his long service as United States minister to Norway elevated him to the status of dean of the diplomatic corps there, and a prominent group of donors had a bust sculpted of him to be placed in the legation.[9]

Swenson painstakingly guided the State Department to purchase its own building in 1924 at 28 Nobelsgate to house the legation. It was a splendid property located on spacious grounds in one of the best residential districts in the west end of the capital city. Built as a private home in 1911, it was one of the larger and finer residences in the city at the time. It served as the American legation (and later embassy) until long after World War II.[10]

While Swenson served in Norway, Helmer H. Bryn continued his long service in Washington as Norwegian minister to the United States. His departure in 1927 was marred by circumstances that put a cloud over his record. His son was in an automobile accident resulting in the death of his passenger. His wife and family stayed on in Washington an inordinantly long time after his departure from his post. But most troublesome, Bryn was involved in a nasty controversy with another foreign service officer over the long-festering ship claims of Christoffer Hannevig against the

United States. Bryn emerged from the episode honorably and was appointed Norwegian consul general ad interim in Montreal. But it was an unfortunate way to close out his long service in the United States.[11]

Both Bryn in the United States in 1927 and Swenson in Norway in 1930 were succeeded by diplomats who had already had long careers as foreign service officers. The new Norwegian minister to the United States was Halvard H. Bachke, who served in Washington from 1927 to 1934; the new American minister to Norway was Hoffman Philip, who served in Oslo from 1930 to 1935.

During his seven years in Washington Bachke arranged the purchase of land at the corner of Massachusetts Avenue and Thirty-fourth Street, on which Norway constructed a new legation building. The present chancellery was built many years later, but partly on land that Bachke and the Norwegian government had purchased in 1930. In 1934 Bachke departed his post in the United States to become Norway's minister and consul general in Paris.[12]

Swenson was in no hurry to leave Oslo, and Philip was in no hurry to go there. Philip had had a long and honorable career in the foreign service before being named minister to Norway, most of it spent in the Middle East and in Latin America. Personal matters in the United States, health difficulties (emphysema), increasing age, and approaching retirement absorbed much of Philip's attention during his tour in Norway. He found it necessary to be absent from his post frequently during his nearly five years as minister to Norway. He performed his duties responsibly, but he revealed little of the love of Norway so apparent in his predecessor nor much of the enthusiasm and fascination with Norway and its people evidenced by his immediate successors there. In 1935 Philip was named United States ambassador to Chile, his last position before he retired from the foreign service in 1937.[13]

Bachke's successor as Norway's minister to the United States was Wilhelm T. von Munthe de Morgenstierne. He represented Norway in the United States, first as minister and later as ambassador, from 1934 to 1958, longer than anyone else. Born in 1887 and educated at the University of Oslo, he began his career in the Norwegian foreign service in 1910 as attaché at the legation in Washington. Over the years the lean, active Morgenstierne had assignments in various countries as well as in Oslo. But always his responsibilities brought him back to the United States—as counselor of the legation, as consul general, and in a variety of special assignments before he became minister. He developed friendships with many in all walks of life in the United States. Morgenstierne kept in touch with developments in Norway through regular visits to his home country. His wife (a Canadian) and his daughters, however, knew America much better than they knew his native land. As the years passed, some in Norway worried that he might be becoming more American than Norwegian. But he served Norway's interests and Norwegian-American relations exceedingly well over a very long time.[14]

In 1935 President Franklin D. Roosevelt appointed Anthony J. Drexel Biddle, Jr., of Philadelphia to succeed Hoffman Philip as minister to Norway. Wealthy, young, handsome, energetic, athletic, and outgoing, Biddle quickly became unusually popular in Norway. Tennis was his game, but Norwegians skied, and he was a dashing skier. That pleased his hosts. In a remarkably short time he visited many parts of Norway and won an army of friends and admirers. When he left in 1937 to become ambassador to Poland, the only significant criticism was that his service in Norway ended so soon. During World War II, when the Norwegian government was in exile in London, President Roosevelt appointed Biddle to serve as minister (later ambassador) to governments in exile there, including Norway's.[15]

In 1937 President Roosevelt appointed Florence J. Harriman (Mrs. J. Borden Harriman) to replace Biddle in Oslo. She had a hard act to follow, but she did it very well. A native of New York and a widow with one daughter, Mrs. Harriman had been active in the Democratic party and in public service. Though in her midsixties and functioning in a traditionally male role, she quickly became accepted and respected in leadership and diplomatic circles. She entertained graciously, traveled widely, and won friends and acquaintances in a wide range of social strata in Norway. It was her misfortune to be serving in Oslo when Nazi Germany launched its surprise attack on Norway on April 9, 1940. Her performance throughout was courageous and responsible. It was entirely appropriate for King Haakon to award her the Grand Cross of the Order of Saint Olav, the highest decoration he could bestow on her.[16]

AMONG the more persistent issues to test the skills and patience of those diplomats between the two world wars concerned the Norwegian merchant marine. The huge Norwegian fleet of merchant ships had been depleted terribly by losses to submarines and mines during World War I. But Norwegian shipping companies quickly set about rebuilding. Five years after the fighting stopped, Norway's merchant marine totaled more than thirty-seven hundred ships with over 2.6 million gross tons. A decade after the war it had greater total tonnage than the merchant marines of Denmark, Sweden, and Finland combined, and Norway's tanker tonnage was five times that of the three other Scandinavian countries. In 1934 Norway's fleet had over four million tons, making it the fourth largest in the world and perhaps the most modern.[17]

All that development was accomplished by private enterprise, with the government keeping its hands out of the operation for the most part. Though Norway did not discriminate against foreign shippers, American merchant ships rarely stopped at Norwegian ports. Most trade between the United States and Norway was carried in Norwegian or other non-American ships. The Great Depression hurt the Norwegian merchant marine severely, as it did those of other countries. The income derived from Norway's carrying trade, however, played an important role in helping to fill the exchange gap between its substantial imports and its much smaller exports.[18]

One particular matter relating to the merchant marine troubled relations between the United States and Norway. That matter concerned claims growing out of United States expropriation of ships under construction in America during World War I, particularly the so-called Hannevig claims. After the United States declared war in 1917, Congress authorized the president to commandeer ships under construction in American shipyards.[19] Among those expropriated by the United States Shipping Board Emergency Fleet Corporation under the authority of the president were ships contracted by, or under construction for, Norwegian companies. After the war Norway submitted claims for losses suffered because of American expropriation. With Emil Stray conducting the negotiations for Norway, the two countries reached an agreement in 1919 that required the United States to pay $34.5 million to settle certain of the claims.[20]

Under the terms of a Norwegian-American agreement signed June 30, 1921, another smaller group of claims went to arbitration in the Hague. In October 1922 the arbitral tribunal, by a vote of two to one (with the American member dissenting), awarded nearly twelve million dollars plus interest to the Norwegian claimants. The United States promptly paid the amount due.[21]

The Stray settlement and the Hague arbitral award represented most Norwegian claimants – but not all. The conspicuous exception was Christoffer Hannevig and the corporations he organized and controlled. He had come to the United States in 1915 and organized or developed three American shipbuilding corporations, which consolidated under the name Pusey & Jones Company. When the United States entered the war in 1917, his companies had contracted for, or had under construction, various ships in America. Hannevig had invested some $6.7 million in shipbuilding yards and in ships under construction. The United States seized them during the war. In 1920 the Emergency Fleet Corporation, under the United States Shipping Board, had offered Hannevig and his companies a settlement. But when assets, liabilities, claims, and counterclaims were totaled, the "offer" showed that Hannevig owed the United States about three million dollars. That outcome was not exactly what he had in mind. When the war began, Hannevig was a wealthy man. By the middle of 1921 both Hannevig and Pusey & Jones were bankrupt.[22]

In a series of lawsuits Pusey & Jones reached a compromise settlement with the United States in 1926. But Hannevig persisted. He made all sorts of promises in his efforts to win support from influential circles in Norwegian government and society. He persuaded the Norwegian government to press his claims in 1926 and again in 1935 (under a new Labor government). The United States insisted that Hannevig had no legal ground for further action, so Norway tried to win a friendly settlement on the ground of equity rather than law, but to no avail.[23]

Finally in 1940, less than two weeks before Nazi Germany attacked Norway, the United States and Norway reached an agreement on procedures to be used in settling the Hannevig claims and a much smaller claim by George R. Jones against Norway (though legally the two cases were not related and were not alike in details). Neither country thought the claims of the other were justified, but both wanted to remove distracting irritants in their relations at a time when war abroad gave them much more important matters to treat.[24]

But even the 1940 agreement did not end the matter. The Senate did not approve the treaty until eight years later, and Norway and the United States did not exchange ratifications until November 1948, long after World War II had ended. Another decade was to pass before the claims were settled. In 1959 the courts (acting in accord with the 1940 agreement) concluded that the United States did not owe Hannevig's estate anything. Both Hannevig and Jones had long since died.[25]

A controversy consuming countless thousands of hours of the time of innumerable people in both Norway and the United States, and filling hundreds of despatches and documents in both countries over the course of more than four decades, finally came to a close. The episode was annoying, but it never was allowed seriously to disrupt amicable relations between those two democracies.

A MATTER having less to do with wealth and more to do with the lives of ordinary people concerned immigration. Norwegian immigration to the United States, so massive during the last twenty years of the nineteenth century and the first decade of the twentieth century, had declined a bit just before World War I and dropped substantially during the war. After the war, however, hard times in Norway and prosperity in America encouraged a resurgence of emigration.[26]

In 1925 both in Norway and in the United States, festivities commemorated the beginnings of Norwegian immigration to the United States a century earlier. Celebrities in both countries participated in the commemorative events. President Calvin Coolidge traveled to Minnesota to address a large gathering on the occasion, and King Haakon presided over ceremonies in Oslo. The centennial festivities emotionally underscored ties between the two countries.[27] In retrospect, however, those celebrations might be seen as marking very nearly the end of Norwegian immigration to America almost as precisely as they marked the centennial of its beginnings.

Before World War I the United States had not restricted the flow of immigrants from Europe, except for certain categories of diseased, defective, or obviously undesirable people. That policy changed during and after the war. In 1917 Congress passed, over President Wilson's veto, a literacy requirement for immigrants. In 1921, 1922, and 1924 it passed ever more restrictive immigration laws, which established numerical limits and quotas based on the national origins of the American population in specified years.

The laws did not apply to immigrants from countries in the Western Hemisphere, but they flatly barred all immigrants from Asia. The quota systems had the effect—and the intent—of discriminating against potential immigrants from the Latin countries of southern Europe and from the Slavic countries of eastern Europe. But they put caps on the number of immigrants to be admitted from the countries of northern and western Europe as well, including Norway. In its final phase in 1929 the legislation allowed a maximum of 150,000 immigrants each year, with national quotas based on the national origins of the American population in 1920. The implementation of the restrictions fell most heavily on the shoulders of American consular officials in the countries from which the immigrants came.[28]

Under the quotas provided in the laws of 1921 and 1922 a total of 12,202 Norwegians were allowed to immigrate to the United States each year. Those quotas may not have reduced the number of Norwegians going to America greatly below the level that might have been reached if there had been no restrictions.[29]

The Immigration Act of 1924 allowed 6,453 Norwegians to immigrate to America each year until 1929. That was considerably fewer than would have gone if there had been no restrictions. The waiting lists and the waiting time for potential immigrants grew longer and longer. Fearful of the restrictions, Norwegians flocked to apply for immigrant visas. The American consul general in Oslo from 1921 to 1928, Alban G. Snyder, was convinced that "many applicants have no actual intentions of ever immigrating to America but apply simply to have a place on the waiting list should unexpected developments create a desire for a change of surroundings or render such change desirable." He believed that if the quota restrictions were removed, the waiting list could be reduced by 20 to 40 percent. Nonetheless, in 1927 he reported that the waiting list for his consulate general was between twenty-five thousand and twenty-six thousand.[30]

In its final phase in 1929 the law allowed 2,377 Norwegians to immigrate to the United States each year. The American consul general in Norway at that time, Thomas H. Bevan, estimated that the reduced quota would extend the waiting period for potential immigrants from three years to seven years. And since, under the law, preference would go to Norwegian relatives of Americans and to skilled farm workers and their families, nonpreference applicants might have to wait more than ten years before their turns came under the quota.[31]

To keep those patterns in perspective, one should note that because of the massive Norwegian immigration to America earlier and the large number of persons of Norwegian descent living in the United States, Norway had comparatively large quotas for its small population. Other countries with larger populations had smaller quotas (Spain, for example), and some that had larger quotas than Norway had quotas that represented much smaller percentages of their total populations. For example, in 1931 France had a quota of 3,086 and Russia a quota of 2,701 – both larger than Norway's but at the same time representing much smaller percentages of the vastly larger population of each of those two countries. The largest quotas by far went to Great Britain, Germany, and Ireland.[32]

The quotas made the processes of immigrating to America more complicated, more difficult, less pleasant, and sometimes almost humiliating. In the 1920s America's consular offices in three cities (Oslo, Bergen, and Stavanger) handled immigration matters in Norway. Their small staffs and cramped quarters were inadequate for their increased responsibilities. The Oslo office had acquired additional space in the middle of the decade but had no waiting room. As a result, according to Consul General Bevan:

> Under the present arrangement, the immigrants who can not be seated in the visa office are required to wait in a long narrow passage, which has no ventilation whatever. As this passage is not wide enough for chairs, a number of small wooden stools have been placed along the corridor for the immigrants to sit on. On busy days there are as many as forty people, including men, women, small children, and nursing babies packed in this corridor. As it has no ventilation, the odor at times becomes most offensive. . . . Business men and all other callers must pass through this evil smelling crowded passage to get into the Consulate General. It is needless to say that such an entrance creates a very bad impression on callers.

The State Department authorized rental of three additional rooms, but the difficulties did not entirely disappear.[33] The consul in Bergen asked the State Department to authorize purchase of a sturdy swinging door between the main waiting room and the immigrant waiting room "to keep out the noise and unwholesome odors of immigrants and their crying babies."[34]

Most consular officers tried earnestly to perform their duties responsibly. But under the pressures of long hours and endless streams of people even well-meaning officers could become curt and insensitive at times. And there were those whose compassion and sensitivity to the human element may have been slight in the first place and quickly diminished in the process. Complaints and grumbling by potential immigrants became common, and the press and political leaders added their voices to the tumult. American Consul General Snyder bitterly complained about his lot in Norway.[35] He came under particularly severe criticism from Norwegians.

Carl J. Hambro, Conservative party leader and president of the Storting, ranked second only to the king in the Norwegian political hierarchy. He visited the United States many times and had affection for the country. But in a speech before the Storting in 1929 he exploded against the treatment accorded Norwegians by

American consular officers. Hambro contended that there was no reason to extend courtesies to Americans if they were not reciprocated by the United States. The uproar following the speech embarrassed both Hambro and other government officials. But as American Minister Laurits Swenson phrased it, "The disrepute into which Mr. Snyder brought the Consulate General at Oslo has made that branch of our Service more or less a byword in Norway." Hambro continued to be "deeply concerned about the ill-will growing from the arrogance and insolence shown by the subordinates in the consulate to all Norwegians appearing before them." He found Snyder's administration of the consulate general "notorious." He wrote of "a current running very strongly against the brutality and lack of civility shown." Though less strident in his tones, the Liberal party leader, Johan Mowinckel, sharply criticized the American immigration laws as they applied to Norwegians.[36]

Norwegians also warned against the deteriorating conditions that immigrants would suffer when they reached America. One disillusioned Norwegian who had returned after ten years in the United States found little to praise and wrote of "the hollowness of American morals." The author of an article in the major conservative Oslo newspaper, *Aftenposten*, emphasized the need for emigration from their "barren little viking land." But he sympathized with the immigrant's "pain which grips the heart of the stranger when he gets off at the last dismal prairie station to meet the unknown." An editorial in a Bergen newspaper warned that the position of new immigrants in America was "considerably more difficult than it was 25 years ago." It pointed out that the "dividing wall" between immigrants and Americans had "grown higher and higher." It warned of employment discrimination against older workers, and of low pay and high prices. It concluded by advising Norwegians, "Stay at home!"[37] Then things got worse.

The Great Depression of the 1930s made America less appealing to potential immigrants than it had been earlier. High unemployment increased pressures within the United States to prevent an influx of new immigrants, who would compete in the sharply depleted job market with unemployed Americans or who would further strain the limited resources of America's primitive welfare programs.

Consequently in 1930 the Department of State pointed out to American diplomatic and consular officers that the Immigration Act of 1917 barred aliens who were likely to become public charges. Given the acute and persistent unemployment in the United States, the State Department directed consular officers to presume that a person was likely to become a public charge unless he could "show good reason to the contrary." At the discretion of the consul, such an alien could be refused immigrant visas unless he could demonstrate that he had "other sources of income or support" and would not become a public charge. Even persons in preferential categories, such as wives and children of people in America, were to be barred unless current evidence indicated that "the resident alien relative is employed or otherwise able to support them." Since those considerations might increase the demand for nonimmigrant and nonquota visas, the State Department directed consuls "to examine with great care applicants for such visas." Those instructions were to "be effective until canceled by the Department."[38] They were never canceled during the decade of the 1930s before World War II. In practice those restrictions, rooted in the severe depression in America, limited immigration to the United States from Norway even more severely than the continuing quotas did. The Hoover administration initiated those policies, and the Roosevelt administration continued them.

Unavoidably a certain amount of discretion rested with individual consular offices in implementing the instructions. It was difficult to have consistent standards worldwide; it was even difficult to maintain them among the three consular posts in Norway. Early in the decade both the consulate at Stavanger and the one at Bergen were relieved of their immigrant visa duties. By September 1932 all American immigration responsibilities for Norway were consolidated at the consul general's office in Oslo.[39] Throughout the 1930s, however, American consular officials in Norway interpreted the "LPC" (likely to become a public charge) rules very rigidly.

The possession of a certain amount of money was not considered sufficient guarantee that the individual would not become a public charge: "He may lose the money or spend it foolishly or have it stolen or lose it through swindlers. Furthermore it may not be sufficient to last throughout the hard times." Each case had to be decided on its own merits, "the burden of the proof being on the immigrant, who must convince the consular officer that he will not become a public charge subsequent to his arrival in the United States." When the potential immigrant would be dependent for support on relatives or others in America, it must be shown that the interested persons are not only financially able to assume the support of the aliens, but that they can be relied upon to do so for an indefinite period in case of necessity. Where there is no direct obligation on the part of the interested persons to assume support of the aliens, more convincing evidence is naturally necessary to establish that the support of the aliens would be assured in view of the possible change in attitude which might occur after the arrival of the aliens in the United States."[40]

Inevitably the number of persons who successfully qualified for immigrant visas to the United States shrunk sharply. Norway's immigration quotas had always filled until the 1930–31 depression restrictions went into effect; those quotas never filled during the remainder of the depression decade. From 1902 through 1907 slightly more than twenty-two thousand persons emigrated from Norway each year, most of them going to the United States. In 1930 there were 3,673 Norwegians who emigrated, in 1931 the number was 825, and in 1932 only 436 emigrants left Norway. Of those 436, only 315 of them went to the United States. At the same time the American commercial attaché in Oslo reported, "Every ship coming from the United States brings back hundreds of Norwegians who intend to settle in Norway."[41]

In the 1930s Norway accepted only a tiny number of refugees from central Europe (mostly Jewish refugees fleeing Nazi anti-Semitism). In 1939 America's consul general in Oslo wrote, "Although the individual Norwegian sympathizes genuinely with the plight of these unfortunates, there is an almost fierce determination to prevent any considerable immigration into Norway." In response to an inquiry, he explained that America's immigration laws "contemplate no discrimination between applicants based on their national or religious status and that refugees are given equal consideration with Norwegians in the issuance of visas." Those refugees who were admitted to Norway temporarily, hoping to get

immigrant visas to the United States, generally – like Norwegians--
could not qualify. In any event, they could not do so in the short
time (sixty days) they were allowed to remain in Norway.[42]

When in 1939 the American consul general in Vienna (then a
part of Nazi Germany) sought help in Oslo to facilitate immigration
of German Jews to America by using part of the Norwegian quota,
the American consul general in Oslo described the practices
routinely followed in handling Norwegian applicants for immigrant
visas. The consul general in Vienna responded that if those practices were applied in Germany, they "would result in the refusal of
nearly every one of the more than 200,000 applicants now regis-
tered in Germany." He wrote that "none of the thousands of refugees to whom visas have been issued by this office, and others in
Germany, has been refused admission in the United States on
L.P.C. grounds." There never was any allegation that the United
States discriminated against Norwegians in the issuance of immigrant visas. But for Norwegians requirements for visas to immigrate to the United States were more stringent in the 1930s than
they were for potential Jewish refugees from Nazi Germany.[43]

Substantial Norwegian immigration to the United States has
never revived since World War II. The dramatic adventure of that
migration lasted a little more than a century. Immigration laws and
quota systems sharply reduced the flow of immigrants in the
1920s; the Great Depression of the 1930s and the requirement that
potential immigrants prove that they were not likely to become
public charges very nearly put an end to it. Ultimately the exhaus-
tion of supplies of productive public lands in America, the urban-
ization of American society, good government and welfare systems
in Norway, and the growth of Norwegian prosperity and standards
of living combined to bring that great migration to a close.[44]

DURING the two decades between the wars immigration consumed
the largest part of the time and energies of American consular
officials in Norway. A traditional and equally important part of
their duties, however, involved the promotion of American trade
with that country. Consular officers were required to seek out business, trade, and investment opportunities for American business-

men and to assist those merchants and bankers in a variety of ways.

Consuls reported trade opportunities, provided reports for the World Trade Directory in Washington, submitted required annual and monthly reports on commerce and industries in their areas, and prepared special reports requested by the Department of State. When time permitted, they compiled voluntary reports focusing on particular economic developments or opportunities. Consuls responded as helpfully as they could to letters of inquiry from American businessmen and to letters from Norwegians seeking business contacts in the United States. They conferred with American businessmen visiting or traveling in Norway and advised them on economic conditions and business practices there. State Department officials in Washington monitored the commercial work by consuls in the field and prodded them to greater effort when they thought it necessary. Consular officials, in turn, tried to persuade their superiors in Washington that they were doing everything possible to promote American business.[45] All those activities were standard operating procedure in the American consular service throughout the world (and in the consular services of other countries, including Norway).

The minister to Norway and his legation staff helped promote American business there. In the 1920s, under the vigorous direction of Secretary of Commerce Herbert Hoover, commercial attachés performed similar functions.[46]

So far as Norway was concerned, however, those commercial efforts did not produce particularly impressive results. Immediately after World War I, when Norwegians were prosperous and European producers were recovering from the war, American exports to Norway increased. But as dollars became scarce, as European producers stepped up production, and as Norway slipped quickly into its postwar depression, Norway's trade fell into patterns not radically different from what they had been before the war.

Most of Norway's trade was with Europe. As in earlier years, Great Britain commanded substantially more of that trade than any other country. Germany was second, generally the United States was third, with Sweden close behind. Norway had unfavorable balances of trade with most of its leading trade partners; that is, it imported more from them than it exported to them. The United States sometimes was an exception, buying more from Norway than it sold there. Norway imported from the United States quantities of motor vehicles and accessories, petroleum products, textiles, tobacco, fresh and dried fruits, meat and meat products, and rubber products. Its exports to the United States included wood pulp and cellulose, fish and fish products, whale oil, cod-liver oil, ferromanganese, and aluminum.[47]

America's standing in Norwegian foreign trade was important to the economy of that small Scandinavian country, but Norway played only a tiny role in the total foreign trade of the United States. American manufacturers generally did not think the small Norwegian market worth much effort; businessmen often did not act on trade opportunities that consular officers brought to their attention.

In the 1920s American banks and investment houses arranged loans of millions of dollars to the royal government of Norway and to the governments of various Norwegian cities, including Oslo and Bergen. Norway had an excellent credit rating and the Department of Commerce under Secretary Hoover had no objections to the loans.[48] There was, however, little direct American investment in businesses and properties in Norway. There were no branch offices of American banks in Norway, and Norwegian laws restricting the role of foreign businesses in the Norwegian economy discouraged them.

It was entirely appropriate that immediately after the war the United States closed its consulates at Kristiansand and Trondheim as well as the one it had established briefly at Vardö. The importance to the American economy of those two small cities and that remote northern outpost was almost nil. The United States even closed its consulate at Stavanger in 1933.[49] Norwegian trade with the United States slackened during the decade of the 1920s and declined still further during the depression decade of the 1930s.

In extended and careful negotiations from 1922 to 1928 the United States and Norway worked out terms for a new Treaty of Friendship, Commerce, and Consular Rights to replace the earlier Treaty of Commerce and Navigation of 1827. The new agreement included an unconditional most-favored-nation clause rather than the conditional one in the earlier agreement. It also included provisions on consular rights not covered in the earlier treaty. On June 5, 1928, Secretary of State Frank B. Kellogg for the United States and Minister Bachke for Norway signed the new agreement and exchanged letters clarifying the American tariff treatment of Norwegian sardines. Norway promptly ratified the treaty, but the United States Senate did not approve it until nearly four years later. The two governments exchanged ratifications on September 13, 1932, late in the Hoover administration.[50] It was a carefully drafted document, similar to agreements the United States negotiated with other governments at the same time. But it had no striking impact on evolving trade patterns between Norway and the United States.

And then there was the whale oil controversy. Whale oil was to Norwegian-American trade relations in the 1930s what Hannevig was to ship claims and what quotas and LPC rules were to immigration. Whaling in Norway was as old as history. But in the 1920s it expanded spectacularly with the development of huge factory ships that greatly increased the Norwegian take of whales in the Antarctic and the production of whale oil. Norway became the world's leading whaling country, with only Great Britain providing substantial competition. The Norwegian whaling industry employed some eleven thousand men, and perhaps forty thousand people depended on the industry for their livelihood. The United States imported large quantities of whale oil directly from the Norwegian ships on their return from the Antarctic. Nearly all the whale oil was used for the manufacture of soap, particularly by the Proctor and Gamble Company.[51]

America imposed a tariff on whale oil, but competing palm oil entered the United States duty free. Consequently in 1933 Norway approached the United States about the possibility of reducing or eliminating the tariff on whale oil. Both President Roosevelt and Secretary of State Cordell Hull favored reciprocal tariff reductions, so the Norwegians had reason to hope that their suggestion might be received favorably by the new administration.[52]

But Congress put a stop to Norwegian hopes. The Revenue Act of 1934 imposed a tax of three cents per pound on whale oil imported into the United States. It was a prohibitive tax that in practice produced no revenue and barred the import of all whale oil. Agricultural interests had pressed for the tax, fearing competition for their vegetable and fish oils. The Roosevelt-Hull administration opposed the tax, but it passed nonetheless.[53] Morgenstierne, Norway's minister to the United States, later said that except for the war years he did not know of any action that so dislocated Norwegian-American trade as the whale oil tax.[54]

Norway lost its valuable American market for whale oil. The United States imported tallow from other countries to supply the market the Norwegians had lost. Unable to sell their whale oil in the United States, Norwegians had to sell where they could. That turned out to be Germany – at substantially lower prices. Germany, however, insisted on clearing agreements that required Norway to take payment for the whale oil in German products. That arrangement meant that Norway had to buy more from Nazi Germany (and less from the United States). That affected various products, but particularly automobiles.[55]

Norway pressed earnestly and persistently in its efforts to persuade the United States to repeal the tax on whale oil. Most prominent in those efforts were Minister Morgenstierne and Hans Bull-Ovrevik of Bergen, who functioned as spokesman for Norwegian whale oil interests. Late in 1937 even Norway's scholarly foreign minister, Dr. Halvdan Koht, pressed the Norwegian case on a visit to the United States.[56] Secretary of State Hull, Assistant Secretary of State Francis B. Sayre, and, to a lesser extent, President Roosevelt responded sympathetically (but ineffectively) to the Norwegian overtures.

Sayre was tremendously impressed by Morgenstierne's efforts. He wrote that Morgenstierne had "probably visited the Department to discuss whale oil a greater number of times than the importance of the question would ordinarily warrant." But rather than "being annoyed at his persistence," the department had "felt a profound sympathy for a man striving hard to bring to a successful conclusion the one big issue in the first part of his incumbency." Sayre considered Morgenstierne "a fine gentleman who has with all propriety worked extremely hard in this case and who has at this stage done all that any diplomatic representative could do."[57]

Among the various remedies they explored, the most direct was the bill introduced in 1935 by Congressman Richard J. Tonry of New York (H.R. 7373) that would have repealed the whale oil tax. Secretary Hull wholly approved the bill and urged the president to give it his support. Roosevelt was concerned about the possible harmful effects it might have on the American whaling fleet and its workers. Hull insisted, however, that so few Americans were involved in whaling that it did not justify the major harm the tax was doing to Norway and to Norwegian-American commercial relations.[58] Secretary of Agriculture Henry A. Wallace advised the president "that the repeal of the excise tax on whale oil would probably not be seriously felt by any branch of domestic agriculture and would be definitely beneficial to some branches." With that, the president gave his support to the Tonry bill.[59]

Nonetheless, the effort to repeal the whale oil tax failed both in the House of Representatives and in the Senate. Congressman Schuyler Bland of Virginia, Senator Walter George of Georgia, and Senator Robert LaFollette of Wisconsin, among others, led the opposition. Among the special interests behind that legislative opposition were the American Farmers' Union, the National Dairy Union, the National Grange, and tallow, cotton seed oil, and fish oil interests. Representative Bland particularly represented Virginia's fish oil industry. Those special interests prevailed in Congress over the wishes of the administration, even though Roosevelt's Democratic party commanded overwhelming majorities in both houses.[60]

Neither the administration nor the Norwegians gave up, however. In 1936 they tried again. That time they attempted to reduce opposition from agricultural and fishing interests by proposing that whale oil admitted to the United States be "so denatured, under Customs supervision at the port of entry, as to render it unfit for edible purposes." That would not hurt the American market for Norwegian whale oil because nearly all of it was used in the manufacture of soap. It would, the administration hoped, reduce opposition from Americans whose products were used largely as edible fats. At the same time Hull pointed out that the tax, by forcing Norway to sell its whale oil in Germany, had sharply cut the German market for American lard; the tax was, Hull contended, actually hurting American agricultural interests rather than helping them. But that effort failed too: the Senate rejected the amendment to exempt denatured whale oil from the tax.[61]

The administration kept trying. But so did the opposition, particularly American fisheries, fish products companies, whaling interests, and maritime workers.[62] That opposition prevailed. Despite their earnest efforts, Secretary Hull and his associates (and the Norwegians) were never able to persuade Congress to repeal the whale oil tax during the Roosevelt administration. That whale oil controversy also managed to kill all efforts to accomplish a Norwegian-American reciprocal trade agreement during the Roosevelt years.

Under the leadership of Secretary Hull, and with the president's support, Congress passed the Reciprocal Trade Agreements Act in June 1934. It authorized the administration to conclude bilateral trade agreements in which the United States could reduce its tariff rates by as much as 50 percent in return for comparable reductions by other countries. Each of those agreements was to include an unconditional most-favored-nation clause extending the tariff reductions to other countries that did not discriminate against the United States in their tariffs.

The governments of both Norway and the United States favored tariff reduction, so it was reasonable to assume that they would quickly conclude a reciprocal trade agreement under the authority of the new law. Norway initiated conversations with the United States looking toward the negotiation of such an agreement as early as 1933, even before Congress passed the Reciprocal Trade Agreements Act. Later it renewed its inquiries along those lines many times. The United States would not undertake negotiations so soon, but it left the door open. And in July 1934 the State Department informed Norway that the United States was prepared to begin negotiations on a reciprocal trade agreement when Morgenstierne returned to the United States in September from a visit to Norway.[63] Diplomats and statesmen on both sides attempted initiatives to get the negotiations under way. Both the State Department and the Norwegian foreign office made detailed preparations for such negotiations.

But those efforts were never able to overcome the huge obstacle that the whale oil tax threw in their path. The tax was so high that it would still be prohibitive even if it were reduced by the 50 percent allowed under the Reciprocal Trade Agreements Act. Consequently Norway saw no advantage in undertaking general reciprocal trade negotiations until or unless the whale oil difficulty was resolved. It proposed that the United States and Norway initiate limited negotiations on whale oil and a few other items. If those negotiations were successful, it might then be possible to negotiate a general trade agreement. Hull and the State Department did not like that idea. If Norway got what it wanted on whale oil in a limited agreement, it might not feel much incentive to make other trade concessions to the United States in the broader negotiations later.[64]

In 1934 the Norwegian government prohibited the importation of motor vehicles except by special import license. Though the Norwegian government denied it, many Americans believed that Norway hoped to use that licensing regulation as a bargaining device to win concessions from the United States on the whale oil tax.[65] Norway also suggested the possibility of a bilateral barter agreement, such as Norwegian whale oil for American wheat. But that conflicted with Hull's preference for multilateral reductions represented by the unconditional most-favored-nation clause in his reciprocal trade agreements.[66] That proposal and other proposals for breaking the log jam all failed. The probing for openings continued without success throughout the decade until war erupted in Europe in 1939.

It was ironic and rather sad that two democracies friendly toward each other, both headed by governments that favored tariff reduction and both eager to negotiate an agreement, failed completely in those efforts. From 1935 onward Norway's Labor government was handicapped by its politically essential alliance with the Agrarian party. That small party opposed tariff concessions on agricultural products from the United States. On the other side of the Atlantic, Secretary of State Hull was passionately committed to multilateral tariff reduction through reciprocal trade agreements. He had the support of the powerful president under whom he served, and the Roosevelt-Hull Democratic party commanded huge majorities in both houses of Congress. But shifting minority interests (agricultural, fishing, and whaling), drawing support from both major parties, successfully blocked repeal of the whale oil tax in any form.

The combination of the continuing Hannevig controversy, severe immigration restrictions, the prohibitive tax on one of Norway's most valuable export products, and the resulting inability to negotiate a mutually satisfactory reciprocal trade agreement traced a troubled pattern for relations between Norway and the United States in the 1930s. There were understandable reasons for the positions taken on both sides on all the issues. But the essentially negative positions taken by the powerful United States blocked courses of action pressed by the weak Scandinavian state.

In a 1934 despatch American minister Hoffman Philip described Norway as "a stout, nationalistic-minded little country with an equable population of frugal, hard-headed folk, temperamentally ready to make great sacrifice for a matter of conceived principle or injustice, but generally amenable to reason in important questions if approached with tact and intelligent consideration."[67] Those qualities were not enough for a weak state contending with a major power. They were not enough in World War I, and not enough between the wars. Few should have been surprised to discover that they would not be enough as the clouds of war once again loomed on the horizon.

IN the 1920s and 1930s both Norway and the United States, in their separate and independent ways, were dedicated to peace and non-involvement in foreign wars. Each shaped its policies to accomplish those goals in different ways. Norway was a member of the League of Nations throughout its stormy history; the United States never joined the League. Most people in all parties in both countries opposed involvement in foreign wars. Each country determined to guard its independence in shaping its foreign policy.

Both Norway and the United States were parties to multilateral approaches designed to preserve peace, including the Nine Power Pact of 1922 and the Kellogg-Briand Pact of Paris of 1928. Neither of those pacts involved commitments to collective security responsibilities. Both Norway and the United States sent delegates to major conferences concerned with disarmament or peace, including the World Disarmament Conference at Geneva in 1932, and the Brussels Conference in 1937. For the most part, however, Norway and the United States shaped their policies independently of each other.

As war drew near, Norwegians and their leaders from all parties united in their determined commitment to neutrality and non-involvement. In the United States opinion was not quite so united or so determined. But the dominant view in both political parties favored neutrality and noninvolvement. President Roosevelt and Secretary Hull wanted the United States to play a larger and more positive multilateral role in trying to preserve peace and security. They were restrained, however, by noninterventionist sentiments that dominated American public opinion. Most people in both the United States and Norway favored neutrality and noninvolvement in the wars that erupted in Asia in 1937 and in Europe in 1939.[68]

The United States, in the person of Secretary of State Charles Evans Hughes, took the lead in calling the Washington Conference of 1921–22. The Five Power Naval Treaty it negotiated limited the tonnage of capital ships of the world's leading naval powers. That conference also concluded the Nine Power Treaty endorsing the Open Door policy for China in East Asia. Norway did not participate in the conference, but it formally adhered to the Nine Power Treaty, as did the United States.[69]

In 1928, in response to a French proposal, the United States took the lead in negotiating the multilateral Kellogg-Briand Pact of Paris outlawing war as an instrument of national policy. Norway was one of many countries from all over the world that ratified the pact. It did so with enthusiasm and with praise for the United States in initiating that peace effort.[70]

In 1929 Norway and the United States concluded a new bilateral Treaty of Arbitration to replace the one that had expired the year before.[71] Both countries sent delegates to the World Disarmament Conference at Geneva, which began its long deliberations in 1932. And both shared in the failure of that conference to accomplish arms limitation.[72]

There were many in the United States who deeply regretted the failure of the Senate to approve American membership in the League of Nations. They included Franklin D. Roosevelt, who as the Democratic vice presidential candidate in 1920 campaigned for joining the League. After that election, however, neither party and none of America's presidents – Republican or Democratic – proposed American membership.[73]

Norway had joined the League of Nations at the close of World War I. The failure of the United States to join, and the absence for some time of other major states including the Soviet Union and Germany, reduced Norwegian optimism about its likely effectiveness. During the 1920s and early 1930s the Labor party opposed the League.[74] And as the League proved ineffective in the increasingly alarming international crises of the 1930s, Norwegians grew more pessimistic about its capacity to preserve peace.

Nonetheless, Norway remained a member of the League of Nations throughout. It sent its most distinguished statesmen to represent its interests in League deliberations, including Dr. Fridtjof Nansen, Dr. Christian L. Lange, Liberal party leader Johan L. Mowinckel, Conservative party leader Carl J. Hambro, and (after the Labor party won control of the Norwegian government in 1935) Dr. Halvdan Koht, foreign minister in Nygaardsvold's Labor government.[75] In 1930 Norway won a nonpermanent seat on the Council of the League of Nations.[76]

The League wrestled with a wide range of problems in world affairs. One of the alarming crises directly endangering world peace, the Italian-Ethiopian war of 1935–36 in east Africa, demonstrated the League's ineffectiveness. For Norway it made clear both the risks involved in, and the harmful consequences of, its participation in economic sanctions that the League imposed on Italy. That eye-opening experience (and perhaps Labor party reservations all along about the League) moved Norway to reconsider the roles it would, and would not, play in the League's peacekeeping efforts.

In October 1935, in accord with the League's decisions, the Norwegian government, under Prime Minister Nygaardsvold and Foreign Minister Koht, forbad the export to Italy of the articles covered by League sanctions. That list was very similar to the list of products embargoed independently by the United States for export to Italy and Ethiopia under provisions of the American Neutrality Act of 1935. League sanctions did not directly affect Norwegian exports to Italy very much; Norway did not export significant quantities of arms or war goods to Italy or to any other country. And tankers in Norway's merchant marine profited from carrying oil to Italy.[77]

The indirect consequences for Norway, however, were harmful. Mussolini's Italy retaliated by banning the sale of Norwegian fish and fish products in Italy. Fishermen in northern Norway depended heavily on the Italian market for dried and salted fish. The whole experience hurt Norwegian fishermen economically. Moreover, the League action did not prevent Mussolini's fascist Italy from conquering the primitive African country of Ethiopia. As American Minister Biddle wrote, "Professor Koht considers that Norway will be more adversely affected by sanctions than any of the other Scandinavian countries and has perhaps gone further than any of them in adhering to the principles of the League in the application of sanctions."[78]

That unpleasant experience led Norwegians of all political complexions to have second thoughts about their role in the League of Nations. They became aware that sanctions could be a two-edged sword, hurting the countries that imposed the sanctions as well as the country against which they were directed. Dr. Koht of the Labor party, Mowinckel of the Liberal party, and Hambro of the Conservative party all agreed that Norway should remain a member of the League of Nations. They agreed that Norway should encourage the League in its peaceful efforts to prevent war. But they also agreed that Norway would never share in any League of Nations military sanctions. They became disillusioned about the effectiveness and wisdom of economic sanctions. Norway remained in the League of Nations, but it was unlikely that it would cooperate with any League sanctions in the future.[79]

A whole succession of alarming international crises in Europe in the last half of the 1930s further demonstrated the ineffectiveness of the League of Nations and the growing danger of war. The remilitarization of the Rhineland by Hitler's Nazi Germany in 1936, the Spanish civil war from 1936 to 1939, the Anschluss incorporating Austria into greater Germany early in 1938, the Munich conference in the autumn of 1938 when Britain's Neville Chamberlain appeased Hitler by yielding Czechoslovakia's Sudetenland to Nazi Germany, and Hitler's dismemberment of the rest of Czechoslovakia in March 1939 in violation of his promises at Munich each produced terrifying headlines that warned that another horribly destructive world war could be in the offing.

The League of Nations played only a negligible role in coping with those crises. Leading statesmen bypassed it, ignored it, or made only token gestures in its direction. The foreign ministers of the Scandinavian governments met from time to time to discuss matters of common concern, but they carried little weight and were particularly preoccupied with preserving their own neutrality in the event of war.[80] The "Oslo states," including both Scandinavia and the Low Countries of northwestern Europe, held various meetings. But they focused largely on trade and tariff concerns rather than on political, diplomatic, or military defense matters.[81]

President Roosevelt and Secretary Hull wanted to have the United States play an active and positive role in helping to preserve peace. They were handicapped, however, by the timidness of European leaders, who gave them little to work with abroad, and by isolationist strength in America, which limited their freedom of action in proposing or carrying through peacekeeping initiatives. Within those severe limits Roosevelt and Hull groped ineffectively for actions they might undertake that would reduce the likelihood of war in Europe. Their various initiatives encouraged some Europeans to hope that under Roosevelt the United States might one day play a larger peacekeeping role. But both individually and in their totality the American gestures were feeble and futile; they did not slow Europe's march toward war.[82]

In 1935, 1936, and 1937 Congress passed, and President Roosevelt signed into law, neutrality acts designed to keep the United States out of foreign wars by restricting both America's economic involvement and the president's freedom of action in the face of foreign wars. Though opinions were divided, in the 1930s most Americans preferred such legislative action to assure noninvolvement rather than the administration's efforts to prevent war abroad. The so-called "permanent" Neutrality Act of 1937 was law when World War II began in Asia in 1937, and it was still law when World War II began in Europe in 1939.[83]

In Norway the people and their leaders in all major parties

were united in their general foreign policy views. In speech after
speech, statement after statement, Norwegian leaders reempha-
sized their determination to remain neutral and stay out of any war
that might erupt. Many assumed that Britain would protect them
in the event of war. On May 31, 1938, after the Anschluss but
before Munich, the Storting's Foreign Affairs Committee proposed
the adoption of a neutrality declaration upholding "the right of the
country to maintain complete and unconditional neutrality in any
war which it does not endorse as an action of the League of Nations." Koht, Mowinckel, and Hambro, from the three leading parties, all endorsed the statement. Foreign Minister Koht told the
Storting that "Norway has both right and duty to state that this
country will not be involved in any particular conflict and that we
ourselves will decide whether we will participate in any action of
the League of Nations." The Storting promptly passed the declaration unanimously.[84]

When Nazi Germany invited the four Scandinavian countries
to enter into nonaggression pacts in 1939, Norway (after conferring with the other Scandinavian governments) politely declined
on the grounds that it did not feel threatened by Germany. In its
determination to maintain neutrality it would not conclude nonaggression pacts with any country. Norway's leaders and people were
almost desperately determined to guard their country's neutrality
at any cost and to give no country the slightest justification for
war.[85]

OVER the years the royal family had won a highly respected and
much-loved status in Norway. King Haakon expressed his views
freely in private but never involved himself in Norwegian politics.
He genuinely believed in democracy, abhorred pomp and ceremony, was unpretentious and open in his style, and had good judgment. Many Labor party leaders had opposed the monarchy earlier, but they, too, were won over and gained real respect and
affection for the king.

Reflecting her English background and the experience of
World War I, Queen Maud was strongly anti-German. King
Haakon shared her general attitude but was a bit more detached.

The king thought England's appeasement policies under Prime Minister Chamberlain would not produce satisfactory results. In his opinion Hitler's government could not be relied on. According to Mrs. Harriman he believed that "a policy of neutrality is the only one compatible with the safeguarding of Norwegian interests." In dozens of conversations over the years King Haakon made abundantly evident his friendly attitude toward both England and the United States.[86]

In 1938 Queen Maud died in London following an operation. Mrs. Harriman, who had known her both officially and informally, represented the United States at the funeral services. The queen was buried in a mausoleum under the chapel of the historic Akershus Fortress in Oslo.[87]

President Roosevelt at various times had invited King Haakon's son, Crown Prince Olav, and his wife, Crown Princess Märtha, to visit the United States. Prince Olav was as well liked as his father. Educated at the Military School in Norway and at Balliol College at Oxford University in his mother's England, he was handsome, friendly, and athletic. He loved skiing and was exceptionally skilled at sailing. More important, he shared his father's values and his qualities of character. His marriage in 1929 to Princess Märtha of the Swedish royal family was well received in Norway.[88]

Through Mrs. Harriman, President Roosevelt again invited the crown prince and princess to visit America in 1939, on the occasion of the world's fairs in both New York and San Francisco. In extending the invitation, President Roosevelt specifically expressed the belief "that democracies of the world [should] keep in close personal and official touch with each other—and Norway and the United States have always had close associations." The royal couple accepted the invitation.[89]

After detailed preparations they set out aboard the *Oslofjord* on their great adventure to the United States (which neither had visited before), arriving in New York on April 27. They were guests of President and Mrs. Roosevelt at their home in Hyde Park. (Activities included an informal picnic with hot dogs and potato salad.) Later the president received them at the White House in Washington. During their two and a half months in the

United States the young couple traveled across the country to the Pacific coast and back. They covered some fifteen thousand miles and visited thirty-four states. They especially toured those parts of the United States where many Norwegian-Americans lived, including Michigan, Wisconsin, Minnesota, Iowa, the Dakotas, and Washington State. Everywhere they were received warmly, and they left good impressions wherever they went. They, in turn, received highly favorable impressions of the United States, the American people, and especially President Roosevelt. Both the crown prince and his father warmly thanked the president for the hospitality they had enjoyed in America.[90]

Over that delightful adventure, however, and over all the world that summer of 1939, hung the ominous dark cloud of approaching war. At the dinner given at the palace on the occasion of the return of the royal couple, Mrs. Harriman was the only diplomat present. Prince Olav personally escorted her to her place, and she was seated next to Foreign Minister Koht. That distinguished Norwegian scholar and historian was, according to Mrs. Harriman, "very pessimistic about the European situation." He predicted that "there will be war in September." Unfortunately he was correct. King Haakon, too, was disturbed by the international outlook.[91]

Their concerns were fully justified. Less than six weeks later, on September 1, 1939, Nazi Germany invaded Poland, and World War II became a terrible reality in Europe. Both the Norwegian and the American traditions of neutrality and noninvolvement in European wars were soon to be brought to a violent end.

*May 13, 1942, Wilhelm T. de Munthe de Morgen-
stierne, Norway's first ambassador to the United
States, presents his credentials to President Franklin
D. Roosevelt. Also present are H.R.H. Crown Prince
Olav (left) and Prime Minister Johan Nygaardsvold.
(Norwegian Official Photo. Courtesy of Mrs. Solveig
Morgenstierne Padilla)*

August 3, 1942, Norwegians worldwide celebrate King Haakon's seventieth birthday. In London's Hyde Park, King Haakon, with Crown Prince Olav and Crown Princess Märtha, salutes a parade of Norwegian forces. (Norwegian Official Photo. Courtesy of Mrs. Solveig Morgenstierne Padilla)

*Laurits S. Swenson, U.S.
Minister to Norway, 1911–
1913 and 1921–1930.
(Courtesy of Amb. Robert. D.
Stuart, Jr.)*

*Florence J. Harriman, U.S.
Minister to Norway, 1937–
1940. (Courtesy of Amb.
Robert D. Stuart, Jr.)*

Anthony J. D. Biddle, Jr., U.S. Minister to Norway, 1935–1937 and 1941–1942; U.S. Ambassador to Norway, 1942–1944. (Courtesy of Amb. Robert D. Stuart, Jr.)

Charles Ulrick Bay, U.S. Ambassador to Norway, 1946–1953. (Courtesy of Amb. Robert D. Stuart, Jr.)

4

Oslo and Pearl Harbor

BOTH Norway and the United States had long traditions of neutrality and noninvolvement in European wars. Norwegians united in their determination to preserve that tradition when World War II erupted in Europe in 1939. Most Americans similarly hoped they could stay out of the war. Both counties failed in those efforts. Both were forced violently into the war through surprise attacks by Axis states: Nazi Germany attacked Norway at Oslo and other points on April 9, 1940; Japan attacked the United States at Pearl Harbor in Hawaii on December 7, 1941. Those attacks brought war to both countries and shattered their cherished traditions of noninvolvement. Neither could ever go back to these traditions again.[1]

The two countries had much closer relations with Great Britain during World War II than they had with each other. Nonetheless, the separate but shared experiences of Norway and the United States during World War II drew those two North Atlantic democracies closer together. World War II destroyed much, but it changed even more than it destroyed. Among the changes were those in relations between Norway and the United States and in the roles of both of those democracies in world affairs.

BOTH the Norwegian and United States governments proclaimed their neutrality at the beginning of World War II. Both were neutrals from the time the fighting began on September 1, 1939, until Nazi Germany attacked Norway more than seven months later on April 9, 1940. Sympathies in both democracies were with Great Britain and the other victims of German aggression. The circumstances of the two countries, however, and the tone and style of their policies differed.

Norway was small, weak, and vulnerable. Even if it had marshaled its maximum power and military capacity, it could not have made much difference in the course of the war. The possibility that one or another of the major belligerents might take preemptive military action against Norway was very real. Maintaining its neutrality was a bit like walking a tightrope in a tornado. But Norwegians united in their determination to preserve Norwegian neutrality.

Foreign Minister Halvdan Koht was a brilliant scholar and learned historian. He had traveled widely in both Europe and America. He was almost desperately determined to preserve Norwegian neutrality at whatever cost. He would do nothing that might provoke attack or give any of the belligerents the slightest cause to question or challenge Norway's neutrality. In his efforts he had the united support of the Norwegian people despite their differences on other matters.[2]

Americans, too, wanted to stay out of the European war. Millions were as determined in their noninterventionist convictions as Dr. Koht was in his. Despite modern military technology, the oceans still provided a substantial geographic barrier, which complicated matters for any potential military assailant. America's large population, its highly productive economy, and its power, both actual and potential, further reduced its vulnerability to military attack.

At the same time, however, that population, productivity, and power made it obvious that the United States could make a difference in the war. Belligerents had to take the United States and its possible policies into consideration in shaping their courses of action. Such considerations made it inevitable that the British and French would seek American aid or involvement. It led Axis leaders to try, within limits, to avoid any provocation that might draw the United States into the war against them.

The awareness that the United States could make a difference was shared by many in America. Consequently American commitment to neutrality and noninvolvement was less united and, for many, less determined than in Norway. President Roosevelt proclaimed American neutrality, but he did not call for neutrality in thought, as Wilson had done twenty-five years earlier. From the beginning Roosevelt considered the defeat of Nazi Germany essential to world—and American—peace and security. He hoped it could be accomplished without American military involvement in the war. But within the limits set by public and congressional opinion he determined to use America's resources to help the British and French defeat Hitler. In that determination the president had the support of much of the leadership elite in the urban Northeast and of a large part of the Democratic South.[3]

During the early months of the war Roosevelt was cautious in his efforts to aid the allies and he masked his efforts behind secrecy and paeans to peace and noninvolvement. As the Axis challenges grew more menacing, as the United States built its own power, and as the allies suffered alarming reverses, Roosevelt's language and actions became bolder. The American people followed his lead—all the while continuing to oppose an American declaration of war.[4]

In September 1939 the Norwegian government called a special session of the Storting, and President Roosevelt called a special session of Congress. In Norway the government took various actions to conserve needed supplies. There was talk of the possibility of a coalition government. But the king's speech from the throne emphasized that "Norway must preserve absolute neutrality in this war." Few dissented from that conviction.[5]

In the United States President Roosevelt asked Congress to revise the Neutrality Act by repealing the arms embargo and by reenacting cash-and-carry that had expired three months earlier. He urged those actions in the name of American noninvolvement. But repeal of the arms embargo would have—and did have—the practical effect of allowing Britain and France to buy arms and munitions in the United States. British command of the seas made certain that those arms and munitions would not go to Britain's enemies. Though Roosevelt did not identify it in those terms at the time, revision of the Neutrality Act was an early step in his efforts to aid the allies short-of-war.[6]

While Congress deliberated on revision of the Neutrality Act (and before cash-and-carry was reenacted), a drama unfolded on the seas involving three neutrals (the United States, Norway, and the Soviet Union) and two belligerents (Germany and Great Britain). On October 5, 1939, a German pocket battleship, the *Deutschland*, sank the British S. S. *Stonegate* off Newfoundland and took its crew on board. Four days later, on October 9, the *Deutschland* stopped a five-thousand-ton American freighter, the *City of Flint*, en route from the United States to England. It carried a cargo of tractors, grain, fruit, oil, leather, wax, and other commodities. The Germans considered the cargo contraband, put a twenty-one-man prize crew on board along with the thirty-eight crew members of the *Stonegate*, and sent it on its way to Hamburg, Germany. The officer in command of the German prize crew informed the captain of the *City of Flint*, Joseph A. Gainard, that there would be no difficulties if they carried on as usual; if there were any trouble, he would put them in lifeboats and sink the ship. There was no violence.[7]

Instead of going to Hamburg, however, the *City of Flint* sailed to Norway. Before it reached that neutral country, the German crew painted over the name of the ship with a new name, *Alf*, and replaced the American flag with a German flag. On October 20 the ship put in at the harbor at Tromsø, on the northwest coast of Norway. The Germans turned over the crew of the *Stonegate* to the British consul there, took on water and other supplies, and departed the next day, October 21.[8]

As the Department of State explained it, under international law as spelled out in the Hague Convention of 1907, "a prize may be brought into a neutral port only on account of unseaworthiness, stress of weather or want of fuel or provisions, and is required to leave as soon as the circumstances that justified its entry are at an end. Failure to leave puts upon the neutral power the obligation to release it with its officers and crew and to intern the prize crew." The Norwegian foreign office described its handling of the matter as "correct in every respect. It was correct to permit the boat to enter Tromsø and to refuse it permission to remain there for a longer period." The British captain believed that the Norwegian authorities were responsible for winning release of the English crew in Tromsø.[9]

Instead of continuing on to Hamburg, however, the *City of Flint* on October 22 sailed to Murmansk in the northern Soviet Union, a neutral country. The Soviet officials handled the matter much less expeditiously, efficiently, and courteously than the Norwegian officials had. Not until October 28 did the *City of Flint* depart with both its American crew and the German prize crew on board.[10]

After departing Soviet waters, the *City of Flint* moved south along the coast within Norwegian territorial waters past Tromsø and Bergen to Haugesund, where the officer in charge of the prize crew believed he had been ordered to anchor. Sixty-two-year-old Rear Admiral Carsten Tank-Nielsen handled matters for the Norwegians by telephone from his home in Bergen. He was from an old seafaring family and had had wide experience at sea. With the *City of Flint* in neutral Norwegian territorial waters, under international law the admiral had authority to free it. On Friday evening, November 3, he waited until the last of the many newspaper reporters had abandoned their watch and the German officer and his prize crew were asleep. At midnight he sent a party of thirty sailors under an officer and petty officers from the nearby Norwegian ship, *Olav Tryggvason*, to board the *City of Flint*. They quietly and efficiently took over the ship, arrested the prize crew, and transferred them to the *Olav*. Not a shot was fired.[11]

The American seamen had been aboard the *City of Flint* continuously throughout the entire episode. All were restive, and a few were almost rebellious. Under orders from the owners, and with tactful assistance from Mrs. Harriman, all the members of the crew signed a statement that the ship was properly equipped to proceed on its voyage. Eventually the cargo of the *City of Flint* was unloaded and warehoused at Haugesund. The ship took on a cargo of iron ore at Narvik for ballast and returned to the United States under German assurances of safe passage. Norway released the prize crew to Germany.[12]

With the exception of a few of the more troublesome crew members of the *City of Flint*, all the Americans and Norwegians involved in the episode conducted themselves magnificently, including Captain Gainard, Mrs. Harriman, and Maurice P. Dunlap, the American consul in Bergen. Rear Admiral Tank-Nielsen and Commander Dynsnor and his sailors, who took over the *City of Flint* that night in Haugesund, also performed commendably. Both Norway and the United States had, with dignity and in accord with accepted international law, preserved their neutrality. Not a life was lost in the incident. Haugesund experienced momentary prosperity from the money spent there. Stavanger complained that apples from the cargo of the *City of Flint* destroyed its local market for home-grown apples.[13]

Captain Gainard was awarded the Navy Cross for his distinguished service in the episode. In 1943, in the midst of the war, a German submarine torpedoed the *City of Flint*, killing seventeen crewmen. Later that year Captain Gainard, in command of a navy transport, was himself killed in action.[14]

Even as the *City of Flint* episode was reaching its final phases, war in Europe was taking new alarming forms for Norway. After Germany (and the Soviet Union) completed the conquest of Poland, the war in central and western Europe quieted into what was called a "phony war" or "sitzkrieg." But at that very moment the Soviet Union took actions in eastern Europe and the Baltic that kept war fears alive. As part of its efforts to build its strength against a possible German assault later, the Soviet Union made demands and brought pressures on the Baltic countries of Latvia, Lithuania, and Estonia that eventually destroyed their independence and incorporated them in the Soviet Union.

Finland bravely resisted Soviet demands. In November 1939 the Soviet Union threw its massive military forces against that small Scandinavian country in an undeclared war. The Finns fought back fiercely. Not only was Finland a fellow Scandinavian state and a member of the "Oslo states" that included Norway, but also it had a common boundary with Norway's Finnmark region in the far north. The Soviet aggression against Finland pointed in Norway's direction.

Most people in Norway rejected communism. But many socialists and some liberals viewed the Soviet Union as representing an ideology that at least had laudable humanitarian and working-class concerns. Those sympathies evaporated quickly, however, when Norwegian national interests and security were endangered. Norwegians wholly sympathized with Finland against the Soviet Union. Young men in Norway volunteered to fight for Finland against Russia. Norwegians provided Red Cross and other aid to Finland. Press editorials praised the Finns and denounced Soviet aggression.

Norway did not abandon its commitment to neutrality, but Norwegians were much less inhibited in objecting to Soviet aggression in Finland than they had been in objecting to Nazi aggression when Germany gobbled up Austria, Czechoslovakia, and Poland. From the Norwegian perspective the differences in the two situations did not rest with ideology; they rested, instead, with conceptions of Norwegian national interest and survival.[15]

Americans, too, felt great sympathy for Finland. Its independence, accomplished in 1917, was consistent with Wilson's commitment to the right of self-determination. Moreover, Americans saw Finland as the only European country that did not default on payment of its "war debts" to the United States. President Roosevelt, members of Congress, and the press warmly praised the courageous Finns and favored aid for their struggle to resist the Soviet assault.[16]

American aid, however, was "too little and too late." American isolationism was still strong. Most sympathized with Finland, but not to the extent of risking involvement in a European war.[17] Ironically Norwegians, who tenaciously guarded their own neutrality no matter what happened to weak countries that fell victim to Hitler's aggression, were terribly unhappy when the United States persisted in its noninterventionist policies in the Russo-Finnish war. They wanted the United States to extend much more substantial aid to the Finns—and to do it quickly.

In a letter to Crown Prince Olav, President Roosevelt clearly explained his—and the American—perspective on the Russo-Finnish war. He lamented the Soviet Union's "brutal attack on Finland," but "the only ray of light" he could see was "the magnificent defense that is being put up by Finland." He reminded the crown prince "how difficult" it was in the United States "to take a more concrete and practical part in helping Finland—or, for that matter, in helping Norway, Sweden and Denmark in the event that they, too, are attacked." There was "almost solid sympathy for Scandinavia in the United States," and Americans wanted "to be helpful." But even in the case of Finland, which had "paid her debt with regularity," FDR was "still confronted by the isolationists who talk much of their sympathy but throw every obstacle into the way of anything that goes further than Red Cross aid." He wrote that if "things should go from bad to worse," and the crown prince and princess should think it advisable to send their children out of Norway, he hoped they would consider sending them to America for the Roosevelts to look after. He promised that they "could make them very happy and safe at Hyde Park." In the meantime, however, Roosevelt concluded that "all we can do is to pray that things will grow no worse and that before the year is over we shall have a return to peace."[18] The president's prayers may have won long-term response, but in the short run—"before the year is over"—things went from bad to worse for Norwegians and for many others.

The president's letter explained things much as they were so far as American aid was concerned. But he may have been a bit too eager to blame the isolationists. Hugh S. Cumming in the Department of State wrote to Mrs. Harriman that "even among the higher officers of the Department there are some who are quite strongly opposed not only to proposals for loans or credits for the purchase of armaments by Finland, but also the sale to Finland or to Sweden of military supplies from American Government stocks." Even action on a proposed Export-Import Bank loan to Norway moved slowly.[19] That delay elicited sharp criticism from Norwegians.

Mrs. Harriman was troubled by "the bitter feeling" in Norway that was "being expressed in the Press, and by people in general, towards America." She wrote that Norwegians seemed to believe that the United States had "let Finland down by not giving it quicker and more effective help." She received "scores of letters every week, and visits every day, from people begging" her to ask the president "to come to Finland's rescue before it is too late!" Among Mrs. Harriman's visitors was "a member of the Storting, the editor of a newspaper, and others who should have more understanding of the situation in the United States than they have." Even

Carl J. Hambro, president of the Storting, criticized the "small amount of money that has gone to Finland." Mrs. Harriman thought it was "an hysterical condition here caused by the fear of Russia's moving on to Norway if Finland should fall." She complained that "much of the criticism is founded on radio news which seems to originate in England"—a frequent allegation among Americans in Norway.[20]

To one Norwegian critic of America's policies Mrs. Harriman explained that "ninety-eight percent of the people of the United States are in sympathy with Finland, but there are laws that must be observed, and democracies of the size of the United States move slowly." She noted the irony that "most of the opposition to the loan in Congress came from the States where Scandinavians predominate." She conceded that America had its faults, "but a lack of generosity cannot be counted as one of the American people's shortcomings."[21]

To a friend in the State Department Mrs. Harriman wrote that Norwegian criticism of the United States for its policy toward the Russo-Finnish war was "the attitude of a frightened child, calling for help to the biggest person he knows, and not understanding why everything isn't done at once, and to the full extent of his hopes." She understood "their terror that Norway will be drawn in, or attacked," but she thought their abuse of the United States was "impolitic, to say the least." She regretted that nothing was published about what the United States sent through Norway in the way of munitions and airplanes, and again she complained that "most of the erroneous reports seem to have originated in London and Brussels."[22] Norwegians were impatient and intolerant of American neutrality and noninterventionist policies, even as those same Norwegians tenaciously persisted in their own neutrality relative to Hitler's war in Europe.

The Soviet Union triumphed over Finland in the spring of 1940 and took what it wanted. Finland survived as a sovereign state, and Soviet troops did not cross the Norwegian border. But the whole terrifying episode underscored a matter that Norway had neglected for years. Modern Norway had never maintained formidable military forces. Both Liberal and Labor governments had neglected military preparations. Not until the latter part of the

1930s did the Norwegian government set in motion efforts to modernize and expand its armed forces. Those efforts were speeded by the alarm caused by the Russo-Finnish war.

Defense preparations by the Labor government under Nygaardsvold and Koht moved slowly, however.[23] Bernt Balchen was an American of Norwegian descent active in Norwegian aviation. He was a representative in Norway for the United Aircraft Export Corporation of Connecticut. In 1936 he visited the United States to study the products of American military aviation, and he returned to Norway enthusiastic about certain aircraft. But nothing much happened. In 1935 and again in 1936 Colonel Trygve Klingenberg, chief of the Norwegian Army Air Service, also visited American factories and facilities. He, too, was favorably impressed. But like Balchen, he got no action.[24]

The death of Colonel Klingenberg in 1937 interrupted the progress of the defense efforts. Colonel Thomas H. Gulliksen succeeded him and shared his attitudes. But he was no more effective in getting action.[25]

Near the end of 1937 Norway bought six Gloster-Gladiator planes from England; later it bought six more. In 1938 it bought four Italian twin-engine Caproni planes and six German Heinkel planes. But none of those airplanes was suitable for modern military combat. They were either obsolete or appropriate for little more than training and observation purposes.[26]

Early in 1939 various Norwegian military officers spoke out publicly on Norwegian defense and its requirements. Their comments were not encouraging. As Mrs. Harriman reported their views, "There was a possibility of a surprise German attack on Norway for the purpose of establishing a naval and air base against an English blockade. There was an equal possibility of a similar move on England's part to block such a German objective." As she reported their views, "Norway was powerless to defend itself against such attacks. With the meager Norwegian Navy and the inadequate coastal defense existing today, a foreign power could establish itself in the fortifications in the outer Oslo fjord and Kristiansand and Bergen, in fact in any strategical spot along the Norwegian coast, without firing a shot. The Navy Yard at Horten and the Sola Air Field at Stavanger were equally defenseless. The

Air Force was an illusion." She pointed out that the Norwegian government had "opposed armament on any scale broader than what one can regard as a 'neutrality guard', what is clearly inadequate under present uncertain world conditions." It was voting only comparatively small increases for national defense – "considered completely insufficient by the parties in opposition to the Government, and by senior military officials." Mrs. Harriman concluded that "Norway has not the financial capacity to expend sums sufficient to provide defense for a country with a long and difficult coast line or, for that matter, to protect its principal commercial asset, its merchant marine." As she understood it, "The control of the air has now become a factor of military importance. Thinking Norwegians fear that despite their efforts to maintain neutrality, the broadened scope of a future European war may quickly and inevitably involve them with unforeseeable and possibly disastrous consequences for themselves."[27] That gloomy analysis was absolutely correct at the time, and it was still correct a year later.

In the summer of 1939, just before the war erupted in Europe, Norway ordered twelve Curtiss P-36 pursuit planes in the United States. Mrs. Harriman wrote to FDR near the end of 1939 asking about the possibility of having the United States sell Norway some of its old destroyers. The president replied, however, that the United States had none to spare and that sale of destroyers was "prohibited by law."[28] Eight months later President Roosevelt gave fifty overage destroyers to England in exchange for bases in British possessions in the Western Hemisphere.

Early in 1940 the Norwegian government sent a mission under Captain Birger F. Motzfeldt to the United States to buy military airplanes and other equipment for the Norwegian army and navy. King Haakon wrote to President Roosevelt asking his help for the mission, and Mrs. Harriman wrote to General George C. Marshall, Army Chief of Staff, seeking his help. President Roosevelt drew in Henry Morgenthau's Department of the Treasury and its procurement division, much as he had done for a French purchase mission earlier. Captain Motzfeldt and his colleagues won a warm reception in the United States and were shown what they wanted to see. By the end of March 1940 the Norwegians had placed orders for various military airplanes, airplane engines, and other equipment—including more P-36 single-engine pursuit planes. All of that equipment, however, was scheduled for delivery in the latter part of 1940 and early 1941.[29]

Unfortunately Hitler would not delay the German attack on Norway until then. Norway had waited too long to do too little in the way of building up its military defenses. When Nazi Germany attacked on April 9, 1940, Norway was only able to mobilize an army of some seventeen thousand men. Its navy, designed for coastal defense, numbered about 750 officers and men. They manned a fleet of obsolete ships consisting of nine destroyers, nine submarines, a couple of minelayers, a few torpedo boats and patrol craft, and not much else. The Norwegian air force had some three hundred aviators and only 115 airplanes, none of them modern combat planes. Nineteen newly delivered Curtiss P-36s were still in their crates. Another 150,000 men had had some military training, but most of them were never mobilized.[30] Norway's belated military preparations were entirely inadequate.

On March 30, 1940, the American consul in Bergen, Maurice P. Dunlap, attended a dinner given by the German consul general there. The other guests were all Norwegians. In the course of the evening the host proposed a toast to "Peace and Mutual Understanding." The consul general visited at length with Dunlap, emphasizing the German desire for mutual understanding. He hoped that the just-completed diplomatic mission to European capitals by America's Under Secretary of State Sumner Welles might contribute to such understanding.[31]

On April 5 the German minister in Oslo showed "a peace film" to a formal gathering of officials of the Norwegian foreign office that he had invited. The film turned out to be a terrifying documentary of the Luftwaffe's assault on Warsaw. The minister explained that it was designed to show what happened to a country that resisted Nazi attempts to "defend it from England." Norwegian Foreign Minister Koht was not there. He and the French minister were guests at a dinner given by Mrs. Harriman. It had been a hard day for him—he had had sessions with the German, French, and British ministers—but he had no intimation of what was coming for Norway. The next day the German minister invited Mrs. Harriman to dinner on April 19. He also invited Dr. Koht and the

Danish and Swedish ministers and their wives.[32]

On April 8 the British laid mines in Norwegian territorial waters near Narvik, the port from which Swedish iron ore was shipped to Germany. By telephone the American legation in Copenhagen informed the legation in Oslo of the movement of a large German fleet. Norwegians were comforted by the widely held belief that the British navy controlled the seas adjoining Norway. No one suspected that Norway was the destination of the German fleet. That fact did not become apparent until very early the next morning.[33]

AT three o'clock on Tuesday morning, April 9, 1940, Mrs. Harriman was awakened by a telephone call from the British minister to Norway. He provided the first word she had received that German warships were steaming up the Oslo fjord toward Norway's capital city. She promptly telephoned Norwegian Foreign Minister Koht. He confirmed that ships were approaching; he assumed they were German. The American legation notified Washington and Stockholm. Dr. Koht informed her that the Norwegian government was leaving at seven in the morning by special train for Hamar to the north. He invited Mrs. Harriman to go with them.[34]

The American minister could not get ready soon enough to make the train. But as quickly as possible she, a maid, a clerk, and a driver loaded their luggage (and the code book) into a trusty Ford and headed north in pursuit of the fleeing Norwegian government. The wives and children of American legation and consular officers set out for Sweden. American personnel sealed the British and French legations. Raymond E. Cox, first secretary, took over responsibilities for the American legation in Oslo.[35]

Norwegian military forces were weak, unprepared, and surprised. The Germans seized Oslo with no real fight. They had hoped to gain a semblance of legitimacy by capturing Norway's king and government and controlling them with the power of a triumphant German army. It never worked out that way. Aged guns and torpedoes at Fort Oscarsborg surprised the Germans by sinking their heavy cruiser, the *Blücher*, as it steamed up the Oslo Fjord. That resistance delayed the Germans briefly and gave the king and government time to flee from Oslo north to Hamar on their special train.[36]

The Storting, meeting first in Hamar and later in Elverum further east, fully sustained the government in rejecting German demands. It voted unanimously to authorize the Nygaardsvold ministry to govern Norway until such time as it and the leaders of the Storting could summon an ordinary meeting of that body. King Haakon refused the German demand that he dismiss the Nygaardsvold ministry and name Vidkun Quisling to head the government; he threatened to abdicate rather than yield to German demands. The Norwegian government fully supported him. The Germans and Quisling failed in their efforts to give legitimacy to a new German-controlled government. King Haakon and the Nygardsvold ministry, with the support of all parties represented in the Storting, continued to provide leadership for Norway in opposition to the German invaders—even though they had to flee to England to do so.[37]

Not only did the Norwegian government escape the Germans, so did the Norwegian gold reserves. In an incredible sequence of events beginning April 9, the Norwegians took the fifty tons of gold reserves out of the Bank of Norway in Oslo, secreted them in trucks, train cars, and sledges across the country to the northwest coast of Norway, shipped them to England and then across the Atlantic to the United States, and finally placed them in the Federal Reserve Bank in New York, and in Canada. There they were safe until they could be returned to Norway after the defeat of Hitler's Nazi Germany and the triumph of the United Nations.[38]

Mrs. Harriman and her little group tried to keep up with the fast-moving Norwegian government. But the king and his government were moving from place to place as the Germans relentlessly pursued them on land and from the skies. Buildings and whole towns where the king and the government had found temporary refuge were destroyed by German bombers. After a few days Mrs. Harriman, along with the British and French ministers, decided to abandon their efforts to stay close to the fast-moving Norwegian government. Her military aide, Captain William Losey, was killed by German bomb splinters. She and many others turned to neutral Sweden for refuge.[39]

Mrs. Harriman wrote to the President Roosevelt that she was "heartbroken over the fate of my many Norwegian friends." She described the Norwegians as "so simple and honest that they couldn't dream that any one could deceive them." In her memoirs later she wrote, "A hundred years of peace had bred in them kindness, hospitality, and decency. One does not learn suspicion in a day, nor how to meet the wiles of war."[40]

The Norwegians, even with the help of troops from Britain, France, and Poland, could not prevent Hitler's military forces from overrunning Norway. On June 7, 1940, less than two months after the Germans first attacked, sixty-eight-year-old King Haakon VII, Crown Prince Olav, and the Nygaardsvold ministry left Norway and fled to England. Some 350,000 German soldiers enforced Hitler's will on Norway. For five long years Norway and its people remained under Nazi Germany's boot.[41]

But the Norwegians never surrendered. King Haakon and the Norwegian government-in-exile in London symbolized and helped lead the continuing struggle against their Nazi oppressors. The government took over Norway's huge merchant marine, which served in the war against the Axis all over the world. Thousands of young Norwegians trained in England, Canada, and Sweden for the day when they might share in warring against Hitler's Germany. Norwegians at home organized an increasingly courageous and defiant resistance against their German and Quisling overlords. The Germans learned that it was much easier to overrun Norway than it was to conquer the Norwegian spirit. The one they did quickly; the other they never accomplished.[42]

Nominally the United States continued as a neutral for twenty months after Hitler brought war to Norway. It would be more accurate, however, to describe the United States from April 9, 1940, until December 7, 1941, as a nonbelligerent on the side of the allies. The overwhelming majority of the American people and Congress continued to oppose a declaration of war. But under Roosevelt's leadership America's policy of aid-short-of-war became increasingly bold. The destroyer deal with England, the enactment of lend-lease, the occupation of Greenland and Iceland, the patrol system and shoot-on-sight policies in the Atlantic, and the increasing economic squeeze on Japan in the Pacific constituted virtually an undeclared war against the Axis. There was nothing neutral about it. Hitler, Mussolini, and the Japanese leaders could have used the American actions as justification for war if they had thought it in their interests to do so. They did not choose to do so until December 1941.[43]

The United States legation in Oslo and its consular posts in Oslo and Bergen continued to function in occupied Norway after the Germans took over. As they had done earlier when the war first started in Europe, they busily helped Americans return to the United States and tried to locate people stranded in Norway.[44] The German government, however, required the United States to close its legation in Oslo on July 15, 1940.[45] In August the American consul in Oslo moved his offices to the vacated legation building at 28 Nobelsgate. Under Austin R. Preston in Oslo and Maurice P. Dunlap in Bergen the United States consular offices continued to function until Germany required them to close by July 15, 1941.[46]

In Washington, D.C., Wilhelm T. von Munthe de Morgenstierne continued to represent Norwegian interests in dealings with the United States government. He, of course, rejected orders from Norway to represent the Quisling regime, and he ably served under direction from the Norwegian government-in-exile in London. The United States continued to receive him in that capacity and never recognized the puppet government in Norway.[47] Norwegian consuls in America continued to serve. The government-in-exile established a Norwegian Shipping and Trade Mission office in New York, which, along with a similar office in London and lesser offices elsewhere, ran Norway's merchant marine in service to the war against the Axis.[48]

Crown Princess Märtha had fled with her three children to Sweden, and Crown Prince Olav accepted President Roosevelt's invitation to provide them with safe refuge in the United States. The United States sent the passenger ship, the *American Legion*, to Petsamo in northern Finland to bring refugees back to the United States. Among its 895 passengers on that long journey were Crown Princess Märtha, ten-year-old Princess Ragnhild, eight-year-old Princess Astrid, three-year-old Prince Harald, Mrs. Harriman, and the spouses and dependents of American foreign service personnel still serving in Scandinavia.

After arriving in New York on August 28, the Crown Princess and her children stayed for a time at Roosevelt's home in Hyde Park, New York, and then located comfortably in a house at Pook's Hill on the edge of Washington, D.C.[49] At the president's invitation Olav visited his wife and family in the United States in December and on other occasions. He and his aide traveled on the Pan American Clipper posing as Norwegian army officers under the assumed names of Colonel Alexander Carlsen and Lieutenant Colonel Petter Einardsen.[50]

In July 1940 the United States appointed Dr. Rudolf E. Schoenfeld to serve as chargé d'affaires ad interim to the Norwegian government-in-exile in London.[51] In February 1941 President Roosevelt appointed Anthony J. Drexel Biddle, Jr., to serve as United States envoy extraordinary and minister plenipotentiary near the Norwegian government in London (and to other governments-in-exile there). He arrived at his post on March 14 and was received by King Haakon on March 20.[52]

Norwegian-Americans and others wanted to send relief in the form of food and clothing to occupied Norway. The United States government approved the proposal before the end of 1940, but the British objected. They contended that to allow shipment of food and clothing to Norway would "tend to weaken the whole blockade structure." They charged that Germany had "denuded Norway of clothing and that to allow replacements from the United States would directly benefit the German war effort and to that extent would help to prolong the war."[53]

The United States did, however, provide two Lockheed Lodestar airplanes used in transporting Norwegians between Sweden and London.[54] Crown Prince Olav spoke to Norwegian-American groups in America on his visits, as did Morgenstierne. And President Roosevelt kept in touch with the king and the government-in-exile in London.

Though both Roosevelt and the American people felt much sympathy for the Norwegians in their plight, priority in American foreign affairs went to helping the British, the Chinese, and (after June 22, 1941) the Soviet Union in their war against the Axis powers. The Norwegians did not receive much more than sympathy and good wishes from the United States during 1941.

GERMANY brought war to Norway when it invaded on April 9, 1940; Japan brought war to the United States when it launched a surprise attack on Pearl Harbor on December 7, 1941. Under President Roosevelt's leadership Congress, with only one dissenting vote, declared war on Japan on December 8. When Germany and Italy declared war on the United States three days later on December 11, Congress promptly and unanimously voted war on those two European Axis states. The United States and Norway were both belligerents on the same side in the most destructive war in human history.

Under President Roosevelt's leadership the United States gave priority to military preparations and planning for its war against the Axis powers. It worked intimately with Winston Churchill's government in Great Britain in those preparations. It extended massive lend-lease aid to Britain and, to a lesser extent, to the Soviet Union, China, and other countries warring against the Axis. None of the great powers gave Norway top priority as they planned their military operations.

Nonetheless, even more than Wilson in World War I, Roosevelt had a warm concern for Norway, its leaders, and its people in their courageous and continuing resistance to the Nazis. With White House assistance Crown Princess Märtha and her three children continued to enjoy comfortable and safe refuge in the United States. At the president's invitation Crown Prince Olav visited his wife and children in America from time to time. He and his wife made tours speaking to groups of Norwegian-Americans and others about continued Norwegian resistance to the Nazis and about their determination to win freedom for Norway once again.[55]

Similarly Roosevelt sent encouraging and inspiring messages to King Haakon in London. In honor of the king's seventieth birthday on August 3, 1942, the president arranged (via lend-lease) the gift of a 173-foot patrol craft (subchaser) to Norway and named it after the king.[56] In his remarks on the occasion of the formal presentation President Roosevelt said:

> If there is anyone who still wonders why this war is being fought, let him look to Norway. If there is anyone who has any delusions that this war could have been averted, let him look

to Norway. And if there is anyone who doubts the democratic *will* to win, again I say, let him look to Norway.

He will find in Norway, at once conquered and unconquerable, the answer to his questioning.

We all know how this most peaceful and innocent of countries was ruthlessly violated. The combination of treachery and brute force which conquered Norway will live in history as the blackest deed of a black era. Norway fought valiantly with what few weapons there were at hand – and fell.

And with Norway fell the concept that either remoteness from political controversy or usefulness to mankind could give any nation immunity from attack in a world where aggression spread unchecked.

But the story of Norway since the conquest shows that while a free democracy may be slow to realize its danger, it can be heroic when aroused. At home, the Norwegian people have silently resisted the invader's will with grim endurance. Abroad, Norwegian ships and Norwegian men have rallied to the cause of the United Nations. And their assistance to that cause has been out of all proportion to their small numbers.

In concluding his remarks, the president praised King Haakon and expressed the hope that the day would come when this new ship would "carry the Norwegian flag into a home port in a free Norway!" Crown Princess Märtha, in similarly moving terms, accepted the ship on behalf of the king and the Norwegian people.[57] The president's words often were quoted to inspire Norwegians and others to further efforts against the Axis in the course of the war. King Haakon and Crown Prince Olav similarly communicated warmly, appreciatively, and confidently in messages to the president.

Various top officials in the Norwegian government visited the United States at one time or another during the war. Prime Minister Johan Nygaardsvold visited in May 1942.[58] In February 1941 Trygve Lie had replaced Dr. Koht as Norwegian foreign minister. In the spring of 1943 Lie visited the United States and had meetings with Secretary of State Hull and others.[59] C. J. Hambro, Conservative party leader and president of the Storting, spent much of the war in the United States.[60]

In May 1942 the United States elevated Anthony J. Drexel Biddle, Jr., its minister to Norway's government in London, to the rank of ambassador. Roosevelt initiated that change "as an indication of the importance" that the United States attached "to the participation of the Norwegian Government and of Norwegian citizens throughout the world in the war effort of the United Nations." At the same time Norway changed its legation in Washington to an embassy and promoted Morgenstierne to be Norway's first ambassador to the United States.[61]

Tony Biddle served effectively at No. 40 Berkeley Square in London. In January 1944 President Roosevelt reluctantly allowed him to resign that diplomatic position. At Biddle's request, FDR appointed him as a lieutenant colonel to General Eisenhower's staff at SHAEF (Supreme Headquarters Allied Expeditionary Forces) with responsibility for serving as military liaison to the governments-in-exile.[62] Rudolf E. Schoenfeld, who had been counselor of the embassy under Biddle, then functioned as chargé d'affaires ad interim until December 1944. The president then appointed Lithgow Osborne of New York as the new United States ambassador to Norway. Roosevelt had known him since childhood. Osborne had attended Harvard and had served as a career foreign service officer for several years. His wife was a Danish countess.[63]

Norwegian military pilots trained in Canada during the war at "Little Norway" near Toronto, and later near Gravenhurst, Ontario. The Norwegian government purchased in the United States most of the airplanes those pilots flew. After completing their training, they flew for units of the Norwegian Royal Air Force, stationed in England.[64]

A small but important part of that air war in Europe was fought in the skies over Norway. On July 24, 1943, airplanes of the American Eighth Air Force bombed strategic targets as far north as Trondheim (a round-trip flight of nineteen hundred miles). Though the British Royal Air Force had flown earlier missions there, that was the first United States Army Air Force bombing mission over German-occupied Norway during World War II.[65]

Another important American bomber mission over Norway was part of the efforts to stop Nazi German development of atomic weapons. The Norsk Hydro plant at Vemork in the mountains of southern Norway used its abundant supplies of water and hydroelectric power to produce heavy water. Heavy water was essential for German nuclear research and development. Under German control the Norsk Hydro plant increased its production and channeled its product to Germany. Consequently destruction of that plant and its product won high priority.

On September 8, 1942, Major General George V. Strong, head of G-2 intelligence for the United States Army Chief of Staff, wrote a personal and secret message to Lieutenant General Dwight D. Eisenhower in England about the plants at Vemork, their production of heavy water for the Germans, and its importance "for experimental purposes in the development of fission bombs based upon uranium." He noted that both American and British scientists were making progress along those lines and suggested that "whichever nation can put fission bombs of this character in use will have a destructive agent which may determine the final outcome of this war." Since such a development required use of heavy water, he advised that "the designation of Vemork as a bombing objective from the air, or crippling of the plant by sabotage, should seriously be considered." General Eisenhower consulted General Carl Spaatz, his air adviser, and promised to "initiate action, in collaboration with the British, sometime within the next six weeks."[66]

It was not so simple. It required four daring efforts to accomplish the mission. Three (including one failure, one limited success, and one decisive success) were undertaken by courageous young Norwegians trained and directed from England. The first, in November 1942, involving the use of gliders, was a disastrous failure. The second, in February 1943, was a flawless, daring sabotage success, but by the middle of the year the plant was back in production.[67]

The third attempt fell to the United States Army Air Force. On November 16, 1943, in a formidable daylight raid, approximately 150 four-engine B-17 bombers of the Eighth Air Force dropped hundreds of bombs on the Vemork plant. Bombs hit their target, and some by mistake fell on the nearby town of Rjukan. Among the dead left by the attack were twenty-two Norwegians. Despite direct hits, the bombs failed to destroy either the heavy-water supplies or the plant that made them. The Norwegian government in London protested that it had not been consulted and that the loss of Norwegian lives indicated the method used was inappropriate for the task.[68] The Norwegian government wanted to have sabotage replace air raids against important industries in Norway to limit civilian casualties.

The various attempts did, however, convince the Germans to move the plant and its product from Norway to Germany. But when they tried to do so, bold Norwegian saboteurs set time bombs that, on February 20, 1944, sank the ferry on Lake Tinnsjo that was carrying the heavy water. The lake was too deep for recovery efforts. The Norwegians, under British direction, had accomplished through daring, skill, and great courage what the American Eighth Air Force had been unable to accomplish.[69]

Norway's largest contribution to the war effort against the Axis, however, was in the use of its huge merchant fleet to carry men and material for Great Britain and the United States. When Germany attacked Norway, most of the Norwegian merchant ships were at sea or in other parts of the world; very few were captured or bottled up. The Norwegian government took over that fleet and operated it for the United Nations war effort throughout the war. That provided the government-in-exile with substantial income. It also provided Great Britain and the United States with tremendous shipping facilities invaluable for the war effort.

Though Britain, the United States, and Norway shared in using that merchant fleet for the common goal of defeating the Axis, inevitably there were conflicting interests among those three states. There was much tugging and pulling as they tried to work out mutually satisfactory allocation of those shipping resources. The greater part of the Norwegian fleet had been chartered by the British even before Norway and the United States were brought into the war, and before the Norwegian government took over the merchant fleet. The British wanted to keep it that way and bring it even more fully under their own control. The United States acknowledged Britain's tremendous shipping needs but was reluctant to have Norwegian ships drawn away from service in America's Caribbean and Latin American routes. Norway was proud of the contributions its ships and seamen were making to the war effort and wanted to be treated as a full partner in deciding the allocation and use of those ships. It did not want to be left at the end of the war with a few worn-out vessels surviving from the magnificent modern fleet with which it had entered the war. It wanted appropriate compensation, aid, and replacements from the British and Americans during the course of the war so it might have that invaluable resource available for its postwar economic recovery efforts. To make the Norwegian position all the more difficult, there were rarely enough ships—old or new, of any nationality—to meet the insatiable shipping needs of the United Nations war effort.[70]

Inevitably the Norwegian merchant fleet suffered heavy losses at the hands of German submarines and airplanes. It had over 7.5 million deadweight tons initially. By February 1942 more than one-third of that fleet had been sunk; only a little more than 4.5 million tons remained. At the beginning of the war Norway had some 3 million tons of tankers; by the beginning of 1942 that figure had been reduced to 2.3 million tons. By September 1942 Norway had lost more than three hundred ships and the lives of sixteen hundred of its seamen. By March 1943 it had lost 44 percent of its ships and tonnage and was continuing to lose about one ship every three days.[71]

The United States armed Norwegian merchant ships and was helpful in servicing and repairing them. In July 1942 the United States and Norway concluded a master lend-lease agreement and exchanged notes relating to the Norwegian merchant fleet.[72] In the exchange of notes that accompanied the lend-lease agreement the United States recognized the valuable contribution made by the Norwegian merchant marine to the United Nations war effort and the importance of that fleet as a Norwegian asset. It accepted the principle of helping to replace Norwegian ships lost at sea "as soon as conditions permit."[73]

Norwegian leaders believed that the United States and Britain were slow in acknowledging Norway's maritime contributions and losses and in practice were laggard in providing replacements. In 1942 Norway asked for ten new replacement ships. The American War Shipping Administration offered old ships; Norway insisted on new ones. President Roosevelt generally was sympathetic. As he phrased it in late 1942, "They [the Norwegians] have idle men – we have the ships – why not marry them?" But by the end of 1942 not a single American-made merchant ship had been transferred to the Norwegian flag.[74]

Similarly, Norwegian leaders thought they were not being treated by the United States and Great Britain as a full partner in maritime policy-making. As Ambassador Morgenstierne phrased it in a letter to Secretary of State Hull, "My Government feels that the total contribution of the Norwegian Merchant Marine to the solution of the transportation problem justifies Norwegian participation in the direction of the transportation policies of the United Nations."[75]

At the end of January 1943 Norway received its first two merchant ships built in the United States. By the end of May it had received six ships from the War Shipping Administration and had been assured that it would get two more in the near future, for a total of eight.[76] In 1945 the United States and Norway concluded agreements on the maritime problems and differences that arose during the course of the war.[77]

Throughout the war there was a chronic and increasing need for food and clothing in occupied Norway. Ambassador Morgenstierne repeatedly urged President Roosevelt and the Department of State to permit food relief for Norway to pass through the blockade. Various groups in the United States, including the American Friends of Norway (under the chairmanship of Mrs. Harriman), Norwegian Relief, the Federal Council of Churches of Christ in America, and other Norwegian-American and church groups raised money and supplies for relief purposes. Both President Roosevelt and the State Department sympathized with some form of humanitarian relief in Norway.[78]

The British, however, were adamant in insisting that to relax the blockade at all to permit such relief, even with carefully controlled and supervised distribution of relief supplies, would seriously damage the blockade and, to that extent, weaken the war effort. Even FDR's personal approval of a carefully planned relief program in one test district on an experimental basis and an appeal by him personally to Prime Minister Churchill could not weaken the British opposition.[79]

Not until November 1943 did the American and British blockade authorities in London consent to the shipment from Sweden to Norway of 250 tons per month of certain foods, providing shipments of merchandise to Sweden through the blockade were suspended. That pattern was allowed in connection with a carefully planned Swedish government relief program of school lunches for Norwegian children.[80] During 1944 the amount permitted from Sweden for food relief in Norway was increased, first to five hundred tons a month and then to one thousand tons a month. That aid continued despite objections on military grounds by the American Joint Chiefs of Staff to such relief efforts in areas of northern Norway devastated by German troops retreating before Soviet military advances there.[81]

Throughout the war both the Norwegian government in London and the United States government devoted much attention to planning for the postwar era—as that planning related both to foreign affairs and to domestic economy and government. Norwegians also had to anticipate the procedures for freeing their land and people from the German troops. Some expected an allied military invasion of Norway to accomplish that task. The Norwegian resistance movement wanted to coordinate its actions against the Germans to help any such allied military move. Both the Norwegian government in London and General Eisenhower's Supreme Headquarters Allied Expeditionary Forces discouraged premature activity by the Norwegian resistance that might bring violent retaliation by the Germans against the Norwegian people.

The Soviet Union drove Nazi German forces back in eastern and central Europe, and General Eisenhower's American, British, and Canadian forces invaded Europe at Normandy in France on June 6, 1944. In October 1944 military forces of the Soviet Union attacked German forces in Finnmark in the far north of Norway. The Germans followed a "scorched-earth" policy there, destroying everything in the path of the advancing Soviet army and causing terrible suffering for the Norwegian people living in the region.[82]

The German forces stationed in the rest of Norway might conceivably have continued to resist even after the Nazi surrender in Berlin on V-E Day, May 8, 1945. Fortunately they did not do so. It was time for German troops to lay down their arms, for Norway's leaders to return home, and for the Norwegian people to rejoice in the victory and the restoration of freedom.

IN military and diplomatic terms the ending of the war in Norway and the transition there from military to civilian control went forward with impressive orderliness, efficiency, and civility. On May 16, 1944, the United States, Great Britain, and the Soviet Union had all signed identical agreements with Norway to facilitate that transition at the close of hostilities.[83]

The Supreme Headquarters Allied Expeditionary Forces under General Eisenhower named General Sir A. F. Andrew N. Thorne of Great Britain to command the Allied Land Forces in Norway at the close of World War II in Europe. His deputy was Colonel Charles H. Wilson of the United States Army. The Home Front forces in Norway began to take over on May 7 and 8. General Thorne's representatives received the surrender of the German commander in Norway on May 8, 1945, and his forces—British, American, and Norwegian—began entering Oslo on May 10. With only rare exceptions the German troops obeyed orders to lay down their arms and surrender. Crown Prince Olav and an advance party of ministers from the Norwegian government received an enthusiastic welcome when they returned to Oslo on May 13.[84]

Orsen N. Nielsen, counselor of the United States embassy, and L. Milner Dunn, vice consul, were the first two American foreign service officers to return to Norway after the German surrender. They traveled to Oslo in a British Sunderland flying boat. The Norwegian pilot of the huge four-engine airplane, according to Nielsen, was "almost delirious with delight" and put the plane "through all kinds of fancy stunts over every town from Kristiansand to Oslo; then spent 15 minutes above this city." The three Norwegians who had been left as caretakers of the legation (now embassy) at 28 Nobelsgate had performed their duties well and had kept the grounds and lawn presentable. Nielsen and Dunn quickly readied the building for the return of the ambassador. And they eagerly shared with huge throngs of Norwegians in joyous celebration of syttende mai, May seventeenth, the Norwegian national holiday in commemoration of the adoption of the constitution in 1814.[85]

The rest of the Norwegian government, along with American Ambassador Lithgow Osborne, his wife, and the embassy staff, sailed from Liverpool aboard the British S. S. *Andes*, arriving in Oslo at noon on May 31.[86]

Crown Princess Märtha and her children hurried back to England from the United States aboard American Air Transport Command airplanes to accompany King Haakon when he returned to Norway aboard the British cruiser *Norfolk*. Crown Prince Olav met his father, the king, and his family at the entrance to the Oslo Fjord. And many thousands of cheering Norwegians enthusiastically greeted King Haakon when he stepped back on Norwegian soil at Oslo on June 7, 1945 – five years to the day after he had left to go to England and forty years since he had first arrived in Norway to become king. There were speeches, parades, and celebrations. The country was almost deliriously happy to be free again.[87]

As the American ambassador described it in a telegram the next day, "The almost incredible enthusiasm with which [the] King was greeted by all classes and members all political parties upon his return yesterday was clearly genuine and is another indication [that] moderation and reason in solving political questions will prevail. Barring severe economic or food crisis constitutional monarchy and democracy are safe for the foreseeable future in Norway."[88] He was completely correct.

After five terrible years uncertainties and differences inevitably had arisen between the Norwegian government in London and the "Home Front" in Norway. There were questions about the transition from allied military control to Norwegian civilian control, as well as a certain amount of uneasiness about the likely course Prime Minister Nygaardsvold's government would set when it returned. But all went impressively well.

General Thorne, with SHAEF approval, notified the king on June 7 that under the terms of the civil affairs agreement he was returning most authority for civil matters to the Norwegian government. As promised in advance, the Nygaardsvold ministry, which had been in power for a decade, resigned on June 12. Most expected Paal Berg, chief justice of the Norwegian supreme court and highly respected leader of the Home Front during the war, to form a new government. Snags developed, however. Conservatives, led by Hambro, refused to participate in a government that included any members of the wartime ministry, and Berg insisted on including Trygve Lie and Oscar Torp from that ministry. Communists wanted a Labor government rather than a coalition government. Faced with those difficulties, Berg did not persist in trying to form a government.[89]

Consequently the king asked Einar Gerhardsen, deputy leader of the Labor party, to form a government. On June 22 the new Gerhardsen coalition government was announced, including Trygve Lie as foreign minister and Torp as minister of defense. It served until Norway held its first postwar elections on October 8. In those elections the Labor party won a majority in the Storting. Gerhardsen then formed a new Labor government, still including Lie as foreign minister.[90]

The Gerhardsen governments marked a new phase in Norwegian political history. The prewar leaders largely retired or were bypassed. The new ministers were young. Gerhardsen was forty-eight; the youngest was thirty. The average age was less than forty-five. Most had never been elected to the Storting or held high government office previously. The tall, slender, blue-eyed Gerhardsen was of working-class origins and had early become active in the Labor party. During the war he had been active in the Home Front resistance, was arrested by the Germans in 1941, and spent much of the war in concentration camps in Nazi Germany. Others in his government similarly had participated in Home Front resistance during the war.[91] Norway successfully accomplished the transition from wartime government-in-exile and Home Front resistance back to the functioning constitutional monarchy and representative government it had sustained since 1905.

With a minimum of vindictiveness and a maximum of regard for legal procedures, Norway prosecuted those who had betrayed their country to the Nazis. Vidkun Quisling was tried and convicted; on October 23, 1945, he was executed before a Norwegian firing squad.[92] Both Norway and the United States conducted careful investigations to determine the responsibility in their separate governments for the events before and immediately after the Axis attacks that brought each of the two countries into the war.[93]

When SHAEF disbanded on July 14, British forces under General Thorne and American troops under Colonel Wilson stayed on to complete the repatriation of German prisoners and of Russian prisoners the Germans had held in Norway. The last of the United States troops withdrew from Norway before the end of October.[94]

As the American troops departed, King Haakon sent President Harry S. Truman in the United States a telegram thanking "for the invaluable assistance rendered by the United States Army in liberating Norway and restoring the freedom and independence of the country." He praised "the admirable way in which the American forces have fulfilled their mission." The king expressed the conviction that the presence of the American troops in Norway "has further developed the strong ties of friendship and relationship between our two nations to the benefit of both countries."[95]

Ambassador Osborne wrote that, despite a few "unpleasant incidents," he considered his mission "fortunate in having had such a fine body of officers and men representing the United States Army in the liberation and occupation of Norway." Most Norwegian newspapers expressed similar views. As reported in translation by the American embassy, the Norwegian newspaper *Verdens Gang* had editorialized:

> G.I. Joe – the American soldier – comes from all parts (of the U.S.). He is a blond Scandinavian from Minnesota or a Pole from Buffalo, N.Y. He is a dark-haired Italian from Brooklyn or a Japanese from California. He is a Jew from the Bronx or a German from Wisconsin, a Frenchman from New Orleans or a Briton from Massachusetts. A Mexican from New Mexico or a Negro from Mississippi. . . . We hope you have liked it here with us, Joe. And that you will return some time when the war-wounds have been healed and we can meet again – out of uniform and busy with peacetime occupations. You will always be a welcome guest.

The *Morgenposten* editorialized, "We were happy when you came because you were not Germans. We are happy today because we know you are Americans. You will be welcome when you return."[96]

Franklin D. Roosevelt did not live to share in the end of the war, the celebrations of victory, and the return of peace and freedom to both Norway and the United States. He died of a cerebral hemorrhage in Warms Springs, Georgia, on April 12, 1945. But he was by no means overlooked or forgotten either in the United States or in Norway. Ambassador Morgenstierne had served in Washington most of the time Roosevelt was president. When he was interviewed in Oslo in September, he told newsmen:

> President Roosevelt's friendship for Norway was exceptionally warm and sincere. The part played by the Norwegian merchant fleet among other things made a great impression on him. . . . Furthermore he was very much interested in the battles on the Norwegian home front. He also visited Norway in his youth and the mighty nature of Norway made a great impression on him.
>
> From the very first day of the German attack on Norway he showed great sympathy and good-will towards our country. . . . A few days after the attack Roosevelt condemned the nefarious attack in the strongest terms at a great press conference. America was neutral at the time. I was present myself and his words made a deep impression on me.
>
> Later at all the occasions when I was with the president, whether at Hyde Park or in the White House, I had the impression that his interest in Norway was sincere in an extraordinary degree and that he was sure that we would regain our liberty.
>
> I do not believe that Norway has ever had a better and more sincere friend outside of our own country.[97]

In June 1950 Mrs. Eleanor Roosevelt, the president's widow, visited Norway to unveil a monument to her husband in Oslo. Norwegians received her warmly and enthusiastically, a tribute both to her own outstanding qualities and accomplishments and to the memory of her husband's place in Norwegian-American relations.[98]

On July 13, 1951, a royal decree approved and proclaimed the decisions by the Storting and the cabinet to declare that the government considered the war between Norway and Germany terminated.[99] In 1952 Norway, like the United States, ratified the Japanese peace treaty.[100] Both the United States and Norway, however, had new alarming concerns to absorb their mutual attention in international affairs. Those concerns focused particularly on relations with the Soviet Union and on the developing cold war.

5

The Cold War and NATO

AFTER World War II neither the Department of State, the foreign service, the American diplomatic and military presence abroad, nor the quantity of diplomatic communications ever went back to the comparatively small, personal, and uncomplicated character they had had during much of the first century and a half of American history. The foreign service staff and organization at the American embassy at 28 Nobelsgate in Oslo never approached those in London, Paris, or Moscow in size or complexity. But neither did they ever return to the highly personalized, informal style they had enjoyed during the first four decades of diplomatic relations between the United States and Norway.

The carefully crafted diplomatic despatches of an earlier, more leisurely day, flawlessly typed on quality letterhead bond, were replaced by floods of hurried telegrams and airgrams. There was little time for the painstaking drafting of voluntary reports on aspects of life in Norway that so enriched the diplomatic and consular correspondence of an earlier time. More "important" matters pressed endlessly on the time and energies of the greatly enlarged, but often shorthanded, American embassy staff. American consulates in Norway were reduced in number and status, while the embassy played a comparatively larger role.

More often than not American ambassadors to Norway after

the war continued to be political appointees, as the ministers had been earlier. But they were bolstered by larger staffs of career foreign service officers and by professionals from other agencies involved in American foreign affairs. After World War II there was an ever-changing parade of military officers, information specialists, economic assistance officials, commercial and agricultural attachés, and intelligence agents attached to the embassy in one capacity or another. Though tiny in comparison with the rapidly expanding government service in Washington, the operation under the American ambassador in Oslo began to justify use of the word *bureaucracy* in ways it rarely had earlier.[1]

In July 1946 Charles Ulrick Bay of New York replaced Lithgow Osborne as United States ambassador to Norway. A self-made engineer, businessman, and financier, Bay was the first American of Norwegian descent to serve as chief of mission in Oslo since Laurits S. Swenson had left that post more than a decade and a half earlier. Bay stayed on as the American representative to the government of Norway for seven years, long enough for him to become dean of the diplomatic corps in Oslo, as Swenson had been earlier. Serving through most of the presidency of Harry S. Truman, Bay's tour of duty in Norway did not end until July 1953, when he was replaced by L. Corrin Strong, a political appointee of the new Republican administration of President Dwight D. Eisenhower.[2]

Wilhelm T. von Munthe de Morgenstierne continued to represent Norway to the United States government in Washington, as he had done since 1934, first as minister and then, after 1942, as ambassador. The Norwegian staff in the embassy at Thirty-fourth Street and Massachusetts Avenue was not so large as the American staff in Oslo. It was much larger than it had been before the war, however, and in time it became the largest embassy staff that the Norwegian government maintained in any foreign capital.[3]

Beginning in 1941 Trygve Lie served as Norway's foreign minister in the government of Prime Minister Johan Nygaardsvold until that government resigned after the war. He then continued as foreign minister in the postwar Labor government of Prime Minister Einar Gerhardsen until he resigned early in 1946 to become the first secretary-general of the new United Nations organization in New York. Born in Oslo and educated in law at the University of Oslo, Lie was a strong, hard working, prominent Labor politician. He spoke English well and was favorably inclined toward Great Britain and the United States. At his initiative the Norwegian government in London during the war began careful planning for its postwar foreign policy.[4]

In February 1946 Halvard M. Lange succeeded Lie as foreign minister in Gerhardsen's Labor government, and he served in that capacity almost continuously for nearly two decades until 1965. Born in Oslo in 1902, Lange was reared in an unusually cosmopolitan and international environment. His father, Christian L. Lange, served as the longtime secretary-general of the Inter-Parliamentary Union and was awarded the Nobel Peace Prize in 1921. The son was reared and educated in Belgium, Switzerland, and Italy, in addition to Norway. He studied at the University of Oslo, the University of Geneva, and the London School of Economics. For a time he worked for the International Fellowship of Reconciliation, a peace organization. He became active in the trade-union movement and in the Labor party. Lange was fluent in several languages, including English and French. He wrote books in his areas of interest, including scholarly histories.

During World War II Lange was active in the resistance movement in Norway. The Gestapo arrested him repeatedly. He spent more than three years in German concentration camps – including several months in solitary confinement – damaging his health in the process. Among his fellow prisoners in Germany were Einar Gerhardsen and others who filled leadership roles in Norwegian governments after the war.

Like Lie before him, Lange had sympathetic views toward Great Britain and the United Nations. He favored building Norway's ties with the Atlantic states in the West. Despite his pacifist views as a young man, World War II and postwar developments persuaded him of the necessity for military defense preparations. Only forty-three years old when he first became Norway's foreign minister in 1946, no one played a larger role than Lange in shaping Norway's policies in international affairs after World War II and in the cold war.[5]

LONG before World War II ended, many in both Norway and the United States began to plan for peace and security in the postwar era. As early as 1940 Trygve Lie urged building a North Atlantic security system after the war. In September 1941 the Norwegian government formally adhered to the Atlantic Charter that President Roosevelt and Prime Minister Churchill had drafted the month before. In January 1942 both Norway and the United States adhered to the United Nations Declaration. In an interview in February 1942 Prime Minister Johan Nygaardsvold emphasized that Norway's traditional policy of neutrality was dead, that it had left the door open to aggressors. In his view an enduring postwar peace would depend on cooperation among states that had common interests and ideals. He thought Norway would share larger interests with Great Britain and the United States than with either Scandinavian or European grouping of states.[6]

In June 1942 Foreign Minister Trygve Lie provided Ambassador Biddle with a confidential memorandum on Norway's foreign policy. That carefully drafted policy statement emphasized that after the war Norway could obtain security only through organized cooperation with others. It acknowledged Norwegian interest in European arrangements but contended that "Norway's strategic, economic and cultural interests are first and foremost linked with Great Britain and the overseas countries." It considered the defense of its extensive coastline to be "Norway's most important future military problem" and asserted that Norway could defend it adequately "only in cooperation with the great Atlantic Powers." At the same time it was "obviously in the interests both of Great Britain and of the United States to prevent any continental power from gaining control of the Norwegian coast. The defense of the North Atlantic seems, therefore, to be the natural common task for the great Atlantic Powers and Norway." The memorandum emphasized that it was "of paramount importance that the United States, which will probably be the strongest military power after the war, should participate in such an Atlantic system from the very outset."[7] Though policies varied from time to time, it is significant that that important Norwegian policy document took that position long before the end of World War II, before the beginnings of the cold war with the Soviet Union, and before the creation of the North

Atlantic Treaty Organization seven years later.

So far as the Soviet Union was concerned, the Norwegian document urged that "friendly cooperation, based on mutual confidence, should be established between the Great Atlantic Powers and Soviet Russia." It promised that Norway would "support all attempts to create a universal League of Nations, and all endeavors to develop positive international cooperation." Until that became possible, however, Norway would have to seek security in regional accord. Consequently it wanted "binding and obligatory military agreements concerning the defense of the North Atlantic."[8]

Americans, too, initiated planning during World War II for postwar peace and security. President Roosevelt, Secretary of State Hull, the leadership elites, and—after the Japanese attack on Pearl Harbor—most of the American people agreed that the United States must turn away from traditional "isolationism" and abandon its opposition to "entangling alliances." Secretary Hull shared in planning the creation of a world organization after the war and in building bipartisan support for American membership in that organization. In 1943 both the Senate and the House of Representatives adopted resolutions urging the creation of such an organization and American participation in it.

President Roosevelt shared those general attitudes but was not utopian in his expectations. He discouraged detailed deliberations during the war on postwar peace arrangements lest they divide the American people and the states warring against the Axis. Flexible, adaptable, and undoctrinaire, Roosevelt was persuaded of the importance of maintaining cooperation in the postwar period among the major states that were working together to defeat the Axis powers. He thought of the great powers (the United States, the Soviet Union, Great Britain, and China) as Four Policemen to guard peace and security. If they could cooperate for peace after the war as they had cooperated for victory during the war, peace and security could prevail. If they failed to do so, no world organization was likely to be effective.[9]

President Roosevelt, along with the Soviet Union's Joseph Stalin and Britain's Winston Churchill, tried to accomplish that unity of the great powers for postwar arrangements at a summit conference at Yalta in the Crimea early in 1945. Roosevelt tried to assuage Stalin's distrust of Western capitalist countries and to find common ground on which the three states could cooperate effectively in the postwar era. To do so, he yielded to arrangements likely to leave the Soviet Union dominant in eastern Europe (though Soviet military successes would have left it dominant there with or without FDR's assent). Despite close Anglo-American relations during the war and his collaboration with Churchill, Roosevelt tried to act sufficiently independently of the British at Yalta to allay Stalin's fears that the Western leaders might gang up on him and on the Soviet Union. Though he had to compromise on many issues, Roosevelt left Yalta hopeful that they had laid the groundwork on which enduring peace could be constructed. He was troubled by differences that developed after the conference, but he continued to hope the great powers could work together effectively to preserve the peace up until his sudden death on April 12, 1945, less than a month before the final German surrender.[10]

In the summer of 1945 both Norway and the United States sent delegates to the San Francisco conference that drafted the charter for the United Nations Organization. Secretary of State Edward R. Stettinius, Jr., led the American delegation. Among Norway's delegates were Foreign Minister Lie, Ambassador Morgenstierne, C. J. Hambro, and historian and adviser Dr. Arne Ording. Both governments ratified the United Nations charter and became active members of the new world organization. In both countries most people earnestly hoped the United Nations could effectively preserve peace and security in the war-torn world.[11]

In August 1945 Foreign Minister Lie, in carefully prepared written responses to an American newsman's questions, wrote: "Norway expects that the United States will make the same mighty contribution to the four freedoms in peace as she did during the war, and that America will never again remain outside the international political scene. The world needs America and cannot endure a recurrence of that which happened after the first world war. With America's marked feeling for individual freedom, we rely on your country also to keep in mind the interests of the small nations." At the same time Lie wrote, "The Norwegian people do not entertain any fear of Russian abuse of power."[12]

Both Norway and the United States, along with countries and peoples all over the world, earnestly explored the paths to peace and security after the war. But the unity among the great powers for which Roosevelt had worked, and on which the United Nations security system was based, failed to develop. Fear, distrust, insecurity, and anxiety about the possibility of renewed warfare in what had become the "nuclear era" intensified on all sides. What one historian referred to as the "Yalta axioms" yielded to more belligerent perspectives. Some blamed that change on the inexperienced new president, Harry S Truman of Missouri. But Truman did try to follow the policies of his predecessor as he understood them. Some of Roosevelt's policy advisers were themselves growing disenchanted with the Soviet Union and were losing confidence in the policies that Roosevelt had initiated. Their guidance for the new president did not always reflect accurately FDR's earlier views.[13]

Similarly, the shift from the Nygaardsvold government to the Gerhardsen government, and later the shift from Trygve Lie to Halvard Lange at the head of the Norwegian foreign ministry, may have affected Norwegian-American relations. All involved felt ideological, economic, and security ties with Great Britain and the United States. None was pro-Communist or identified with the Soviet Union. None wanted the world divided into blocs, and none wanted Norway drawn into power blocs. Lange said he would not make significant changes in Norwegian foreign policy but there may have been differences of degree or style.[14]

By December 1945, some seven months after Norway was freed from the Germans, Ambassador Osborne wrote that the Norwegian government wanted "to orient itself toward the Atlantic powers, not toward Russia, and will do so to the greatest extent that it dares." He explained that "every Norwegian realizes fully that in another world conflict this country cannot possibly remain neutral and will very probably be a battleground. The Norwegian brand of isolationism is dead; but it has been replaced by a jittery determination to stimulate what amounts to a kind of peacetime neutrality." He thought the United Nations Organization would "have no more sincere advocate or loyal member than Norway, if only because the stronger UNO becomes the less pressure there is apt to be from the East." Ambassador Osborne summed up Norway's foreign policy at the close of 1945 in these words:

1. Pro-UK-US to the greatest extent she dares.
2. Pro-Soviet to the extent she must.
3. Pro-UNO to the greatest extent she can.[15]

At the end of September 1946 Foreign Minister Lange told an American newsman that "Norway's position in international affairs is entirely determined by its desire to offer its services when and where they are needed to assist in the work of maintaining friendly cooperation between all nations." He said that Norway wanted to do its "utmost to promote the spirit of cooperation" between the great powers. Lange wanted Norway to "maintain an independent line of policy," but he wanted that policy "to be kept within the frame of our membership in the United Nations, on which our entire foreign policy is based."[16] Norwegian scholars later referred to the role Norway tried to play after World War II in the early phases of the cold war as "bridge building."[17]

THE most pressing need at the close of World War II was to rebuild war-torn economies. Except in the far north, where the German "scorched earth" policy destroyed everything, Norway did not have to endure the devastation that came with massive military combat and bombings. But no country could experience five years of Nazi military occupation without suffering severe economic hardships. War damage totaled 16 to 18 percent of Norway's wealth. In terms of postwar replacement costs the damage was over $2 billion. Half the Norwegian merchant fleet was at the bottom of the oceans.[18]

The Norwegian government in London began careful planning during the war for postwar economic reconstruction. No country planned its recovery policies in greater detail or implemented them more effectively than did Norway. Despite five years of deprivation at the hands of the Germans, the Norwegian people accepted the necessity for severe austerity policies after the war. Norway had accumulated substantial foreign exchange credits abroad during the war—in pounds sterling and in dollars—from its merchant fleet and from insurance on the ships it lost (though insurance paid much less than replacement costs after the war). In 1945 the government allowed modest importation of consumer goods to meet the most urgent needs. To a striking degree, however, Norway restricted consumer expenditures through import restrictions, severe rationing, high taxes, and price controls. As the chief of the Marshall Plan mission to Norway phrased it, Norway's Labor government "tightened the nation's belt to an austerity level that Americans would find almost unbearable." Indicative of public support for those policies, there was only one major postwar strike—and both workers and the Labor government condemned it. Norway had no black market and little inflation.[19]

While keeping consumer demand low, Norway channeled its foreign exchange resources into rebuilding its battered merchant fleet and increasing its industrial and agricultural production to reduce its needs from abroad and to increase its exports to foreign markets. It increased its available foreign exchange credits by requiring Norwegians to turn over their foreign holdings in return for kroner (Norwegian currency) and by reducing its gold reserves. To supplement those Norwegian resources, it borrowed from abroad.[20]

Norway got a loan of $50 million from the Export-Import Bank in the United States (including $10 million approved in 1940 but almost untouched during the war). The United States required, however, that at least 50 percent of the goods purchased with those credits be carried in United States merchant ships. Though its merchant ships were fully utilized, Norway could have carried those products in its own bottoms and objected to the American restriction. Norway also raised $10 million from bonds marketed through investment bankers in the United States.[21]

By 1947–48, however, Norwegians worried that available foreign exchange resources could be exhausted before the country's merchant fleet and its domestic industries were rebuilt to levels that could sustain continued growth and prosperity. He may have overstated the difficulties, but A. E. Staley, Jr., chief of the Economic Cooperation Administration (ECA) Marshall Plan mission to Norway, phrased the situation in these terms: "By April 1948, Norway had virtually reached the limit of its resources. Its gold and foreign exchange reserves could not be further depleted. It had borrowed money wherever it could and new credits were becoming extremely difficult to obtain. Its domestic resources were strained in its great effort towards recovery."[22] There was, in effect, a race between the rate at which Norway's foreign exchange and credits were being expended and the rate at which Norway's merchant fleet, industries, and productive facilities were growing. Despite heroic efforts, it appeared that Norway's supply of foreign exchange could be exhausted before the reconstruction was sufficiently advanced to sustain the country's economy.[23] Other countries with more extensive war damage and less enlightened policies were in even worse circumstances. At that point the United States came forward with the Marshall Plan.

In a major address at Harvard University on June 5, 1947, Truman's Secretary of State George C. Marshall proposed a comprehensive plan to assist European economic recovery on the basis of both self-help and mutual assistance. Marshall said it was not directed "against any country or doctrine, but against hunger, poverty, desperation, and chaos." America offered that aid to all European countries, including the Soviet Union.[24] The Soviet Union chose not to participate, however, and made certain that countries bound to it in eastern Europe abstained as well. That had the effect of further dividing Europe into eastern and western blocs.

Though it had less acute economic distress than some other European countries, and though it resisted tendencies dividing Europe into blocs, Norway with some reservations went along with the plan. It sent a delegation of highly qualified professional economists to participate in the Paris deliberations shaping the European response to Marshall's offer. The Norwegian government wanted operation of the plan kept on economic rather than political grounds, hoped it would not create a western bloc, and preferred to have it administered through the United Nations rather than by a regional organ. Inevitably there was tugging and pulling in each country between what they wanted, what they really needed, and what they thought the United States Congress could, or would, provide. Norwegians estimated their economic needs conservatively. Their figure of $100 million over the course of the four years of the plan was limited to what they thought

Norway absolutely needed and no more. Knowledgeable Americans suspected that that figure was too low.[25]

Out of that huge multilateral effort came constructive action. The Economic Cooperation Act, debated and passed by the United States Congress, was signed into law on April 3, 1948.[26] Ambassador Morgenstierne promptly informed the United States that Norway wished to participate. Negotiations went forward quickly. After deliberation and debate, on July 3, 1948, the Norwegian Storting voted 108 to 11 to authorize the foreign minister to sign the bilateral Economic Cooperation Agreement with the United States. The eleven Communist members of the Storting cast the negative votes. Less than an hour later Ambassador Bay for the United States and Foreign Minister Lange for Norway signed the Economic Cooperation Agreement between the two countries. It went into effect immediately.[27]

Secretary of State Marshall named A. E. Staley, Jr., an Illinois manufacturer and businessman, to head the Economic Cooperation Administration mission to Norway. Staley took over his duties in Oslo late in August 1948 and served until the next spring, when he returned to his manufacturing business. He was succeeded by John E. Gross, a labor leader from Colorado who had been labor adviser to the ECA missions to both Norway and Denmark. The ECA special mission to Norway functioned until it was superseded by the Mutual Security Agency on November 1, 1951.[28]

Inevitably there were differences and difficulties in implementing the program. Norwegian Communists attacked it as evidence of American imperialism. Some in Norway thought a rumored ECA staff of twenty-five would be too large and would demonstrate Communist allegations of American economic control. By the middle of 1951 the ECA staff in Norway under Gross was twice that size—half of them Americans and half of them Norwegians. Norwegians disliked the requirement that half of ECA aid had to be carried in American merchant ships. Americans were uneasy about the possibility that Norway might channel ECA funds into construction of an uneconomic Norwegian steel plant at Mo i Rana. Norway preferred grant aid to credit aid that had to be repaid later. Tensions developed between Ambassador Bay and ECA's Gross.[29]

A fundamental difference arose between ECA officials in Washington and Paris, and Norwegian policy-makers in Oslo. (The American ECA mission in Oslo sided with the Norwegians.) Norway complained that some countries were channeling too much Marshall Plan aid into consumer goods and even luxury items rather than into increased production and capital goods. Early in 1949 Norway's minister of commerce, Erik Brofoss, complained that the French and Belgian "emphasis upon rapid improvement in the volume of goods available to domestic consumers" would "increase the ultimate cost of the recovery program to American taxpayers," and could have "adverse effects upon the rate of recovery of other participating countries which thus far have sought to use ECA funds to the utmost for the purpose of procuring industrial equipment and raw materials." Brofoss concluded that "the French and Belgian Governments apparently are continuing in the belief that American aid indefinitely will be forthcoming as long as those Governments successfully raise the bogey of Communism."[30]

In contrast ECA officials in Washington and Paris insisted that Norway was channeling more into capital investments than could be sustained without substantial aid. To keep resources from being diverted from capital investments to consumer spending Norway was restricting imports of consumer products manufactured by other European countries. That policy clashed with America's emphasis on removing trade restrictions and promoting multilateral free flow of goods and services. The Norwegians were, in effect, continuing the priorities they had pursued throughout their postwar efforts at economic recovery. American ECA officials in Oslo applauded the Norwegian sacrifices and constructive efforts; American ECA officials in Washington and Paris saw the Norwegian policies as economic nationalism contrary to America's policies promoting free flow of goods and services. Richard M. Bissel of the ECA in Washington insisted that the Norwegians "start immediately on reduction of investment expenditures by spreading [their] program over [a] longer period." He made it quite clear that if Norway did not conform, the result could be reductions in ECA aid to that country.[31]

Officials in Washington complained that the ECA mission in Oslo seemed "to be acting more often in the role of apologist for the Norwegian Government than as the local exponent of the views of ECA Washington." One ECA officer in Washington urged "a change of the ECA Mission Chief at Oslo at the earliest possible opportunity."[32] Not surprisingly, Norway found it necessary to compromise and reduce its ambitious investment policies.

In addition to those varied differences and difficulties, cold war and security considerations increasingly influenced foreign aid policies – even in the Economic Cooperation Administration.[33]

The United States Congress appropriated a total of $17 billion for ECA aid to European countries over the four-year life of the program. Altogether Norway received $426.5 million in ECA Marshall Plan assistance from April 1948 through December 1951. The total of all United States economic aid, grants, loans, and credits to Norway from 1945 to August 1953, not counting military aid, came to nearly $530 million – just over a half billion dollars.[34] By the time the program ended, war damage in Norway had been repaired. The Norwegian merchant marine and industrial and agricultural production surpassed prewar levels. As a Mutual Security Agency publication phrased it early in 1952, "The Norwegians have contributed the bulk of efforts and resources behind the drive toward recovery in Norway. American aid, in terms of percentages, is small. But the Norwegians are the first to insist that without assistance from the United States the Norwegian economy could not make such progress toward recovery as it now is making." It was entirely appropriate that the Norwegian committee awarded the 1953 Nobel Peace Prize to George C. Marshall.[35]

THE developing cold war between the Communist countries led by the Soviet Union and the Western countries led by the United States and Great Britain increasingly dominated world affairs – and relations between Norway and the United States. Substantial friction between the Soviet Union and the West was evident even during World War II. It grew more acute and alarming in the years following the war. Both Norway and the United States, in varied degree, tried to keep alive the "Yalta axioms," and to negotiate East-West differences amicably. Those efforts often failed.

Russia converted states in eastern Europe into Soviet-dominated satellites. It tried unsuccessfully to get control of northern Iran, pressured Norway for a larger role in Spitsbergen, and frustrated efforts to negotiate postwar peace treaties. It used its veto to block action in the Security Council of the United Nations and used that world organization as a propaganda forum. It established the Cominform. States on all sides wondered about the limits of Soviet expansionist ambitions. They were troubled by Communist agitation and subversion, and many worried that World War III might erupt before the world had fully recovered from World War II.

On February 22, 1946, George F. Kennan at the American embassy in Moscow sent a long telegram to the Department of State analyzing Soviet actions and advising on policies for coping with them. Circulated at the highest government levels, that telegram helped reshape American thinking on policy toward the Soviet Union. On March 5, 1946, Britain's Winston Churchill, with President Truman beside him, told an American audience in Fulton, Missouri, "From Stettin in the Baltic to Trieste in the Adriatic, an iron curtain has descended across the continent." Early in 1947 Great Britain dropped the problem of support for Greece and Turkey into America's lap. It warned that without substantial aid Communist guerrillas might triumph in Greece and Turkey might succumb to Soviet pressures. Consequently President Truman asked Congress for $400 million to aid Greece and Turkey. In his key statement, which came to be known as the "Truman Doctrine," the president said: "It must be the policy of the United States to support free peoples who are resisting attempted subjugation by armed minorities or by outside pressures." In June 1947 the secretary of state made his speech at Harvard that led to the Marshall Plan and the European Recovery Program. In July 1947 the distinguished journal *Foreign Affairs* published an article by Kennan, then policy planning adviser in the Department of State, calling for "a long-term, patient but firm and vigilant containment of Russian expansive tendencies." The cold war was on!

How did Norway react to these developments? How did those developments affect Norwegian-American relations? What would they do to Norwegian efforts to "build bridges" between East and West and to avoid alienating either side in great-power confrontations? How would they affect Norway's cautious "on-the-fence" role?

Norway persisted in its efforts at amicable relations with the Soviet Union and never gave them up entirely. By the autumn of 1947, however, Norwegian leaders were losing their patience and were turning more toward the West in foreign affairs. Norwegian reaction to the Truman Doctrine was mixed and cautious. Conservatives generally applauded it, but most Norwegians were uneasy about its sweeping language and divisive impact. Early Norwegian responses to the Marshall Plan were guarded. Norwegians worried that the plan and the Soviet response to it would have divisive consequences and would lead to the formation of opposing political blocs.[36]

In October 1947, as Foreign Minister Lange prepared to depart Oslo to head the Norwegian delegation to the United Nations General Assembly session in New York, he expressed deepening pessimism about the growing antagonism between the great powers. He complained that Americans had already given up in their efforts to reconcile differences with the Soviet Union. He conceded that the Soviets were difficult, perhaps impossible, to get along with; everyone's patience was wearing thin. But he thought American patience had been exhausted before abandonment of all hope was fully justified.

Lange's patience was reaching its limits, too, however, and his fundamental sympathy with the West was manifesting itself. He told the American chargé d'affaires ad interim, Cloyce K. Huston, that if the November meeting of the Council of Foreign Ministers in London "should lead to a definite impasse or break, which I fear, I feel we *must* enter into a complete reconsideration of Norwegian foreign policy." Huston interpreted Lange's statement to mean that Norway could "no longer continue to ride two horses in case it becomes clear that the horses are definitely going in opposite directions." Huston concluded that Lange was "now contemplating the possibility of abandonment of Norway's past policy of seeking at all costs to avoid being drawn into one or another of two blocs" and that the time was approaching "when Norway may find it necessary to abandon its middle-of-the-road policy and align itself more definitely with the Western powers."[37] Conversations with other top figures in the Labor government, the foreign office, and the military made clear that others involved in Norwegian policy-making processes were moving in the same direction.[38]

When Foreign Minister Lange returned from the General Assembly session in New York, and after the breakup of the meeting of the Council of Foreign Ministers in London, the patterns were those that Lange—and Huston—had anticipated. Terje Wold was then chairman of the Foreign Affairs Committee in the Storting and a member of the Norwegian delegation to the United Nations. Previously the Americans had considered him sympathetic with the Soviet Union. After his return from New York, however, he told Huston, "Your country is performing a great service for the world. I have tremendous admiration for American policy, particularly now that it has become firm. You *must* be firm with those fellows; it is the only way to deal with them." After a conversation with Lange, Huston concluded that the foreign minister's remarks were "more clearly critical of the Soviet Union and openly favorable to the United States than any he has made in our past conversations."[39]

Huston was a career foreign service officer with substantial experience in Norway. In December 1947, in his impressively detailed and informative "Survey of Soviet Interests and Activities in Norway," Huston summarized:

> Norwegian policy has been undergoing a slow but definite metamorphosis during recent months and . . . there is an increasing tendency among Norwegian officials to recognize that Norway's fate is tied to the West. This tendency probably began, almost imperceptibly, at the time of the emergency of the "Truman Doctrine" last winter and received fresh impetus when the Marshall Plan for European recovery was announced a few months later. . . . Norway must be considered as being essentially pro-Western. The Embassy is convinced that all of the country's important leaders . . . will unhesitantly turn to the West in the event of an emergency. . . . The former on-the-fence policy is already changing.[40]

Huston was correct. The "emergency" that he anticipated came early in 1948 in the form of the Communist coup d'état in

Czechoslovakia, pressure on Finland to sign a "pact of friendship" with the Soviet Union, and reports from various sources in Europe that Norway was next on the Soviet list.[41] Those developments provoked very serious concern, approaching alarm, in Norwegian policy-making circles. Norwegian leaders were concerned whether the United States and Great Britain would require peacetime cooperation as a price for their support if actual war threatened or erupted.

On February 17, 1948, Norwegian Defense Minister Jens C. Hauge queried the American naval and air attachés in Oslo at length to find out about the "possibilities and probable character of American assistance to Norway in case of war." The attachés forwarded the defense minister's inquiry to Washington, where it was routed to the Joint Chiefs of Staff for their consideration.[42] On February 29 Prime Minister Gerhardsen, in a speech to a Labor party meeting, strongly condemned Communist plotting against democratic societies.[43] Foreign Minister Lange made unequivocally clear to both British and American representatives that Norway would reject any defense or security pact that the Soviet Union might propose.[44] Early in March Lange pointedly asked both Ambassador Bay and the British ambassador to Norway what policies their two governments might follow on aid to Norway if the Soviet Union threatened.[45] Lange also conferred with the foreign ministers of Denmark and Sweden to determine what support those Scandinavian countries might provide for Norway against the Soviet Union. In mid-March the Norwegian Storting voted 100 million kroner for an extraordinary appropriation to increase military preparedness. Only the eleven Communists and one pacifist Labor party member voted against the appropriation. On March 15 all leaves for Norwegian army and navy personnel were canceled. Early in April the Storting created a special committee to consider foreign relations and military affairs. The new committee excluded Communists, who had representation on the Storting's regular Committee on Foreign Affairs.[46]

Norwegian alarm helped trigger action in Great Britain and the United States that led to creation of the North Atlantic Treaty Organization. British Foreign Minister Ernest Bevin was already in the process of forming the Brussels Pact military accord, composed of Britain, France, Belgium, the Netherlands, and Luxemburg—not including Norway and the United States. In a highly secret communication to the United States on March 11, however, Bevin indicated that he thought there was "ground for Norwegian apprehensions and that Soviet demands on Norway will in fact be made shortly." He suggested that American and British representatives in Oslo "be instructed to do their best to infuse some courage into the Norwegian Government." He recognized that the Brussels Pact countries "could not by themselves effectively defend Scandinavia against pressure." Bevin contended that "the most effective course would be to take very early steps, before Norway goes under, to conclude under Article 51 of the Charter of the United Nations a regional Atlantic Approaches Pact of Mutual Assistance." He believed Britain and the United States "should study without any delay the establishment of such an Atlantic security system." The alternative, he thought, would be "to repeat our experience with Hitler and to witness helplessly the slow deterioration of our position, until we are forced in much less favourable circumstances to resort to war in order to defend our lives and liberty."[47] Conceivably Bevin may have been "using" Norway's concerns to draw the United States more fully into European security arrangements. If so, his tactic worked.

After conferring with President Truman and Secretary of Defense James Forrestal, Secretary of State Marshall promptly responded to Bevin that the United States was "prepared to proceed at once in the joint discussions on the establishment of an Atlantic security system." He suggested that British representatives come to Washington "early next week" to discuss the matter.[48] At the same time Marshall directed Ambassador Bay to tell Foreign Minister Lange that the United States was "giving most urgent consideration to question of Norwegian security," and that "if Soviet demands are made on Norway, in our opinion it is imperative that Norway adamantly resist such demands and pressure." He informed Lange that the United States was in communication with the British government "about Norwegian situation."[49] On March 17 President Truman delivered two important speeches urging that "the determination of the free countries of Europe to protect themselves . . . be matched by an equal determination on our part to help them protect themselves."[50]

One should not exaggerate Norway's role in the background of the creation of NATO. But Trygve Lie had proposed the general idea at least as early as 1940 and had advanced it in a formal Norwegian policy document two years later. Norwegian security concerns vis-à-vis the Soviet Union early in 1948 played a central role in triggering British and American initiatives that led directly to the negotiation of the North Atlantic Pact and to the creation of NATO.

In mid-April 1948 Norway submitted to the United States a list of military equipment it particularly needed to build up its military strength. It included tanks, radar, antiaircraft ammunition, clothing and boots, and jeeps and other vehicles. The Department of State advised Secretary of Defense Forrestal that it attached "great importance, from the political viewpoint, to the fulfillment of the Norwegian request to the greatest extent practicable."[51]

At the same time Foreign Minister Lange continued to speak out, making it unequivocally clear that Norway would reject any Soviet-proposed pact, that Norway clearly identified with the Western democracies, and that it could not "remain indifferent to the ideological war between democracy and totalitarianism."[52] Also in April Dag Bryn, Norway's undersecretary of defense, and Gunnar Jahn, director of the Norges Bank, traveled to Washington to discuss Norway's military needs. The State Department made certain that Bryn and Jahn had opportunities to discuss their needs with appropriate military and civilian officials in the United States.[53]

On June 14 Secretary of Defense Forrestal informed Secretary of State Marshall that the Joint Chiefs of Staff had concluded "that the United States should provide equipment first to strengthen Norway's military posture as a deterrent to Soviet armed aggression, and second to enable the Norwegian forces to resist actively an actual attack." He indicated that a small amount of surplus military equipment should be furnished promptly to encourage the Norwegian government but that further equipment would depend on appropriations, on the needs of other countries, and on worldwide military priorities. Marshall concurred in the recommendation and informed Ambassador Bay to that effect.[54]

In July 1948 the United States began top secret exploratory

talks that ultimately culminated in the North Atlantic Pact. Norway was not included in those early deliberations, but Marshall assured the Norwegians that he had the "problem of Norwegian and Danish security much in mind."[55]

Throughout 1948 and into early 1949 Foreign Minister Lange also conducted negotiations with the foreign ministers from Denmark and Sweden. Some (not including Lange) considered a Scandinavian military defense accord a viable alternative to a North Atlantic pact. But differences among the three Scandinavian countries proved insuperable. Sweden wanted a Scandinavian defense pact that would be neutral in the cold war and independent of any security ties with the North Atlantic powers; Norway would have welcomed a Scandinavian defense pact providing it was tied to North Atlantic security arrangements in the West; Denmark was torn between the two positions but drew closer to Norway in the deliberations. Sweden would not compromise its position of neutrality, and Norway would not back off from its insistence that any Scandinavian pact must be linked with North Atlantic security arrangements. Lange realized very early that the differences between Norway and Sweden could not be reconciled. He also realized, however, that many in Norway – especially in his own Labor party – would turn away from a Scandinavian accord only with great reluctance. It was a domestic political reality that he had to handle with great care. Consequently he persisted in protracted Scandinavian negotiations even after he was convinced that a viable compromise was impossible.[56]

In July 1948 Secretary of Defense Forrestal responded to the Norwegian request for specified military equipment. He wrote Secretary Marshall that "in view of important legal and logistic considerations we are unable to provide more than a token assistance at the present time." He thought the Norwegian request, along with comparable requests from other governments, made it clear that the United States should develop "a carefully planned and comprehensive approach to military assistance in general."[57] The State Department informed Norway of the response to its request for military equipment. The Norwegian government decided not to take the token obsolete tanks and rocket launchers that the United States had been willing to release. Instead Norway hoped that "perhaps at a later date it might be possible for the U.S. Government to reconsider the question of military equipment for Norway."[58]

Early in September the secretary of state provided the American embassy in Oslo with a National Security Council report on American policy toward Scandinavia, a report approved by President Truman. That NSC 28/1 report viewed the Scandinavian countries as "strategically important both to the United States and the USSR." It believed that "the chief threat to the Scandinavian nations arises from the possibility of direct Soviet action against one or more of them in the form of severe diplomatic pressure or outright attack." It noted that both Norway and Denmark had "now determined forcibly to resist any Soviet armed attack and actively to suppress further communist infiltration." It specifically mentioned that "the Norwegians have, in fact, officially stated their determination to defend themselves if attacked and their unequivocal refusal, if approached, to negotiate a military pact with the Soviets." Though Norwegian military forces were much too weak to offer effective prolonged resistance to a Soviet attack, the NSC report "believed that with a relatively small amount of added equipment, they are capable of maintaining internal security, and might, if properly organized and strengthened by outside aid, constitute some deterrent to attack." The report concluded that it was "in the security interests of the United States that Norway, Denmark and Sweden remain free from Soviet domination." It recommended that the United States try to "strengthen the present tendency of Norway and Denmark to align themselves with the Western Powers." It advised the United States to support Norway and Denmark by extending economic aid, by providing military equipment, and by combating Communist propaganda through an intensified United States information program. It also recommended supporting Norway in maintaining its sovereignty over Spitsbergen.[59]

In late September the Department of State informed Norway in general terms of the progress that had been made in the negotiation of a North Atlantic pact. It made clear that other countries in the North Atlantic area would be consulted before drafting the final pact to determine whether they were prepared to accept the responsibilities that might go with membership.[60]

At the end of 1948 Ambassador Morgenstierne impatiently asked the State Department when Norway would be approached to participate in the ongoing negotiations. He was assured that the United States planned "to arrange so that Norway will have an opportunity to comment on the draft and make appropriate suggestions for alterations in it."[61]

The year 1948 had not brought formal Norwegian involvement in any Western alliance system. Norway continued its Scandinavian negotiations and was not yet included in the negotiation of the North Atlantic Pact. But the die was already cast. Whatever the other Scandinavian countries might do, Norway under its Labor government was prepared to join forces with the United States and the West in the cold war against the Soviet Union and the Communist bloc.

That policy had the support of all the parties represented in the Storting except the Communists and a segment of the Labor party. According to public opinion polls it had the support of the majority of the Norwegian people. It won its strongest support in conservative circles. With the Labor government providing positive leadership, however, even a majority of Labor supported it.[62]

In January 1949 the Soviet Union submitted a demarche to the Norwegian government labeling the projected Atlantic pact aggressive, in conflict with the United Nations, and endangering world peace. Norway promptly responded that, given the ineffectiveness of the United Nations, it felt its security required regional cooperation for defense. It assured the Soviet Union that Norway would never cooperate in aggressive policies and would not allow military bases for foreign powers on its territory so long as it was not threatened by attack. It noted that Norway and Russia had long lived peacefully as neighbors, and Norway hoped to have friendly relations with all peace-loving countries.[63]

Much of Norway's whole consideration of the North Atlantic Pact and of Norway's relation to it came together during February 1949, one year after the Communist coup d'état in Czechoslovakia and Soviet pressure on Finland had ignited Norway's concerns. By February negotiations for a Scandinavian pact had broken down over the conflicting positions of Sweden and Norway on the relation of such a pact to the major North Atlantic states. On February 5 the Soviet Union directed a second major communication to the Norwegian government, proposing a nonaggression pact. At the same time Foreign Minister Lange, Oscar Torp of the Labor party in the Storting, and Undersecretary of Defense Dag Bryn traveled to the United States to inform themselves better on the issues involved in the pending North Atlantic Pact and Norway's relations to it.[64]

After a confidential conversation with a member of the foreign service staff of the Norwegian embassy in Washington, Charles E. Rogers of the Department of State Division of Northern European Affairs summarized the situation in these terms:

> The impact of the breakdown of Scandinavian negotiations in Oslo and of the two Soviet demarches upon the Norwegian population has been very great. This impact was particularly felt within the Labor Party which has been split on the issue of Norway's adherence to the North Atlantic Pact. The Norwegian Government now considers that it requires all-out support from the United States in order to save itself, and the decision of Norway which can no longer be postponed depends upon that support. The Norwegian Delegation intends to lay all its cards on the table and hopes for similar treatment from us.[65]

The Norwegians wanted to know American attitudes toward a Scandinavian pact. They were concerned about Norwegian security between the time it might sign the North Atlantic Pact and the time it might receive arms from America – an interval that Secretary Marshall had said might be as long as a year.[66]

Secretary of State Dean Acheson, who had replaced Marshall in January 1949, in consultation with President Truman, concluded that Norway must decide for itself whether it would join the North Atlantic Pact or a Scandinavian pact; the United States would not advise the Norwegians or press them on the matter. They also agreed that they would not exert pressure on Norway by promising or withholding military supplies.[67]

Secretary of State Acheson also consulted Secretary of Defense Forrestal to get guidance from the Joint Chiefs of Staff on the relation of Scandinavia to the North Atlantic Pact. The Joint Chiefs of Staff considered Scandinavia of major strategic importance defensively; it was "in the security interest of the United States that Norway, Denmark, and Sweden remain free of domination by the USSR." A neutral Scandinavian pact could share that view but would be too weak and ineffective to be able to prevent Soviet aggression or domination. The Joint Chiefs of Staff much preferred Norwegian and Danish membership in the North Atlantic Treaty Organization rather than rely on any independent Scandinavian pact.[68]

Foreign Minister Lange met with President Truman while he was in America, and Lange and his colleagues had their final meeting with Secretary of State Acheson on February 11. The Americans had earnestly tried to respond helpfully to the Norwegian queries and had tried to avoid bringing any kind of pressure on Norway. Lange, in turn, was open in his discussions with the Americans. He made clear that Norway could not countenance foreign troops based on Norwegian soil except in case of attack or threatened attack.[69] At the same time the Soviet Union sternly warned Norway against joining the North Atlantic Pact.[70]

On February 19, 1949, the Labor party congress united to approve Norway's adherence to a North Atlantic pact. The initial vote was 329 to 35 in favor.[71] On February 24 Foreign Minister Lange asked the Storting to authorize the government to participate in the negotiation of the North Atlantic Pact.[72] On March 3 the Storting voted 118 to 11 to authorize the Norwegian government to accept an invitation to participate in the Washington negotiations on the pact. The abstentions were largely by members of the majority Labor party who disagreed with the decision.

The United States immediately invited Norwegian participation, and on March 4, 1949, Ambassador Morgenstierne joined in the deliberations. Norway was the first country outside of the original seven to participate.[73] In addition, on March 3 Norway formally responded to the Soviet note of February 5. The Norwegian response was friendly, but it rejected the invitation to conclude a nonaggression pact with the Soviet Union.[74]

On March 29 the Storting voted 130 to 13 to authorize the government to sign and ratify the final North Atlantic Pact. The eleven Communists in the Storting and two members of the Labor party cast the negative votes.[75] On April 4, 1949, at an official ceremony in Washington, D.C., representatives of twelve governments formally signed the North Atlantic Pact. With President Truman at his side, Secretary of State Acheson signed for the United States. Foreign Minister Lange and Ambassador Morgenstierne signed for Norway. The United States Senate approved the treaty by a vote of 82 to 13 on July 21. Ratifications were exchanged, and the treaty went into effect on August 24, 1949.[76]

The North Atlantic Pact was the first formal European alliance to which the United States was a party since it had ended its alliance with France nearly a century and a half earlier. Norway was the only one of the twelve original members of the North Atlantic Treaty Organization to have a common border with the Soviet Union. The members of NATO agreed to consult whenever the "territorial integrity, political independence or security" of any one of them was threatened. The pact provided that "an armed attack against one or more of them in Europe or North America shall be considered an attack against them all," and that in the event of such an attack they would "assist the Party or Parties so attacked by taking forthwith, individually and in concert with the other Parties, such action as it deems necessary, including the use of armed force, to restore and maintain the security of the North Atlantic area." NATO developed complex organizational and planning machinery that a simple alliance could not provide. With American and Norwegian adherence to the North Atlantic Pact, both countries formally ended their long traditions of neutrality and nonalignment in European security affairs.[77]

The choice of General Dwight D. Eisenhower to be the first NATO supreme allied commander Europe (SACEUR) was popular both in the United States and in Norway. His three visits to Norway in 1951 in his capacity as SACEUR were huge successes. The visits were ceremonial, but the general and his staff also played constructive roles in helping to iron out difficulties that inevitably arose in the implementation of the North Atlantic Pact.[78]

AFTER the accomplishment of the North Atlantic Pact much of the focus in relations between the United States and Norway centered on United States military aid. The United States Congress, after heated debate, adopted the Mutual Defense Assistance Program, which President Truman signed into law on October 6, 1949. It provided an initial sum of $1 billion for military assistance to states in the North Atlantic Treaty Organization.[79] On January 27, 1950, in Washington, D.C., representatives of the United States and Norway signed the bilateral Mutual Defense Assistance Agreement. The Norwegian Storting unanimously approved the agreement on February 21. It went into effect three days later on February 24 when King Haakon and Foreign Minister Lange signed the proclamation approving and ratifying the agreement.[80]

The United States named Rear Admiral Ralph E. Jennings to head the Military Assistance Advisory Group (MAAG) in Norway. He and his top officers arrived in Oslo on February 21 to take on their duties.[81]

From the beginning there were differences between the Americans and the Norwegians over the size of the MAAG staff. The Americans wanted at least sixty persons, while the Norwegians wanted no more than twenty-two. A conspicuous American military presence could play into the allegations by Norwegian Communists that the United States was "taking over" their little country. Ambassador Bay explained the difficulty:

> The Norwegians—due to such factors as the smallness of their country, the harsh experience of the German occupation in recent years, and their known traits of individuality—are a proud and sensitive people. They do not have a military tradition, and have always been characterized by a peaceful and at times even a pacifistic outlook in international affairs. Hence the presence of a group of foreign military personnel in their midst, from no matter how friendly a country, represents a political problem to the Norwegian Government.[82]

After tactful negotiations the Norwegians and Americans worked out ways of masking the size of the American MAAG staff in Norway. By counting only the commissioned and warrant officers as part of the group, they were able to say the number was kept at twenty-two. The administrative assistant for the Mutual Defense Assistance Program in Norway, six enlisted men, and six civilian secretaries all were carried on the embassy roster as "embassy support personnel." The MAAG staff of twenty-two was in fact a staff of thirty- five. At the same time the Norwegians agreed to accept special missions and mobile training teams on temporary assignment in Norway.[83]

By the middle of 1953 the public figure for the MAAG staff was thirty-three. The actual total at that time was ninety-three, when one added the thirty-one noncommissioned military personnel and nine civilians that were carried as "embassy administrative support," plus twenty technical representatives on "temporary duty" with MAAG. Norway continued to be sensitive about making public the actual size of the MAAG staff in their country.[84]

There was a chronic problem of finding living quarters and office space for the expanding American personnel in Oslo. Early in 1950 the Norwegian government obtained forty-four rooms for office space for the MAAG by requisitioning the Hotel Terminus. Locating housing for the Americans and their families was not accomplished so expeditiously.[85]

The first shipment of arms from the United States to Norway (three hundred tons of small arms and ammunition) reached Oslo on April 20, 1950. Except for the distribution of some Communist handbills, and hostile headlines and editorials in the Communist newspaper, *Friheten*, the occasion went smoothly. Norwegian newspapers, Norwegian government officials, Admiral Jennings, and the Department of State International Information and Educational Exchange Program (USIE) all helped give favorable publicity to American military aid. Norway's defense minister, Jens Christian Hauge, said: "We cannot develop an effective defense alone; this assistance will strengthen our efforts to avert war and secure peace."[86]

The first airplanes furnished to Norway by the Mutual Defense Assistance Program (MDAP) (two twin-engine C-47 cargo airplanes) arrived on May 20.[87] As shipments of military equipment began to arrive more frequently, Admiral Jennings encouraged giving more publicity to the operations.[88] All of that was accompanied by Norwegian actions to increase and improve Norway's own military preparations.[89]

Among the Norwegians visiting the United States was Prime

Minister Gerhardsen, who spent two weeks traveling there in May 1951. He lunched with President Truman when he was in Washington. Shortly after his return to Norway an American congressional delegation, headed by the chairman of the House Foreign Affairs Committee, visited Oslo.[90] On September 10, 1951, with General Eisenhower present, there was a colorful ceremony at Sola Air Base outside Stavanger on the occasion of the delivery of the first five Thunderjet fighter-bombers to Norway. Accompanying Eisenhower was Lieutenant General Lauris Norstad, whose Norwegian grandparents had emigrated from Stavanger to America.[91]

Admiral Jennings was pleased with the arrival of the military equipment from the United States and with the publicity given that assistance. He was not pleased, however, with the Norwegian capability to receive, use, and maintain that equipment. The end of World War II had found Norway almost without organized military forces. Norway had a highly literate and able population, but its military forces in the cold war had a shortage of professional military officers and technical personnel. It depended heavily on young men drafted for short-term military training and service. It did not have a strong modern military tradition. Norwegians did not rank the military high in their scale of values, and able young men rarely chose to make careers as officers in the armed forces. Norwegian individualism, the maritime and agrarian economy, and the comparatively sparse population were not conducive to the development of a sophisticated bureaucratic organization.

As early as May 7, 1951, Admiral Jennings wrote to the Norwegian defense minister that "equipment is now being received in volumes which in many cases are overtaxing accounting and maintenance facilities, and the situation will continue to worsen until competent personnel in adequate numbers are placed in custodial units. The MAAG is now recommending that action be taken to postpone the shipping of equipment items which are clearly liable to be neglected for lack of proper maintenance." He recommended further training of both commissioned and noncommissioned officers and an increase in the period of national service to a minimum of eighteen months.[92]

In July Admiral Jennings wrote to the Director of the Joint American Military Advisory Group recommending "that no further allocations be made to Norway until requested by this MAAG except for a limited number of items in quantities which are required for maintenance and training."[93] Ambassador Bay concurred in the admiral's recommendation because of the "inadequate personnel program of Norwegian Defense Ministry." He advised, however, that a decision be delayed until the Norwegian cabinet MDAP committee looked into the matter.[94] Gross of the ECA advised moving with less haste.[95] On August 6 Ambassador Bay wrote Foreign Minister Lange about the problem: "Norway's conscriptees cannot, in general, be depended upon for continuity of maintenance and periodic operation of the more complicated types of equipment for the reason that, by the time they have completed their basic training and their apprenticeship in maintenance procedures, they are mustered out."[96]An official study in London concluded:

> A 12 month conscript period, the lack of a regular army, an acute shortage of trained officers and NCOs, an inefficient administrative system, the lack of supporting establishments, and a defense philosophy based upon the mobilization of forces only upon the outbreak of war make it unlikely that the Norwegians will actually produce effective fighting units of the size publicly announced, even by 1954. Partly responsible for these conditions is Norway's meager military tradition which results in a complete lack of experience in modern military operations and the requirements for those operations. Thus the Norwegians have not comprehended the magnitude of their undertaking, and have not yet felt the necessity to undertake correcting deficiencies not apparent to them. It is of primary importance that Norway establish a fulltime, regular force of sufficient size to meet her commitments.[97]

On August 16, 1951, Ambassador Bay, Admiral Jennings, and the MAAG met with the Norwegian Cabinet MDAP Committee. That was the first opportunity the Americans had had to present to members of the cabinet, other than Defense Minister Hauge, the seriousness of the Norwegian deficiencies. At a second meeting on September 7 Hauge reluctantly conceded that the MAAG recommendations for postponement of deliveries should be acted on.[98]

In May 1952 Admiral Jennings's tour as chief of the MAAG in Norway ended. He was succeeded by Rear Admiral James Foskett.[99] In a final report to Ambassador Bay, Jennings wrote that the Storting still had "not taken effective corrective action." He pointed out that "no Norwegian units, except the training brigade in Germany, have been allocated or even earmarked for assignment to SHAPE [Supreme Headquarters, Allied Powers, Europe] either in peace or war." He concluded that "The failure of the Norwegian Government to face up to the personnel program squarely and to take corrective action has in my opinion resulted in a delay of about one year in the progress toward the attainment of their Medium Term Defense Plan goals."[100]

The United States Information Service in Norway used the departure of Admiral Jennings as the occasion for more publicity about the Mutual Defense Assistance Program and the functions of the MAAG. As a part of that publicity it arranged an interview of the admiral, which was published in *Militaer Orientering*, a magazine for military officers published by the Norwegian Ministry of Defense. The article described Jennings as "modest and quiet-spoken" but with "definite opinions." The admiral complained of "the lack of sufficient personnel to handle the matters in connection with the modernization of the defenses and the increase of men in the armed forces." He emphasized that "the quality of Norwegian youth is good enough," but they needed longer training and "more permanent personnel." He emphasized two key words for his Norwegian colleagues: "Personnel—Quality."

While underscoring the difficulties, Admiral Jennings also provided specific information on the magnitude of American military aid to Norway during the more than two years he had served there:

> Norway had received a total of 118,000 tons of military supplies and equipment. The shipments have, among other things, included jet fighter planes, C-47 transport planes, modern radar, radio, and electronic equipment, all types of military vehicles, tanks, 75 and 57 mm. recoilless rifles, Garand rifles, bazookas, field artillery and anti-aircraft artillery, MTB's and other smaller type naval vessels. In addition,

Norway has received spare parts, special tools, and other things necessary to maintain the equipment.

The U.S. Army has trained approximately 500 officers and enlisted men in communications, artillery, infantry and various courses in schools both in the United States and in the U.S. zone of Germany. The United States Navy has trained 30 officers and enlisted men in schools in the U.S., while U.S. technical training teams have trained another 400 Norwegian Naval personnel in Norway. The United States Air Force has trained 635 Norwegians as pilots, aircraft maintenance, armament, electronics, communications, and supply personnel, while another 200 have been trained by the U.S. 12th Air Force in Germany. The United States Army has also supplied a number of training teams to train personnel in Norway, and to aid in the solution of various problems.[101]

In the midst of all that activity Norway changed prime minister and defense minister. Though he was to return for longer service as prime minister later, Einar Gerhardsen resigned for "personal reasons" in November 1951. Oscar Torp replaced him as prime minister in the Labor government. Torp's style and temperament were different from Gerhardsen's, but he fully shared the foreign policy and defense views of his predecessor. Lange continued as foreign minister in the government, but Torp dismissed Hauge as defense minister early in 1952. In August 1952 Torp visited the United States, as his two predecessors as prime minister had done earlier. While in the United States he met with President Truman, Secretary of State Acheson, and other officials and traveled extensively in the country.[102]

The Labor government under Torp earnestly tried to make changes and reforms to correct the deficiencies that Admiral Jennings had pointed out. In reporting on the actions of the Storting in the summer of 1952, the American chargé d'affaires ad interim in Oslo, William P. Snow, wrote, "This illustrates what the Government can and will do with a difficult issue in its own way and at its own speed, once it is convinced that it is in Norway's interest. It also reflects creditably upon the good sense of the Norwegians in general and their support of NATO, even if in our eyes they should have put some of those things through a year or more ago." Those changes were adopted at a time when the Soviet military threat seemed less immediate in Norwegian eyes than it had appeared earlier. Snow advised the State Department that the Norwegians were "apt to find advice from outside distasteful on these matters but they resist it less when it comes from multilateral sources." He recommended that "our tactics in order to win the cooperation of the Norwegians should be mainly to afford them as much of a genuine sense of participation as is possible."[103]

On December 10, 1952, the MAAG United States Information Service arranged a ceremony on the occasion of the arrival of the 150,000th ton of MDAP deliveries to Norway. The cost of that military equipment to the United States was more than $115 million and was in addition to the cost of training and services for Norway.[104]

In 1954 Rear Admiral John Hazard Carson replaced Admiral Foskett as chief of the MAAG in Norway.[105] Through those years Norway had continued to press ahead in its military preparations and reforms. By 1954 Ambassador L. Corrin Strong was able to conclude, "While there are many points at which improvements could be desired, the Norwegian defense build-up has, on the whole, been developing satisfactorily." In his view, "Bearing in mind Norway's lack of experience in the defense field and the traditional antipathy of her people to military matters as such, I am impressed by Norway's sustained effort and the extent of its progress as a member of NATO."[106]

RELATIONS between Norway and the United States focused overwhelmingly on Europe and the North Atlantic. From time to time, however, crises in East Asia forced themselves into Norwegian-American concerns and deliberations. Among those crises were the triumph of the Communists under Mao Tse-tung over Chiang Kai-shek's Nationalists on the mainland of China in 1949 and the Korean War from 1950 to 1953.

Both of those dramatic events in Asia involved the United Nations, including both Norway and the United States. Both countries, of course, were represented in the General Assembly. The United States was a permanent member of the Security Council. In the 1949-50 session Norway was one of the non-permanent members of the Security Council. And Norway's Trygve Lie served as secretary-general of the United Nations.

Despite America's support for Chiang Kai-shek, the so-called China White Paper issued in the summer of 1949 by Secretary of State Acheson seemed to point toward possible United States diplomatic recognition of Mao's government of the People's Republic of China.[107] But the Chinese Communists did not make it easy for the United States to follow that course. In addition to its hostile propaganda, Mao's government confined the American consul general at Mukden, Angus Ward, members of his staff, and their families to the consular compound for months. In October 1949 Ward and four members of his staff were arrested, imprisoned, tried, convicted, and sentenced. After formal protests from numerous governments, including Norway, they finally were released and deported near the end of November.[108] Charges by Senator Joseph McCarthy and others of Communist influences in the Department of State made it politically impossible seriously to consider American recognition of the Communist government of China.

Norway generally followed the lead of Great Britain on dealings with China. It severed diplomatic relations with the Nationalist government of China on the island of Formosa. Early in 1950 Norway, like Britain, attempted to extend diplomatic recognition to Mao's government. That government was not at all cooperative, however. Specifically it objected that Norway and other governments had not ousted Nationalist representatives from United Nations organs and had not seated representatives from the People's Republic of China. China sent no diplomatic representative to Norway. Norway's chargé d'affaires ad interim in Peking had only what one foreign service officer called a "quasi-diplomatic status."[109]

Neither American recognition of the Communist government of China nor the seating of Chinese Communist representatives in the United Nations had been accomplished when military forces of Communist-controlled North Korea crossed the thirty-eighth parallel and invaded South Korea on June 25, 1950. The United States promptly arranged to call the Security Council to meet on Sunday. A Soviet veto could have blocked action by the council, but at that time the Soviet Union was boycotting United Nations organs that seated representatives of Nationalist China. Consequently the Security Council adopted a resolution labeling the North Korean action "a breach of the peace," calling for "the immediate cessation of hostilities," demanding that North Korea withdraw its armed forces to the thirty-eighth parallel, and asking all United Nations members "to render every assistance to the United Nations in the execution of this resolution and to refrain from giving assistance to the North Korean authorities." Nine members of the Security Council (including both the United States and Norway) voted for the resolution. The representative from Yugoslavia abstained, and the Soviet representative was absent.[110]

On Tuesday, June 27, the Security Council by a vote of 7 to 1 approved a resolution recommending that members of the United Nations "furnish such assistance to the Republic of Korea as may be necessary to repel the armed attack and to restore international peace and security in the area." Again both Norway and the United States voted for the resolution. Yugoslavia cast the negative vote and the Soviet representative again was absent.[111]

The United States wanted Norway to introduce a resolution in the Security Council on July 7 establishing a unified command of United Nations forces in Korea and authorizing the United States to name the commander (who was certain to be General Douglas MacArthur). Though it did not oppose the action, Norway was reluctant to introduce the resolution. Consequently the British and French representatives did so. Norway and the United States were among the seven members who voted to approve it.[112]

As expected, President Truman named General MacArthur to command the United Nations forces in Korea. Those forces drew support from various member countries of the UN, but most of the military personnel were from South Korea and the United States. In the fall of 1950 the United Nations forces checked the North Korean advance, pushed them back to the thirty-eighth parallel, and then drove north toward the Yalu river separating North Korea from China. Late in November, however, Chinese military forces attacked across the Yalu and drove the United Nations forces under MacArthur back across the thirty-eighth parallel. Again the United Nations forces checked the advance by the Chinese and North Korean troops and drove them back across the thirty-eighth.

President Truman and the United Nations wanted the fighting limited to Korea. General MacArthur, however, wanted to expand the war by blockading China, having the Nationalist Chinese invade the mainland, and bombing bases in China north of the Yalu. MacArthur persisted in urging those actions in opposition to his civilian superiors in the United States and in the United Nations. Consequently in April 1951 President Truman relieved MacArthur of his command and replaced him with General Matthew Ridgway.

After prolonged negotiations (and after the death of Joseph Stalin in the Soviet Union and the inauguration of Dwight Eisenhower as president of the United States), United Nations negotiators concluded a truce with the Chinese and the North Koreans in July 1953. More than fifty thousand Americans died during the Korean War. Casualties were greater than in any previous American conflict except the Civil War, World War I, and World War II.

Norway did not provide troops to fight in the United Nations forces in Korea. But the Norwegian government did approve of the American and United Nations actions. The Norwegian representative voted for the Security Council resolutions authorizing United Nations military actions in Korea. Despite apprehensions, Norwegian leaders and most of the press applauded the American course. They were less pleased by President Truman's decision to use America's Seventh Fleet in the Formosa Strait to protect Nationalist China on Formosa.[113]

The massive intervention of Chinese troops alongside the North Korean forces evoked mixed feelings among the Norwegians. Nonetheless, on February 1, 1951, Norway joined with the United States, Great Britain, and other countries in voting for the United Nations resolution branding Communist China an aggressor for its role in the Korean War.[114] In 1951 Norway did not favor allowing United Nations troops to drive north of the thirty-eighth parallel a second time, and Norwegians generally approved when President Truman dismissed General MacArthur.[115]

Though Norway did not provide combat troops to fight in Korea, it did provide a fully staffed field hospital for service there. It also provided a merchant ship, the *Belocean*, for the Military Sea Transportation Service in support of the United Nations operations in Korea.[116] Norwegians were pleased when Korean armistice negotiations got under way in 1951 and when they reached a successful conclusion in July 1953.[117]

Not until 1955, after the Korean War had ended, did the Communist People's Republic of China send a diplomatic representative to Norway and formally acknowledge the Norwegian chargé d'affaires in Peking.[118] The United States and the Communist government of China continued to withhold diplomatic recognition of each other, however. Norway favored seating delegates from the Communist government of China in the United Nations. But partly because of the United States, the United Nations continued to seat the delegates from the Nationalist government of China on Formosa and to deny representation to the People's Republic of China.

The cold war between Communist states and non-Communist states continued unabated both in Europe and in Asia. The policies and actions of the United States and Norway on the containment of Communist expansion were by no means identical. Each had its own distinctive perspectives conditioned by its separate historical experience, geography, values, and power. Understandably Norwegians were more persuaded of the necessity for sharing with the United States in concerted efforts to contain Soviet expansion in Europe than in Asia. Nonetheless, Norway and the United States continued to cooperate on most major foreign policy issues in the cold war, just as they had regularly shared common attitudes on foreign affairs when it really mattered ever since the two countries had first established formal diplomatic relations early in the twentieth century.

6

Toward the Future

THE year 1955 marked the fiftieth anniversary of Norway's separation from Sweden and of its independent constitutional monarchy under King Haakon VII. It also marked the end of the first half-century of formal diplomatic relations between the United States and Norway.

Norwegians in all walks of life joined in celebrating King Haakon's eighty-third birthday in 1955. He was the oldest reigning monarch in Europe and was feeling the weight of his years. Tall, lean, and erect, the king remained mentally keen, however, and he was alert to developments at home and abroad. In June he had welcomed Queen Elizabeth II and Prince Philip of Great Britain on a royal visit to Oslo and presided graciously over the occasion. But shortly after their departure, the king fell down, breaking his thighbone. He never fully recovered and was confined thereafter to his bed and a wheelchair. He died quietly on September 21, 1957, at the age of eighty-five

Over the course of his fifty-two-year reign, in peace and in war, King Haakon VII had won the love and respect of nearly all Norwegians. He was truly "the people's king." Among his treasured contributions to modern Norway were his unwavering commitment to democracy and freedom, his example for the proper functioning of a constitutional monarchy, his devotion to Norway and its well being, his orientation toward Great Britain and the

United States in foreign affairs, and his son, who as King Olav V succeeded him as the reigning monarch.

Tall, sturdy, ruggedly handsome, and athletic, King Olav shared his father's qualities of character, his values, his sound judgment, and his devotion to Norway and its people. His beloved wife Märtha had died in 1954, so he was compelled to reign without her at his side. But in the decades that followed, King Olav won a place in the hearts of the Norwegian people wholly worthy of his father's example.[1]

Early in 1955 Oscar Torp resigned his position as prime minister in the Labor government of Norway. Einar Gerhardsen returned to take up those duties that he had voluntarily relinquished to Torp four years earlier. Gerhardsen was to head the Labor government of Norway for ten years longer until October 1965 (with an interruption when a coalition government won power briefly in 1963). Through those many years Halvard Lange continued as Norway's foreign minister, as he had been since 1946.

Gerhardsen and Lange personified the generation of Norwegian leaders that had been molded, hardened, and tested in the fires of World War II. Both had actively resisted Nazi domination of their country, and both had paid the price for their boldness with long years in German prison camps. They needed no further instruction to understand the inadequacies of Norway's traditional policies of neutrality and noninvolvement in European affairs; they required no coaching to realize Norway's need for strong, reliable, like-minded allies to guard peace and security in the twentieth century.[2]

In the United States in 1955 the Republicans, under Dwight D. Eisenhower, controlled the presidency. John Foster Dulles served as his secretary of state. As a professional military officer Eisenhower had been tremendously popular with Norwegians during and after World War II. And if the American people were determined to put a Republican in the White House, Norwegians preferred Eisenhower to any likely alternative in the party. Dulles commanded greater knowledge and experience in foreign affairs than most of America's earlier secretaries of state. But a Norwegian public that had kept Labor governments in power for twenty years and would do so for decades to come was not likely to be inspired by the conservatism they associated with the Republican party – even under Eisenhower. Norwegians liked Eisenhower better as a general than as a president.[3]

Norwegians were uneasy about the dangers of a resurgent American "isolationism." They were more worried about American "isolationism" than they were about the American "imperialism" that the Communists warned against.[4] The Eisenhower who had commanded United Nations forces in World War II and NATO forces in the cold war was unlikely, however, to be attracted by the traditional American policies of nonintervention and "no entangling alliances." In practice President Eisenhower continued the multilateral policies of his Democratic predecessors in the White House, including an active role in the United Nations, containment, military preparedness, foreign aid, and a leadership role in the North Atlantic Treaty Organization.[5]

RELATIONS between Norway and the United States during the first half of the twentieth century revealed the processes by which those two democracies turned away from their well-established traditions of neutrality and noninvolvement in European wars toward active roles in multilateral collective security approaches in world affairs. A 1950 State Department statement on United States policies toward Norway phrased it in these words: "Both the US and Norway have enjoyed a long background of neutrality and relative isolation from European conflicts. Both have undergone parallel foreign policy revolutions of relatively recent origin as the result of German aggression in the last war and the existing threat of Soviet expansion which has for the first time during peace made relations between the two countries a matter of vital concern to both." Those separate but parallel transitions fundamentally changed the roles of both Norway and the United States in world affairs as well as the relations between the two countries.[6]

Through those fifty years of change and transition the United States and Norway sustained an unbroken pattern of good relations with each other. Differences that inevitably arose between them never were allowed to spoil those amicable relations. The

1950 State Department policy statement correctly asserted, "Relations between the US and Norway have almost without exception been friendly and have been characterized by a virtual absence of serious political issues. Attachment to the same concepts of democracy, mutually profitable commerce, and the presence in the US of large numbers of American citizens of Norwegian descent have contributed to this condition." The statement concluded, "Our post-war policy toward Norway has been and continues to be successful. As long as Norway remains a free democracy and the US remains determined to support free democracies Norway will be a steadfast ally. Our present partnership is based on substantial identity of interest and an absence of serious disagreement."[7]

Charles Ulrick Bay served as United States ambassador to Norway for seven years from 1946, early in the Truman administration, to 1953, the first year of the Eisenhower administration. That tenure was longer than those of most who represented the United States to the government of Norway. His service extended through the early years of the cold war when both the United States and Norway shared in shaping and implementing multilateral containment policies vis-à-vis the Soviet Union. Bay knew Norway, its people, and its policies as well as any American official at that time. He knew the ties and kinship between Norway and America, as well as the differences and difficulties that had arisen between them.

On July 31, 1953, as his last official act before ending his tour of duty in Oslo, Bay prepared an analysis of Norwegian-American relations from the perspective of his seven years as ambassador. He wrote that Norwegians did not distrust American motives but were more inclined than they had been earlier "to question the soundness and stability of our judgment." Norwegians, in his opinion, thought too many Americans had "an unduly emotional and alarmist attitude towards Communism." Though Norwegians were "completely confident of President Eisenhower's basic position and guiding principles," they watched carefully "to see whether isolationist pressures within Congress and also upon Congress are gaining headway." In his opinion the Norwegian government thought the United States should have been more flexible and innovative "in the fluid situation brought about by Stalin's death." They thought America "adhered too rigidly to policy lines adopted long ago to cope with an entirely different situation." For example, they considered American policies toward Communist China "too inflexible." To Norwegians "the names 'McCarthy' and 'McCarran' symbolize a disconcerting development of undemocratic and irresponsible forces" within the United States. According to Bay, many Norwegians believed "that the emotional anti-Communist forces have exercised too great an influence on the foreign policies of the present [Eisenhower] Administration." Though Norwegian government officials had "faith in President Eisenhower," they worried that "conflicting forces within the Republican Party" were "seriously impeding his program."[8]

Prime Minister Torp had emphasized to Bay "that no opportunity should be lost to explore any reasonable possibility looking toward the development of new and better relations with the Soviet Union." Ambassador Bay believed that even more important was "the development and maintenance of understanding and unity on major foreign policy issues among the nations of the Atlantic Community." He thought Norwegians realized "that all freedom-loving nations may seek the same goal and yet pursue somewhat different courses as reflected in their foreign policies."[9]

Indicative of the cooperative and adaptable attitudes of the Norwegian government in its relations with the United States was its support for the admission to NATO of Greece and Turkey in 1952 and of Germany in 1955. Norwegians would have preferred that NATO remain a strictly North Atlantic organization and were not eager to include Mediterranean states. They also had grave misgivings about adding Germany to NATO so soon after Nazi troops had occupied their country. Despite their reservations, however, they realistically approved those additions with remarkably little grumbling. For example, the Foreign Affairs and Constitution Committee of the Storting voted unanimously to recommend admitting West Germany to NATO, and the full Storting voted 126 to 7 to authorize Norway's ratification of the protocol admitting West Germany. The opposition consisted of the three Communist members of the Storting, three members from the Labor party, and one Liberal.[10]

There had been differences between Norway and the United States on foreign affairs in the past, and there would be differences in the future. But the shared interests and values of those two North Atlantic democracies made certain that they would travel together in their separate but shared efforts to build and guard peace, security, freedom, and the good life in the years to come.[11]

United States Presidents and Secretaries of State, 1901–61

President	Party	Dates	Secretary of State
Theodore Roosevelt	Rep.	1901–09	John Hay (1898–1905)
			Elihu Root (1905–09)
			Robert Bacon (1909)
William Howard Taft	Rep.	1909–13	Philander C. Knox (1909–13)
Woodrow Wilson	Dem.	1913–21	William J. Bryan (1913–15)
			Robert Lansing (1915–20)
			Bainbridge Colby (1920–21)
Warren G. Harding	Rep.	1921–23	Charles E. Hughes (1921–23)
Calvin Coolidge	Rep.	1923–29	Charles E. Hughes (1923–25)
			Frank B. Kellogg (1925–29)
Herbert Hoover	Rep.	1929–33	Henry L. Stimson (1929–33)
Franklin D. Roosevelt	Dem.	1933–45	Cordell Hull (1933–44)
			E. R. Stettinius, Jr. (1944–45)
Harry S Truman	Dem.	1945–53	E. R. Stettinius, Jr. (1945)
			James F. Byrnes (1945–47)
			George C. Marshall (1947–49)
			Dean G. Acheson (1949–53)
Dwight D. Eisenhower	Rep.	1953–61	John F. Dulles (1953–59)
			Christian A. Herter (1959–61)

157

Norwegian Prime Ministers and Foreign Ministers, 1905–55

Prime Minister	Party	Dates	Foreign Minister
Christian Michelsen	Coal.	1905–07	Jörgen Lövland
Jörgen Lövland	Lib.	1907–08	Jörgen Lövland
Gunnar Knudsen	Lib.	1908–10	Wilhelm C. Christopherson
Wollert Konow	Cons.	1910–12	Johannes Irgens
Jens Bratlie	Cons.	1912–13	Johannes Irgens
Gunnar Knudsen	Lib.	1913–20	Nils C. Ihlen
Otto B. Halvorsen	Cons.	1920–21	Christian F. Michelet
Otto A. Blehr	Lib.	1921–23	Arnold C. Raestad (to 1922)
			Johan L. Mowinckel
Otto B. Halvorsen	Cons.	1923	Christian F. Michelet
Abraham Berge	Cons.	1923–24	Christian F. Michelet
Johan L. Mowinckel	Lib.	1924–26	Johan L. Mowinckel
Ivar Lykke	Cons.	1926–28	Ivar Lykke
Christopher Hornsrud	Labor	1928	Edvard Bull
Johan L. Mowinckel	Lib.	1928–31	Johan L. Mowinckel
Peder Kolstad	Agr.	1931–32	Birger Braadland
Jens Hundseid	Agr.	1932–33	Birger Braadland
Johan L. Mowinckel	Lib.	1933–35	Johan L. Mowinckel
Johan Nygaardsvold	Labor	1935–45	Halvdan Koht (to 1941)
			Trygve Lie
Einar Gerhardsen	Labor	1945–51	Trygve Lie (to 1946)
			Halvard M. Lange
Oscar Torp	Labor	1951–55	Halvard M. Lange

Ministers and Ambassadors, 1905–57

Norwegian Ministers to U.S.	U.S. Ministers to Norway
Christian Hauge (1905–07)	Charles H. Graves (1905–06)
Ove Gude (1907–10)	Herbert H. D. Peirce (1906–11)
Helmer H . Bryn (1910–27)	Laurits S. Swenson (1911–13)
	Albert G. Schmedeman (1913–21)
	Laurits S. Swenson (1921–30)
Halvard H. Bachke (1927–34)	Hoffman Philip (1930–35)
Wilhelm Morgenstierne (1934–42)	Anthony J. D. Biddle, Jr. (1935–37)
	Florence J. Harriman (1937–40)
	Anthony J. D. Biddle, Jr. (1941–42)

Norwegian Ambassador to U.S.	U.S. Ambassadors to Norway
Wilhelm Morgenstierne (1942–57)	Anthony J. D. Biddle, Jr. (1942–44)
	Lithgow Osborne (1944–46)
	Charles Ulrick Bay (1946–53)
	L. Corrin Strong (1953–57)

Notes

CHAPTER 1

1. Henry Bordewich to William McKinley, January 25, 1897, M. J. Dowling to William McKinley, February 24, 1897, Applications and Recommendations for Appointment to the Foreign Service, 1901–1924, Inspection of American Consular Office at Christiania by Horace Lee Washington, November 23, 1907, Inspection of American Consular Office at Christiania by H. W. Harris, October 14, 1909, and Inspection of American Consular Office at Christiania, Norway, by H. W. Harris, October 19, 21, 1911, Record Group 59, Department of State Central Files, National Archives. For photographs of Bordewich see photograph folder, Henry Bordewich Papers, Norwegian-American Historical Association Archives.

2. Sofus Arctander to Henry Bordewich, June 7, 1905, RG 84, Post Records of American Consul General, Christiania, National Archives.

3. W. W. Thomas to John Hay, March 25, 1903, RG 84, Diplomatic Post Records, Stockholm, National Archives.

4. John Midgaard, *A Brief History of Norway*, 8th ed. (Oslo: Tanum-Norli, 1982), 98–104; Tim Greve, *Haakon VII of Norway: The Man and the Monarch* (New York: Hippocrene Books, 1983), 13–36; *Papers Relating to the Foreign Relations of the United States, 1905* (Washington, D.C.: Government Printing Office, 1906), 295–97, 853–65.

5. A diplomat is the official representative from the government of one sovereign state to another and generally resides in the capital city of the foreign state. A consul is an economic and social agent of a government sent to serve the interests of compatriots living, traveling, or doing business abroad. Consuls are assigned to major population and business centers abroad—not just to capital cities.

6. Bordewich to Francis B. Loomis, June 8, 1905, Bordewich to Charles H. Graves, June 8, 1905, Graves to Bordewich, June 9, 1905, RG 84, Post Records of American Consulate, Christiania, National Archives; Alvey A. Adee to Graves, September 19, 1905, Graves to Secretary of State, June 10, 21, July 27, September 20, October 18, 28, 1905, and enclosures, RG 84, Diplomatic Post Records, Stockholm, National Archives.

7. Root to Graves, November 2, 15, 17, 1905, Graves to Secretary of

State, November 14, 1905, Graves to Minister for Foreign Affairs, Christiania, November 14, 1905, RG 84, Diplomatic Post Records, Stockholm, National Archives; Theodore Roosevelt to Haakon VII, June 27, 1906, Root to Peirce, July 2, 1906, Peirce to Robert Bacon, August 10, 1906, Peirce to Root, December 31, 1907, RG 84, Diplomatic Post Records, Christiania, National Archives; telegram, W. H. von Munthe de Morgenstierne to Secretary of State, July 1, 1910, File 701.5711/32, RG 59, Department of State Central Files, National Archives; *Foreign Relations of the United States, 1905*, 853–74; *Papers Relating to the Foreign Relations of the United States, 1907* (Washington, D.C.: Government Printing Office, 1910), 925–26. Christian Hauge had been chargé d'affaires and secretary of the Swedish and Norwegian legation in Washington before being named by Norway to represent its interests there.

8. Among the many reports describing Norway, its geography, its culture, its economy, and its government to be found in United States archives, the following are representative and helpful: [Maj. Paul M. Atkins], "Norway," [June 1927], enclosed with Atkins to Col. Stanley H. Ford, June 10, 1927, RG 165, Military Attaché Reports, National Archives; Post Report enclosed with Hoffman Philip to Secretary of State, February 10, 1932, File 124.57/7, and Post Report enclosed with despatch 832, February 19, 1940, File 124.57, RG 59, Department of State Central Files, National Archives; Lt. Col. Sverre Petterssen, "Norway and the War," June 1942, RG 165, G-2 Regional File, 1933–44, Washington National Records Center (WNRC); C. Ulrick Bay to Secretary of State, April 11, 1947, RG 84, Oslo Legation and Embassy Confidential File, 1945–49, WNRC. See also Arne Selbyg, *Norway Today: An Introduction to Modern Norwegian Society* (Oslo: Norwegian University Press, 1986), 9–46; and Greve, *Haakon VII of Norway*, 15–39. For an excellent scholarly study of the Norwegian constitution and government see James A. Storing, *Norwegian Democracy* (Boston: Houghton Mifflin, 1963).

9. P. C. Knox to John C. Walker, December 3, 1912, File 711.572/1, Inspection Report on Bergen Consulate by Ralph J. Totten, January 10–12, 1916, Inspection Report of Trondhjem Consulate by H. W. Harris, October 16, 1909, Benjamin F. Chase to Secretary of State, November 17, 1921, File 125.9522/17, RG 59, Department of State Central Files, National Archives; Charles Adams Holder to Secretary of State, October 3, 1912, and attached "Report on Information Concerning Archives," File 125.66, and Berne Reinhardt to Henry Bordewich, May 1, 1908, RG 84, Post Records of American Consulate, Christiania, National Archives. For a scholarly history of United States relations with the dual monarchy before Norway separated from Sweden see Brynjolf J. Hovde, *Diplomatic Relations of the United States with Sweden and Norway, 1814–1905* (Iowa City: University of Iowa Studies in the Social Sciences, 1921).

10. Ingrid Semmingsen, *Norway to America: A History of the Migration* (Minneapolis: University of Minnesota Press, 1978), 7; Sigmund Skard, *The United States in Norwegian History* (Westport, Conn.: Greenwood Press, 1976), 14–15.

11. Lawrence Higgins, "Norwegian Migrations," December 22, 1934, and Annexes, File 857.55/8, RG 59, Department of State Central Files,

National Archives; Odd S. Lovoll, *The Promise of America: A History of the Norwegian-American People* (Minneapolis: University of Minnesota Press, 1984), 8–30; Semmingsen, *Norway to America*, 7–120; *USA Today*, June 1, 1983, 1A, 6A. The classic scholarly works on this subject are Theodore C. Blegen, *Norwegian Migration to America, 1825–1860* (Northfield, Minn.: Norwegian-American Historical Association, 1931), and Blegen, *Norwegian Migration to America: The American Transition* (Northfield, Minn.: Norwegian-American Historical Association, 1940).

12. The best and most thoughtful scholarly study on this subject is Skard, *The United States in Norwegian History*.

13. Richardson Dougall and Mary Patricia Chapman, *United States Chiefs of Mission, 1778–1973* (Washington, D.C.: Department of State, 1973), 114, 146; Graves to Secretary of State, November 14, 1905, RG 84, Diplomatic Post Records, Stockholm, National Archives; *Foreign Relations of the United States, 1905*, 870.

14. Root to Graves, November 22, December 6, 1905, January 2, 1906, Theodore Roosevelt to Haakon VII, [May 17, 1906], August 8, 1906, RG 84, Diplomatic Post Records, Stockholm, National Archives; Herbert H. D. Peirce to Robert Bacon, August 27, 1906, RG 84, Diplomatic Post Records, Christiania, National Archives; *Papers Relating to the Foreign Relations of the United States, 1906* (Washington, D.C.: Government Printing Office, 1909), 1190.

15. Graves to Secretary of State, May 21, June 8, July 2, September 10, 1906, RG 84, Diplomatic Post Records, Stockholm, National Archives; *Foreign Relations of the United States, 1906*, 1189–91; Greve, *Haakon VII of Norway*, 9–11, 45–48.

16. Root to Peirce, July 2, 1906, Bacon to Peirce, August 13, 1906, Peirce to Root, December 17, 1906, and Peirce to Andrew Carnegie, May 10, 1909, RG 84, Diplomatic Post Records, Christiania, National Archives; Peirce to the President, September 18, 1893, H. C. Lodge to the President, October 12, 1893, William E. Russell to Daniel S. Lamont, March 5, 1894, Andrew D. White to Ethan Hitchcock, August 26, 1897, unsigned and undated memo headed "PEIRCE, HERBERT H. D. of Massachusetts," Peirce to Secretary of State, December 17, 1906, Peirce to the President, March 7, 1913, Peirce to William Phillips, January 4, 1915, and Applications and Recommendations for Appointment to Foreign Service, 1901–1924, RG 59, Department of State Central Files, National Archives. The latter file contains a photograph of Peirce.

17. Bacon to M. Marshall Langhorne, July 11, 1906, and Peirce to James B. Townsend, September 15, 1909, RG 84, Diplomatic Post Records, Christiania, National Archives.

18. Peirce to Bacon, August 10, 13, 1906, and enclosed text of Peirce's speech to the king, RG 84, Diplomatic Post Records, Christiania, National Archives.

19. Peirce to Bacon, August 11, 1906, RG 84, Diplomatic Post Records, Christiania, National Archives.

20. Peirce to Bacon, August 30, 1906, Peirce to Root, November 10, 1906, January 11, 1907, August 3, 1908, Peirce to P. C. Knox, April 1, 1909, RG 84, Diplomatic Post Records, Christiania, National Archives;

Peirce to Secretary of State, March 28, 1911, File 124.571/1, A. G. Schmedeman to Secretary of State, June 3, 1916, File 124.571/5, Schmedeman to Secretary of State, May 14, 1921, File 124.571/30, Laurits S. Swenson to Secretary of State, February 6, 1924, File 124.571/53, RG 59, Department of State Central Files, National Archives.

21. Peirce to Bacon, October 4, 1906, February 27, 1909, RG 84, Diplomatic Post Records, Christiania, National Archives.

22. *Foreign Relations of the United States, 1906*, 1191-93; Peirce to Root, December 12, 1906, Root to Peirce, December 14, 1906, Peirce to M. Woolsey Stryker, May 21, 1909, Langhorne to Knox, January 10, 1910, Peirce to Johannes Irgens, April 30, 1910, Charles D. White to Gustav Vigeland, May 4, 1910, Peirce to Knox, May 13, 1910, Schmedeman to Bryan, December 17, 1913, RG 84, Diplomatic Post Records, Christiania, National Archives; Richard W. Leopold, *Elihu Root and the Conservative Tradition* (Boston: Little, Brown, 1954), 53.

23. P. C. Knox to John C. Walker, December 3, 1912, File 711.572/1, Alvey A. Adee to I. S. Bygland, June 26, 1918, 711.57/-, RG 59, Department of State Central Files, National Archives.

24. Bacon to Peirce, July 23, 1908, RG 84, Diplomatic Post Records, Christiania, National Archives; H. H. Bryn to W. J. Bryan, May 22, 1913, File 711.5712/7, Bryan to Woodrow Wilson, June 17, 1913, File 711. 572/9A, Bryan to Bryn, February 27, 1914, File 711.5712/9a, Bryn to Bryan, April 6, 1914, File 711.5712/9a, Robert Lansing to Bryn, May 3, 1918, File 711.5712/17, Charles E. Hughes to Bryn, December 24, 1923, File 711. 5712/26B, RG 59, Department of State Central Files, National Archives; *Papers Relating to the Foreign Relations of the United States, 1908* (Washington, D.C.: Government Printing Office, 1912), 663-64.

25. Bryan to Laurits S. Swenson, July 8, 1913, Swenson to Bryan, August 13, 1913, Swenson to Nils Ihlen, September 18, 1913, telegram, Bryan to American Legation, Christiania, May 19, 1914, Bryan to Albert D. Schmedeman, July 16, 1914, Robert Lansing to Schmedeman, October 30, 1914, RG 84, Diplomatic Post Records, Christiania, National Archives; *Papers Relating to the Foreign Relations of the United States, 1914* (Washington, D.C.: Government Printing Office, 1922), 970-73.

26. Peirce to Root, May 22, 1907, Alvey A. Adee to Peirce, June 27, 1907, RG 84, Diplomatic Post Records, Christiania, National Archives. For a scholarly history in English of the entire Spitsbergen controversy see Elen C. Singh, *The Spitsbergen (Svalbard) Question: United States Foreign Policy, 1907-1935* (Oslo: Universitetsforlaget, 1980).

27. Root to Peirce, January 24, 1908, and enclosed letter from Frederick Ayer and John M. Longyear to Root, December 31, 1906, Peirce to W. Christophersen, October 19, 1908, Christophersen to Langhorne, November 9, 1908, Peirce to Root, December 12, 1908, Peirce to Christophersen, December 10, 1908, Langhorne to Root, December 28, 1908, RG 84, Diplomatic Post Records, Christiania, National Archives.

28. Christophersen to Langhorne, January 11, 1909, Peirce to Bacon, February 24, 1909, Peirce to P. C. Knox, June 8, 1909, Peirce to Secretary of State, September 4, 1909, Peirce to Huntington Wilson, September 23, 1910, Adee to Peirce, November 3, 1910, Swenson to Knox, February 2,

1912, Schmedeman to Bryan, November 10, 1914, RG 84, Diplomatic Post Records, Christiania, National Archives; *Foreign Relations of the United States, 1914*, 974–81.

29. Langhorne to Root, December 15, 1908, Peirce to Secretary of State, September 15, 1909, Swenson to Knox, July 13, 1912, RG 84, Diplomatic Post Records, Christiania, National Archives; Charles A. Holder, "Norway as a Market for American Goods," April 16, 1913, RG 84, Post Records of American Consulate, Christiania, National Archives.

30. Bordewich to Assistant Secretary of State, January 3, 10, 1907, January 23, 1908, Bordewich to Secretary of State, February 20, 1911, Bordewich to California Development Board, May 1, 1911, Charles A. Holder to Reid, Kindred & Beard, March 5, 1913, Holder to Janss Investment Co., November 29, 1913, RG 84, Post Records of American Consulate, Christiania, National Archives; Langhorne to Root, April 12, 1907, RG 84, Diplomatic Post Records, Christiania, National Archives.

31. Schmedeman to Secretary of State, March 21, May 20, 1914, File 857.607A/8, 10, RG 59, Department of State Central Files, National Archives; Schmedeman to Nils Ihlen, May 12, 1914, RG 84, Diplomatic Post Records, Christiania, National Archives; Greve, *Haakon VII of Norway*, 68–69.

32. Root to Graves, November 2, 1905, RG 84, Diplomatic Post Records, Stockholm, National Archives; Peirce to Root, December 31, 1907, RG 84, Diplomatic Post Records, Christiania, National Archives; telegram from T. Alexander Baxter to Secretary of State, July 1, 1910, File 701.5711/32, W. T. de Munthe de Morgenstierne to P. C. Knox, July 19, 1910, File 7370/40, P. C. Knox to H. H. Bryn, October 24, 1910, File 701.5711/47, Butler Wright to Alexis H. G. O. Lundh, January 26, 1927, File 701.5711/258a, RG 59, Department of State Central Files, National Archives; *Foreign Relations of the United States, 1907*, 925-26; *Papers Relating to the Foreign Relations of the United States, 1910* (Washington, D.C.: Government Printing Office, 1915), 768–69.

33. Charles B. Curtis to Secretary of State, June 16, 1910, File 233.P35/37, Peirce to Secretary of State, August 19, 1910, File 123.P35/39, attached undated memo from C. L. C. to Mr. Hale, Peirce to Secretary of State, October 17, 1910, File 123.P35/42, Knox to American Legation, April 14, 1911, File 123.P35/45a, Peirce to Secretary of State, May 30, 1911, File 123.P35/53, Bryn to Knox, June 30, 1911, File 123.P35/55, RG 59, Department of State Central Files, National Archives.

34. "Peirce, Herbert H. D. of Massachusetts," n.d., Peirce to President, March 7, 1913, Peirce to William Phillips, January 4, 1915, Phillips to Peirce, January 5, 1915, undated confidential memo on Herbert H. D. Peirce, W. J. Bryan to Peirce, February 1, 1915, unidentified clipping from *Post*, December 6, 1916, Applications and Recommendations for Appointment to the Foreign Service, 1901–1924, Lodge to Phillips, September 7, 1914, File 123.P35/66, Alvey A. Adee to Alfred Rapkin and Co., April 14, 1917, File 123.P35/64, Adee to A. Niguet, June 2, 1919, File 123.P35/65, RG 59, Department of State Central Files, National Archives.

35. Dougall and Chapman, *United States Chiefs of Mission*, 40, 114–

15, 148; Laurits S. Swenson to Jacob Preus, April 29, 1908, Preus to Swenson, April 26, 1911, Preus Papers, Minnesota State Historical Society Library; Knox to Swenson, May 3, 1911, RG 84, Diplomatic Post Records, Christiania, National Archives; Swenson to Secretary of State, July 5, 1928, File 123.Sw4/66, RG 59, Department of State Central Files, National Archives.

36. Haakon E. Dahr, Jr., to Secretary of State, March 20, April 26, 1912, Charles Adams Holder to Secretary of State, September 4, 1912, RG 84, Post Records of American Consulate, Christiania, National Archives; clipping from *Granite Falls Tribune*, March 26, 1912, Bordewich Papers, Norwegian-American Historical Association Archives.

37. Peirce to Root, May 22, November 6, 1907, February 12, 1908, RG 84, Diplomatic Post Records, Christiania, National Archives; *Foreign Relations of the United States, 1907*, 926–28.

38. Peirce to Secretary of State, January 26, 1911, File 211.57, RG 59, Department of State Central Files, National Archives; Knox to Peirce, February 28, 1911, Swenson to Knox, September 18, 1911, Swenson to Bryan, September 19, 1913, RG 84, Diplomatic Post Records, Christiania, National Archives.

39. Swenson to Knox, January 24, 1912, RG 84, Diplomatic Post Records, Christiania, National Archives; Greve, *Haakon VII of Norway*, 4–9.

CHAPTER 2

1. The definitive scholarly monograph on Norway's diplomacy during World War I, based on multiarchival research, is Olav Riste, *The Neutral Ally: Norway's Relations with Belligerent Powers in the First World War* (Oslo: Universitetsforlaget, 1965). The best scholarly volume on United States diplomatic background for entering World War I is Ernest R. May, *The World War and American Isolation, 1914-1917* (Cambridge, Mass.: Harvard University Press, 1959). An older but still useful scholarly study of United States relations with Norway in the war is in Thomas A. Bailey, *The Policy of the United States Toward the Neutrals, 1917-1918* (Baltimore: Johns Hopkins Press, 1942), passim, but see especially 102–35. See also Nils Ørvik, *The Decline of Neutrality, 1914-1941: With Special Reference to the United States and the Northern Neutrals*, 2d ed. (London: Frank Cass, 1971), 38–118.

2. The leading scholar on Wilson is Arthur S. Link. He has written and edited many volumes on Wilson, but a good place to start is Arthur S. Link, *Woodrow Wilson: Revolution, War, and Peace* (Arlington Heights, Ill.: AHM Publishing, 1979).

3. The most detailed biography of Bryan is Paolo E. Coletta, *William Jennings Bryan*, 3 vols. (Lincoln, Nebr.: University of Nebraska Press, 1964–69). An older but still thoughtful scholarly study of Bryan and foreign affairs is Merle E. Curti, *Bryan and World Peace* (Northampton, Mass.: Smith College Studies in History, 1931). See also LeRoy Ashby, *William Jennings Bryan: Champion of Democracy* (Boston: Twayne Publishers, 1987).

4. A solid scholarly study of Lansing and Foreign affairs is Daniel M. Smith, *Robert Lansing and American Neutrality, 1914-1917* (Berkeley: University of California Press, 1958).

5. *Who's Who in America, 1940-1941*, 21:2285; Albert Schmedeman, "Scandinavians in Wisconsin," speeches and addresses, 1934 folder, Schmedeman Papers, State Historical Society of Wisconsin Library.

6. Riste, *The Neutral Ally*, 43-44; Greve, *Haakon VII of Norway*, 192; Laurits S. Swenson to P. C. Knox, February 8, 1913, RG 84, Diplomatic Post Records, Christiania, National Archives; A. G. Schmedeman to Secretary of State, June 17, 1920, File 857.00/150, RG 59, Department of State Central Files, National Archives.

7. Riste, *The Neutral Ally*, 44; Greve, *Haakon VII of Norway*, 195; Swenson to Secretary of State, February 8, 1913, File 857.002/4, RG 59, Department of State Central Files, National Archives.

8. W. T. von Munthe de Morgenstierne to P. C. Knox, July 19, 1910, File 7370/40, RG 59, Department of State Central Files, National Archives.

9. May, *World War and American Isolation*, 305-46; Link, *Woodrow Wilson*, 30-35, 52; Daniel M. Smith, *The Great Departure: The United States and World War I, 1914-1920* (New York: Wiley, 1965), 40-49.

10. Riste, *The Neutral Ally*, 52, 77, 83-94; Arthur S. Link et al., eds., *The Papers of Woodrow Wilson*, vol. 34, *July 21-September 30, 1915* (Princeton, N.J.: Princeton University Press, 1980), 188; Michael J. Hendrick, "Traffic Between German and Norwegian Ports," November 21, 1914, File 870. E. Haldeman Dennison, "The British Blockade as it Effects Norway," August 25, 1916, File 711.2, RG 84, Consular Post Records, Christiania, National Archives; Schmedeman to Secretary of State, January 29, 1916, File 711.2/2, RG 84, Diplomatic Post Records, Christiania, National Archives; Schmedeman to Secretary of State, July 23, 1917, RG 182, War Trade Board Records, WNRC.

11. Riste, *The Neutral Ally*, 96-125; Schmedeman to Secretary of State, April 24, 1916, File 350-2, Schmedeman to Secretary of State, January 9, 1917, February 24, 1917, March 14, 1917, File 631-1, RG 84, Diplomatic Post Records, Christiania, National Archives; Dennison, "Norway's Differences with Great Britain," January 31, 1917, File 690, RG 84, Consular Post Records, Christiania, National Archives; Schmedeman to Secretary of State, March 3, 1917, July 23, 1917, RG 182, War Trade Board Records, Records of Executive Office, Executive Country File, WNRC.

12. May, *World War and American Isolation*, 113-67; Link, *Woodrow Wilson*, 38-48; Riste, *The Neutral Ally*, 64-71, 126-43; Schmedeman to Secretary of State, May 4, 1916, File 711.6-1, RG 84, Diplomatic Post Records, Christiania, National Archives; Dennison, "Norway's Shipping Losses," November 13, 1916, File 857.85/11, Schmedeman to Secretary of State, April 4, 1917, File 857.857/137, RG 59, Department of State Central Files, National Archives.

13. Schmedeman to Secretary of State, October 18, 1916, File 711.1-4, RG 84, Diplomatic Post Records, Christiania, National Archives.

14. Link, *Woodrow Wilson*, 38-46; May, *World War and American Isolation*, 137-67.

15. May, *World War and American Isolation*, 404-15.

16. Link, *Woodrow Wilson*, 65-71; May, *World War and American Isolation*, 416-37; Riste, *The Neutral Ally*, 171-75, 179-80.

17. Riste, *The Neutral Ally*, 179-84; Schmedeman to Secretary of State, February 2, 1917, File 880-1, February 7, 1917, File 710-1, April 4, 1917, File 711.2-5, telegram from Schmedeman to Secretary of State, February 5, 1917, File 701-1, RG 84, Diplomatic Post Records, Christiania, National Archives.

18. Schmedeman to Bryan, December 28, 1914, telegram from Schmedeman to Secretary of State, February 16, 1917, File 711.2-2, RG 84, Diplomatic Post Records, Christiania, National Archives; Captain N. A. McCully, "General Conditions in Scandinavia," August 1917, RG 38, Naval Attaché Reports, National Archives; *Papers Relating to the Foreign Relations of the United States, 1914 Supplement, The World War* (Washington, D.C.: Government Printing Office, 1928), 52, 60, 151, 159-61, 465, 472-73.

19. Telegram from Walter Hines Page to American Legation, Christiania, December 7, 1916, RG 84, Diplomatic Post Records, Christiania, National Archives; *Foreign Relations of the United States, 1914 Supplement*, 465-66.

20. Schmedeman to Secretary of State, May 24, 1916, File 711.6-1, RG 84, Diplomatic Post Records, Christiania, National Archives; *Papers Relating to the Foreign Relations of the United States, 1916 Supplement, The World War* (Washington, D.C.: Government Printing Office, 1929), 112, 121-22.

21. Telegram from Schmedeman to Secretary of State, February 5, 1917, Schmedeman to Secretary of State, February 7, 1917, File 710-1, RG 84, Diplomatic Post Records, Christiania, National Archives; Arthur S. Link, et al., eds., *The Papers of Woodrow Wilson*, vol. 40, *November 20, 1916-January 23, 1917* (Princeton, N.J.: Princeton University Press, 1982), 46-48, 81.

22. Hendrick, "Possibilities for Extension of American Trade with Norway," October 3, 1914, File 610, RG 84, Consular Post Records, Christiania, National Archives; Schmedeman to Secretary of State, June 15, 1915, Schmedeman to T. P. Gore, December 17, 1915, RG 84, Diplomatic Post Records, Christiania, National Archives.

23. Schmedeman to Bryan, October 21, 1914, and enclosed translation of clipping from *Dagbladet*, October 16, 1914, RG 84, Diplomatic Post Records, Christiania, National Archives.

24. Schmedeman to Secretary of State, April 12, 1917, File 711-3, August 2, 1917, File 711-3, September 1, 1917, File 711-1, RG 84, Diplomatic Post Records, Christiania, National Archives.

25. Schmedeman to Secretary of State, April 12, 14, 1917, File 711-3, RG 84, Diplomatic Post Records, Christiania, National Archives.

26. Schmedeman to Secretary of State, January 14, 1918, File 800.2-2, RG 84, Diplomatic Post Records, Christiania, National Archives; Schmedeman to Secretary of State, July 20, 1918, File 857.00/31, RG 59, Department of State Central Files, National Archives.

27. *Papers Relating to the Foreign Relations of the United States, 1917,*

Supplement 2, The World War, 2 vols. (Washington, D.C.: Government Printing Office, 1932), 2:903–5, 908–10.

28. C. L. Paus to H. F. Arthur Schoenfeld, July 1, 1917, and enclosed memorandum, File 711.3-1, RG 84, Diplomatic Post Records, Christiania, National Archives.

29. Confidential aide-memoire from Norwegian Legation, Washington, April 23, 1917, Schmedeman to Secretary of State, May 2, 1917, RG 182, War Trade Board Records, Records of Executive Office, WNRC.

30. *Foreign Relations of the United States, 1917, Supplement 2*, 2:1022; Bryn to Robert Lansing, June 26, 1917, File 033.5711/13, Schmedeman to Secretary of State, July 2, 1917, File 033.5711/18, RG 59, Department of State Central Files, National Archives; Aide-memoire from Norwegian Legation, Washington, June 28, 1917, RG 182, War Trade Board Records, Records of Executive Office, WNRC.

31. *Foreign Relations of the United States, 1917, Supplement 2*, 2:1035–36.

32. For two scholarly accounts of the Nansen negotiations see Bailey, *Policy of the United States Toward the Neutrals*, 88–135; and Riste, *The Neutral Ally*, 191–212. For some of the documents on the negotiations see *Foreign Relations of the United States, 1917, Supplement 2*, vol. 2, passim, but see especially 908–10, 1058–1116; and *Papers Relating to the Foreign Relations of the United States, 1918, Supplement I, The World War*, 2 vols. (Washington, D.C.: Government Printing Office, 1933), 2:1081–1181.

33. Riste, *The Neutral Ally*, 193–95, 202–3; Bailey, *Policy of the United States Toward the Neutrals*, 91–94, 115–18; T. D. Jones to American Embassy, London, November 15, 1917, RG 182, War Trade Board Records, Records of Executive Office, WNRC.

34. Telegram from Schmedeman to Secretary of State, July 11, 1917, File 711.3-1, Schmedeman to Secretary of State, July 23, 1917, File 711.3-1, RG 84, Diplomatic Post Records, Christiania, National Archives.

35. Telegram from Schmedeman to Secretary of State, September 4, 1917, File 711.3-1, Schmedeman to Secretary of State, September 15, 1917, October 19, 1917, File 711.3-1, RG 84, Diplomatic Post Records, Christiania, National Archives. Schmedeman's important despatch of September 15, 1917, is also in RG 182, War Trade Board Records, Records of the Executive Office, WNRC.

36. For a few of many possible examples of the British input see Colville Barclay to Lansing, June 27, 1917, Schmedeman to Secretary of State, July 2, 1917, and enclosed memorandum, Eustace Percy to Vance McCormick, September 1, 1917, October 26, 1917, Percy to Thomas D. Jones, November 17, 1917, RG 182, War Trade Board Records, Records of Executive Office, WNRC.

37. Telegram from Schmedeman to Secretary of State, February 25, 1918, RG 84, Diplomatic Post Records, Christiania, National Archives; cablegram from Page to Secretary of State, February 26, 1918, Schmedeman to Secretary of State, February 27, 1918, RG 182, War Trade Board Records, Records of Executive Office, WNRC.

38. Schmedeman to Secretary of State, November 1, 30, 1917, 857.50/2,5, RG 59, Department of State Central Files, National Archives;

telegram from Schmedeman to Secretary of State, April 11, 1918, RG 182, War Trade Board Records, Records of Executive Office, WNRC.

39. Thomas L. Chadbourne, Jr., to Lawrence Bennett, April 30, 1918, and enclosed text of agreement and Nansen letter, RG 182, War Trade Board Records, Records of Executive Office, WNRC. For the text of the agreement see *Foreign Relations of the United States, 1918, Supplement 1*, 2:1170–83.

40. *Foreign Relations of the United States, 1917, Supplement 2*, 2:963–65, 1007–14.

41. L. P. Sheldon to Alexander V. Dye, April 11, 1918, "Report on Meeting Held at the British Legation on April 24, 1918, for the Purpose of Organizing in Christiania an Allied Trade Committee," File 695-5, RG 84, Diplomatic Post Records, Christiania, National Archives.

42. *Who's Who in America, 1940–1941*, 21:825. Most of the documents and dispatches revealing Dye's style and effectiveness are in RG 84, Diplomatic Post Records, Christiania, National Archives, and, to a lesser extent, in RG 182, War Trade Board Records, WNRC.

43. Frank S. Polk to Schmedeman, November 10, 1917, Polk to Dye, November 10, 1917, File 711.3-4, Dye, "Memorandum on Norway," November 22, 1917, File 711.3-17, Dye to Secretary of State for War Trade Board, December 27, 1917, File 711.2-15, telegram from Lansing to American Legation, Christiania, March 30, 1918, File 695, Quarterly Report by Dye, July 15, 1918, File 893.1, Dye to Secretary of State for War Trade Board, February 26, 1919, File 695-1, Schmedeman to Secretary of State, July 1, 1919, File 711.3-6, RG 84, Diplomatic Post Records, Christiania, National Archives.

44. Dye to Secretary of State, June 3, 1919, File 711.3-15, form letter sent to all associations, May 14, 1918, File 631-3, quarterly report by Dye, July 15, 1918, File 893-1, RG 84, Diplomatic Post Records, Christiania, National Archives. Those agreements and declarations are in boxes 440, 441, 442, and 443, RG 182, War Trade Board Records, Records of Bureau of Exports, Records of Trade Distributors Division, Country File, Norway, 1917–1919, WNRC.

45. William Coffin to Secretary of State, June 30, 1917, File 690, Confidential File, RG 84, Diplomatic Post Records, Christiania, National Archives.

46. Dye to Secretary of State for War Trade Board, December 27, 1917, File 711.3-15, RG 84, Diplomatic Post Records, Christiania, National Archives.

47. Telegram from Schmedeman to Secretary of State, May 6, 1918, Beaver White to John Foster Dulles, May 15, 1918, W. H. Owen to L. P. Sheldon, May 25, 1918, RG 182, War Trade Board Records, Records of Executive Office, WNRC; Owen to McCormick, May 25, 1918, telegram from Lansing to American legation, Christiania, May 30, 1918, File 631-3, RG 84, Diplomatic Post Records, Christiania, National Archives.

48. Dye to Sheldon, August 24, 1918, Dye to H. Charles Dick, August 24, 1918, File 631-6, RG 84, Diplomatic Post Records, Christiania, National Archives.

49. Dye to Secretary of State, November 22, 1918, RG 182, War

Trade Board Records, Records of Executive Office, Executive Country File, WNRC; Dye to Secretary of State for the War Trade Board, February 26, 1919, File 695-1, RG 84, Diplomatic Post Records, Christiania, National Archives.

50. Telegram from Schoenfeld to American Legation, Stockholm, September 11, 1918, Schoenfeld to Secretary of State, September 15, 1918, Dye to Secretary of State, November 7, 1918, "Account of the Work of the War Trade Board in Norway," attached to Dye to Secretary of State, June 3, 1919, File 711.3-15, RG 84, Diplomatic Post Records, Christiania, National Archives.

51. Schmedeman to Secretary of State, July 1, 1919, File 711.3-6, RG 84, Diplomatic Post Records, Christiania, National Archives; *Who's Who in America, 1940–1941*, 21:825.

52. W. H. Owen to Chester Lloyd Jones, October 28, 1918, File 711.3-8, RG 84, Diplomatic Post Records, Christiania, National Archives.

53. "Norway. Economic. Exports & Imports," from O. Y. (B. O.), April 29, 1918, Military Attaché Report, RG 165, National Archivest; memorandum, "Effect of the Norwegian-American Agreement on the Commerce of Norway," from Knute E. Carlson to Barrows, September 12, 1918, RG 182, War Trade Board Records, Norway Commerce folder, WNRC; "Commercial-Political Relations with the Central Powers," translated from Norwegian, enclosed with Schmedeman to Secretary of State, October 11, 1920, File 802.1, RG 84, Diplomatic Post Records, Christiania, National Archives.

54. Telegram from Busser to Secretary of State, November 14, 1918, File 857.857/268, Schmedeman to Secretary of State, January 4, 1919, File 857.857/279, Charles B. Curtis to Secretary of State, July 14, 1919, File 857.00/77, RG 59, Department of State Central Files, National Archives.

55. H. F. Arthur Schoenfeld to Secretary of State, August 9, 1918, File 801.45-1, RG 84, Diplomatic Post Records, Christiania, National Archives. For a scholarly account of this episode by a leading Norwegian scholar see Riste, *The Neutral Ally*, 212–24.

56. *Who's Who in America, 1940–1941*, 21:2288.

57. Schoenfeld to Ihlen, August 15, 1918, Schoenfeld to Secretary of State, August 22, 1918, File 801.45-1, RG 84, Diplomatic Post Records, Christiania, National Archives; Riste, *The Neutral Ally*, 219.

58. Riste, *The Neutral Ally*, 221.

59. Schoenfeld to Secretary of State, August 14, 22, 30, 1918, telegram from Lansing to American Legation, Christiania, August 23, 26, 1918, File 801.45-1, RG 84, Diplomatic Post Records, Christiania, National Archives.

60. Schoenfeld to Secretary of State, August 27, 30, September 5, 1918, File 801.45-1, RG 84, Diplomatic Post Records, Christiania, National Archives.

61. Schoenfeld to Secretary of State, September 30, 1918, File 801.45-1, RG 84, Diplomatic Post Records, Christiania, National Archives.

62. Telegram from Lansing to American Legation, Christiania, for

Schoenfeld, October 1, 1918, telegrams from Schoenfeld to Secretary of State, October 3, 9, 1918, File 801.45-1, RG 84, Diplomatic Post Records, Christiania, National Archives.

63. Telegrams from Schoenfeld to Secretary of State, October 8, 10, 1918, File 711-2, Milo A. Jewett to Secretary of State, December 31, 1918, File 893-1, RG 84, Diplomatic Post Records, Christiania, National Archives.

64. Schmedeman to Secretary of State, November 23, December 7, 1918, File 711-21, Schmedeman to Secretary of State, December 14, 23, 1918, File 711-2, RG 84, Diplomatic Post Records, Christiania, National Archives; *Papers Relating to the Foreign Relations of the United States, 1919, The Paris Peace Conference*, vol. 1 (Washington, D.C.: Government Printing Office, 1942), 236–40.

65. Schmedeman to Secretary of State, March 19, 1919, File 711-2, April 4, 1919, File 711-7, February 26, 1919, July 15, 1919, File 715-1, RG 84, Diplomatic Post Records, Christiania, National Archives.

66. Telegram from Schmedeman to Secretary of State, May 11, 20, 1919, File 867.00/47, 48, RG 59, Department of State Central Files, National Archives; Schmedeman to Secretary of State, May 15, 1919, telegram from Schmedeman to Secretary of State, May 16, 1919, File 711-10, Jewett to Schmedeman, May 16, 1919, "Weekly Report," Henry C. A. Damm, May 26, 1919, File 800-11, RG 84, Diplomatic Post Records, Christiania, National Archives.

67. Telegram from C. B. Curtis to Secretary of State, July 7, 1919, Curtis to Secretary of State, August 13, 1919, File 711-10, RG 84, Diplomatic Post Records, Christiania, National Archives.

68. Telegram from Curtis to Secretary of State, September 20, 1919, Schmedeman to Secretary of State, November 20, 1919, December 18, 1919, File 710-2, Schmedeman to Secretary of State, File 711-10, RG 84, Diplomatic Post Records, Christiania, National Archives.

69. Schmedeman to Secretary of State, January 31, 1920, File 803, Schmedeman to Secretary of State, February 7, 1920, File 711, Schmedeman to Secretary of State, February 16, March 5, 1920, File 710, RG 84, Diplomatic Post Records, Christiania, National Archives.

70. Telegram from Schoenfeld to Secretary of State, August 21, 1918, telegram from Lansing to American Legation, Christiania, September 9, 1918, Schoenfeld to Ihlen, September 10, 1918, File 300-16, RG 84, Diplomatic Post Records, Christiania, National Archives.

71. Schoenfeld to Secretary of State, September 14, 24, 1918, File 300-16, RG 84, Diplomatic Post Records, Christiania, National Archives.

72. Schmedeman to Secretary of State, April 27, 1921, Swenson to Secretary of State, March 2, 1922, March 6, 1925, June 13, 1925, Mowinckel to Swenson, February 28, 1925, Swenson to Mowinckel, August 25, 1925, File 703, RG 84, Diplomatic Post Records, Christiania, National Archives.

73. Telegram from American Mission, Paris, to American Legation, Christiania, May 5, 1919, telegram from Schmedeman to American Mission, Paris, May 6, 1919, File 848-2, Schmedeman to Secretary of State, December 8, 1919, File 848-4, telegram from Bainbridge Colby to Ameri-

can Legation, Christiania, September 25, 1920, telegram from Curtis to Secretary of State, September 25, 1920, Schmedeman to Nansen, October 23, 1920, John Ball Osborne to Schmedeman, December 11, 1920, Schmedeman to Charles H. Albrecht, December 13, 1920, Schmedeman to Secretary of State, April 6, 1921, Charles Evans Hughes to Nansen, August 10, 1921, File 711.4, Swenson to Secretary of State, May 11, 1922, File 848, Swenson to Secretary of State, December 28, 1922, File 090, RG 84, Diplomatic Post Records, Christiania, National Archives.

74. Telegram from American Mission, Paris, to American Legation, Christiania, July 15, 1919, Schmedeman to Secretary of State, November 12, 1919, File 715-1, Marion Letcher to Curtis, September 27, 1919, File 893, Schmedeman to Secretary of State, February 20, 1920, File 714, RG 84, Diplomatic Post Records, Christiania, National Archives; Charles E. Hughes to the President, [1923], Swenson to Secretary of State, January 17, 1925, File 857H.01/33, RG 59, Department of State Central Files, National Archives; Doris H. Linder, *The Reaction of Norway to American Foreign Policy, 1918–1939* (Ann Arbor, Mich.: University Microfilms, 1961), 34–43.

75. Schmedeman to Secretary of State, December 13, 1920, Personal Correspondence folder, Schmedeman Papers, State Historical Society of Wisconsin Library.

CHAPTER 3

1. For a thoughtful scholarly interpretation of the United States in the 1920s see William E. Leuchtenburg, *The Perils of Prosperity, 1914–32* (Chicago: University of Chicago Press, 1958). For a concise scholarly history of the New Deal era see William E. Leuchtenburg, *Franklin D. Roosevelt and the New Deal, 1932–1940* (New York: Harper & Row, 1963).

2. Among many reports in State Department records on the Norwegian economy see "Commerce and Industries, September 1921," from Alban G. Snyder, October 18, 1921, and "Commerce and Industries of Norway – 1924," from Snyder and S. Bertrand Jacobson, August 1, 1925, File 600. RG 84, Consular Post Records, Christiania (Oslo), National Archives; A. J. Drexel Biddle, Jr., to Secretary of State, May 29, 1936, and enclosed memoranda, File 857.50/111, RG 59, Department of State Central Files, National Archives.

3. Among many reports in State Department records on Norwegian politics for those years see Laurits S. Swenson to Secretary of State, August 5, 1924, File 857.002/42, Hoffman Philip to Secretary of State, March 26, 1934, File 857.00/267, "Political Parties in Norway," enclosed with Lithgow Osborne to Secretary of State, April 11, 1946, File 857.00/4-1146, RG 59, Department of State Central Files, National Archives; and enclosure no. 2 attached to Philip to Secretary of State, August 11, 1932, File 803, RG 84, Diplomatic Post Records, Oslo, National Archives.

4. C. B. Curtis to Secretary of State, September 23, 1919, File 800-3, enclosure no. 2 attached to Philip to Secretary of State, August 11, 1932, File 803, Biddle to Secretary of State, November 8, 1935, File Number

800, RG 84, Diplomatic Post Records, Christiania (Oslo), National Archives; Schmedeman to Secretary of State, January 28, 1921, and enclosed "Bolshevism in Norway," File 857.00B/27, Swenson to Secretary of State, December 10, 1926, March 20, 1930, File 857.00/233, 247, Benjamin Thaw, Jr., to Secretary of State, March 25, 1935, "Political Parties in Norway," enclosed with Osborne to Secretary of State, April 11, 1946, File 857.00/278, 4-1146, RG 59, Department of State Central Files, National Archives.

5. *Who's Who in America, 1940-1941*, 21:2514; Thomas Murray Wilson, Foreign Service Inspection Report, Oslo, Norway–Legation, August 14, 1929, Swenson to Secretary of State, February 25, 1910, File 123.Sw4, 22758/9, Swenson to Secretary of State, May 13, 1912, 123.Sw4/29, RG 59, Department of State Central Files, National Archives.

6. Matthew E. Hanna, Foreign Service Inspection Report, Oslo, Norway–Legation, July 16, 1927, Thomas Murray Wilson, Foreign Service Inspection Report, Oslo, Norway–Legation, August 14, 1929, RG 59, Department of State Central Files, National Archives.

7. Wilson, Foreign Service Inspection Report, Oslo, Norway–Legation, August 14, 1929, RG 59, Department of State Central Files, National Archives. See also F. R. Dolbeare, Foreign Service Inspection Report, Oslo, Norway–Legation, July 22, 27, 1925, RG 59, Department of State Central Files, National Archives.

8. Swenson to Secretary of State, July 10, 1924, File 801.4, RG 84, Diplomatic Post Records, Christiania, National Archives.

9. Swenson to Secretary of State, June 1, July 5, 1928, File 123.Sw4/ 65, 66, RG 59, Department of State Central Files, National Archives.

10. Swenson to Secretary of State, January 4, 1921, February 6, 1924, July 10, 1926, File 124.571/35, 53, 68, Robert Woods Bliss to Secretary of State, September 13, 1923, File 124.571/47, J. S. Williams to Secretary of State, October 24, 1938, File 124.571/157, RG 59, Department of State Central Files, National Archives.

11. M. O. Eldridge to Charles Lee Cook, January 19, 1927, Butler Wright to Alexis H. G. O. Lundh, January 26, 1927, memorandum by MVB, September 3, 1927, MVB to Mr. Dunn, May 9, 1928, Swenson to Secretary of State, June 23, 1928, File 701.5711/261, 258a, 285, 286, 288, Swenson to Secretary of State, October 1, 1928, File 411.57 H 19/101, Swenson to Secretary of State, March 5, 1929, File 702.5742/2, RG 59, Department of State Central Files, National Archives.

12. Lundh to Frank B. Kellogg, July 29, 1927, Kellogg to Lundh, August 5, 1927, Swenson to Secretary of State, August 12, 1927, January 29, 1930, memorandum from the Royal Norwegian Legation, April 22, 1931, File 701.5711/269, 268, 271, 307, 321, Hoffman Philip to Secretary of State, April 7, 1934, 857.00 P.R./78, RG 59, Department of State Central Files, National Archives.

13. Richardson Dougall and Mary Patricia Chapman, *United States Chiefs of Mission, 1778-1973* (Washington, D.C.: Department of State, 1973), 26, 31, 53, 79, 115, 163; *Who's Who in America, 1940-1941*,

21:2058; telegram from Swenson to Secretary of State, July 12, 1930, memorandum of conversation between Mr. Marriner and Mr. Offerdahl, July 11, 1930, W. J. C. to Mr. Hengstler, August 1, 1930, Philip to Secretary of State, December 27, 1932, February 13, 1935, and attached memorandum by Dr. Edmund L. Gros, December 13, 1934, telegram from Cordell Hull to American Embassy, Santiago, June 28, 1935, Philip to Herbert C. Hengstler, July 12, 1937, File 123P53/330, 332, 340 1/2, 398, 430, 444, 524, RG 59, Department of State Central Files, National Archives.

14. Swenson to Secretary of State, April 20, 1929, Bachke to Henry L. Stimson, May 21, 1929, File 702.5711/430, 432, William Phillips to the President, March 13, 1934, 701.5711/349A, 350, RG 59, Department of State Central Files, National Archives; clipping from *Minneapolis Sunday Tribune*, April 13, 1952, pp. 1,5, Morgenstierne Papers, Norwegian-American Historical Association Archives; *Washington Post*, February 18, 1986.

15. *Who's Who in America, 1958-1959*, 30:235; William Phillips to Anthony J. Drexel Biddle, Jr., July 22, 1935, Biddle to Secretary of State, October 12, 14, November 26, 1935, Jefferson Patterson to Secretary of State, May 26, 1937, and enclosed translations of newspaper clippings, 123 Biddle, Anthony J. Drexel/12, 29, 30, 31, 110, Florence J. Harriman to Secretary of State, July 6, 1937, 123 Harriman, Florence J./23, RG 59, Department of State Central Files, National Archives.

16. *Who's Who in America, 1940-1941*, 21:1171; Florence J. Harriman to Secretary of State, January 21, 1938, File 857.032/45, RG 59, Department of State Central Files, National Archives; Harriman to Roosevelt, April 30, 1940, President's Secretary's File, Norway 1940 folder, Roosevelt Papers, Franklin D. Roosevelt Library; press release from Hans Olav, Royal Norwegian Embassy, Washington, D.C., August 3, 1942, Harriman Papers, Library of Congress. See also Mrs. Harriman's memoir of her experiences in Norway, *Mission to the North* (Philadelphia: Lippincott, 1941).

17. "Norwegian Merchant Marine Statistics, January, 1923," from A. G. Snyder, April 5, 1923, "Comparison of the Fleets of Norway, Sweden, Denmark and Finland on January 1, 1929," from Thomas H. Bevan, January 17, 1929, File Number 885, RG 84. Consular Post Records, Christiania (Oslo), National Archives; Benjamin Thaw, Jr., to Secretary of State, December 15, 1934, File 885, RG 84, Diplomatic Post Records, Oslo, National Archives.

18. "Opportunity for American Vessels to Obtain Cargoes in Oslo," from S. Bertrand Jacobson, September 15, 1925, File 885, "The Foreign Trade of Norway in 1931," from George M. Abbott, January 22, 1932, File 600, RG 84, Consular Post Records, Oslo, National Archives; Bevan to Thomas D. Davis, April 27, 1933, File 885, RG 84, Consular Post Records, Stavanger, National Archives; Thaw to Secretary of State, December 15, 1934, File 885, RG 84, Diplomatic Post Records, Oslo, National Archives; Philip to Secretary of State, April 21, 1933, File 857.00 P.H./54, RG 59, Department of State Central Files, National Archives.

19. *Papers Relating to the Foreign Relations of the United States, 1917, Supplement 2, The World War,* 2 vols. (Washington, D.C.: Government Printing Office, 1932), 1:603–4, 613–16.

20. A. G. Schmedeman to Secretary of State, June 11, 1919, and enclosed translation of article from *Tidens Tegn,* June 7, 1919, Schmedeman to Secretary of State, June 24, 1919, and enclosed translation of article, File 885-4, RG 84, Diplomatic Post Records, Christiania, National Archives.

21. Schmedeman to Secretary of State, February 21, March 23, April 6, 1921, Swenson to Secretary of State, January 22, 1923, File 885, RG 84, Diplomatic Post Records, Christiania, National Archives; Bryn to Hughes, November 18, 1921, File 701.5711/209, RG 59, Department of State Central Files, National Archives; *Papers Relating to the Foreign Relations of the United States, 1921,* 2 vols. (Washington, D.C.: Government Printing Office, 1936), 2:571–99; *Papers Relating to the Foreign Relations of the United States, 1923,* 2 vols. (Washington, D.C.: Government Printing Office, 1938), 2:617–29; Doris H. Linder, *The Reaction of Norway to American Foreign Policy, 1918-1939* (Ann Arbor, Mich.: University Microfilms, 1961), 76–83. Dr. Linder's 1961 Ph.D. dissertation at the University of Minnesota is the best available scholarly history in English on relations between the United States and Norway between the wars.

22. Swenson to Secretary of State, November 19, 1926, File 350-Hannevig, "Preliminary Memorandum on the Fundamental Facts of the Case of Mr. Hannevig," enclosed with Philip to Secretary of State, May 31, 1935, File 350, RG 84, Diplomatic Post Records, Oslo, National Archives; Cordell Hull to the President, April 13, 1940, File 411.57 H 19/389, RG 59, Department of State Central Files, National Archives.

23. Philip to Secretary of State, May 31, 1935, and enclosed "Preliminary Memorandum on the Fundamental Facts of the Case of Mr. Hannevig," Biddle to Secretary of State, February 15, 1936, Hull to the President, April 13, 1940, File 411.57 H 19/140, 157, RG 59, Department of State Central Files, National Archives; Biddle to Secretary of State, March 23, 1937, File 350, RG 84, Diplomatic Post Records, Oslo, National Archives.

24. Hull to the President, April 13, 1940, File 411.56 H 19/389, RG 59, Department of State Central Files, National Archives.

25. Leon L. Cowles to Secretary of State, January 8, 1946, 357.113/1-846, EAG [Ernest Gross] to Mr. Tate, June 15, 1948, Benedict M. English to John Foster Dulles, October 25, 1948, memorandum from the Norwegian Embassy, Washington, D.C., October 31, 1949, File 411.57H19/6-1548, RG 59, Department of State Central Files, National Archives; Linder, *Reaction of Norway to American Foreign Policy,* 107–11.

26. Marion Letcher to C. B. Curtis, September 27, 1919, File 893, RG 84, Consular Post Records, Christiania, National Archives; Schmedeman to Secretary of State, January 10, 1921, File 857.00/194, George K. Stiles, "Over 100 Per Cent Increase in Norwegian Emigration," February 5, 1924, File 857.56/1, Lawrence Higgins, "Norwegian Migrations," December 22, 1934, 19–20, File 857.55/8, RG 59, Department of State Central Files, National Archives.

27. Swenson to Secretary of State, March 19, April 23, 24, May 9, 23, June 18, 29, 1925, File 841.5, RG 84, Diplomatic Post Records, Oslo, National Archives.

28. Oscar Handlin, *The Uprooted: The Epic Story of the Great Migrations That Made the American People* (New York: Grosset and Dunlap, 1951), 287-93.

29. Charles E. Hughes to American Diplomatic and Consular Officers, June 28, 1922, June 30, 1923, and enclosures, Alban G. Snyder to Secretary of State, September 1, 1927, File 811.1, RG 84, Diplomatic Post Records, Christiania (Oslo), National Archives.

30. Telegram from Hughes to the American Embassy, Paris, June 30, 1924, Snyder to Secretary of State, September 1, 1927, File 811.1, RG 84, Diplomatic Post Records, Christiania, National Archives.

31. Thomas H. Bevan to Secretary of State, June 6, 1929, File 125.3116/53, RG 59, Department of State Central Files, National Archives; Wilbur J. Carr to American Consular Officers, June 2, 1930, and enclosure, File 811.11, RG 84, Consular Post Records, Bergen, National Archives.

32. Carr to American Diplomatic and Consular Officers, June 24, 1931, File 811.11, RG 84, Diplomatic Post Records, Oslo, National Archives; Translation of interview article in Bergen *Dagen*, May 6, 1929, enclosed with Swenson to Secretary of State, May 14, 1929, File 711.57/5, RG 59, Department of State Central Files, National Archives.

33. Bevan to Secretary of State, December 20, 1928, telegram from Kellogg to American Consul, Oslo, File 125.3111/32, RG 59, Department of State Central Files, National Archives.

34. Maurice C. Pierce to Secretary of State, June 10, 1929, File 125.1932/70, RG 59, Department of State Central Files, National Archives.

35. Snyder to Secretary of State, February 16, March 9, 1922, Snyder to D. I. Murphy, October 26, 1922, File 123, Snyder to George K. Stiles, December 13, 1923, File 600, RG 84, Consular Post Records, Christiania, National Archives; Snyder to Secretary of State, November 19, 1926, File 125.3113/214, RG 59, Department of State Central Files, National Archives.

36. John A. Gade to William Castle, April 2, 1929, and enclosed clipping from *Washington Post*, March 23, 1929, Swenson to Secretary of State, April 8, 1929, and enclosed translations of letters from Hambro to Swenson, March 22, April 8, 1929, File 711.57/2, 3, RG 59, Department of State Central Files, National Archives; Bevan to Secretary of State, April 3, 1929, File 811.11, RG 84, Consular Post Records, Oslo, National Archives.

37. H. E. Carlson to Secretary of State, November 29, 1922, and enclosed translation, File 000, RG 84, Consular Post Records, Christiania (Oslo); Swenson to Secretary of State, June 9, 1926, and enclosed translation, File 857.56/2, Swenson to Secretary of State, May 14, 1929, and enclosed translation of editorial from Bergen *Dagen*, May 6, 1929, File 711.57/5, RG 59, Department of State Central Files, National Archives.

38. J. P. Cotton to American Diplomatic and Consular Officers, Sep-

tember 15, 1930, File 811.11, RG 84, Diplomatic Post Records, Oslo, National Archives.

39. Bevan to Secretary of State, December 20, 1930, Carr to Julian L. Pinkerton, February 6, 1931, Bevan to Secretary of State, December 23, 1931, File 811.11, RG 84, Consular Post Records, Bergen, National Archives; telegram from Department of State to American Consul, Oslo, July 30, 1932, File 811.11, RG 84, Consular Post Records, Oslo, National Archives.

40. Pinkerton to George Orr, October 23, 1930, Pinkerton to Bevan, October 28, 1930, Bevan to Pinkerton, October 30, 1930, Bevan to Orr, November 5, 1930, File 811.11, RG 84, Consular Post Records, Bergen, National Archives; Dana Hodgdon to Gerald P. Nye, August 28, 1933, File 811.111, RG 84, Consular Post Records, Oslo, National Archives.

41. George M. Abbott to E. Talbot Smith, May 11, 1931, File 811.11, RG 84, Consular Post Records, Bergen, National Archives; Thomas H. Bevan, "Emigration from Norway During 1932," January 20, 1933, File 856, Annex no. 9 to Lawrence Higgins, "Norwegian Migrations," December 22, 1934, File 855, RG 84, Consular Post Records, Oslo, National Archives; weekly report by Marquard H. Lund, December 19, 1932, RG 151, Commercial Attache Reports, National Archives.

42. A. R. Preston to L. E. Wilson, December 29, 1938, William H. Beck to Reidar Hedemann, January 12, 1939, Beck to Cecilia Razovsky, June 6, 1939, File 811.11, Beck to Secretary of State, January 9, 1939, File 800, RG 84, Consular Post Records, Oslo, WNRC.

43. Preston to Leland B. Morris, March 24, 1939, Morris to Beck, April 1, 1939, Beck to Cecilia Razovsky, June 6, 1939, Beck to Morris, June 24, 1939, Morris to Beck, June 28, 1939, File 811.11, RG 84, Consular Post Records, Oslo, WNRC.

44. For an exceptionally able report on the subject see Lawrence Higgins, "Norwegian Migrations," December 22, 1934, and nine annexes, File 857.55/8, RG 59, Department of State Central Files, National Archives. A copy is also in File 855, RG 84, Consular Post Records, Oslo, National Archives.

45. Carr to Snyder, July 8, 1921, March 20, 1922, December 2, 1924, File 600, Carr to Snyder, October 8, 1921, Snyder to Carr, December 21, 1921, Snyder, "Commercial Work: Trade Extension Work at Christiania, Norway," June 15, 1923, File 610, S. Bertrand Jacobson, "Trade Promotion Work at the American Consulate General, Oslo, Norway," May 1, 1925, C. Porter Kuykendall, "Trade Promotion Work of Oslo Consulate General," July 19, 1928, July 11, 1929, File 610.1, RG 84, Consular Post Records, Christiania (Oslo), National Archives.

46. Snyder to George K. Stiles, December 13, 1923, Carr to Snyder, December 2, 1924, File Number 600, Kuykendall, "Trade Promotion Work of Oslo Consulate General," July 11, 27, 1929, File Number 610.1, RG 84, Consular Post Records, Christiania (Oslo), National Archives.

47. Schmedeman to Secretary of State, July 15, 1920, File 600, Philip to Secretary of State, October 23, 1934, Bevan to Philip, May 9, 1934, File 631, RG 84, Diplomatic Post Records, Christiania (Oslo), National Archives; Snyder and S. Bertrand Jacobson, "Commerce and Industries of

Norway–1924," August 1, 1925, Ragnhild Dunker, "Review of Commerce and Industries, Norway, 1928," April 25, 1929, Abbott, "The Foreign Trade of Norway in 1931," January 22, 1932, Abbott, "The Foreign Trade of Norway in 1932," February 21, 1933, File 600, Snyder, "Commerce and Industries 1923," June 6, 1924, File 601, Walter C. Dowling, "Data for Foreign Commerce Yearbook," June 7, 1935, File 610.1, Bevan to Philip, May 9, 1934, File 631, RG 84, Consular Post Records, Christiania, National Archives; Philip to Secretary of State, April 7, 1934, and enclosed report, Biddle to Secretary of State, September 30, 1935, January 15, 1936, and enclosed reports, File 857.00 P.R./78, 114, 121, RG 59, Department of State Central Files, National Archives.

48. Grosvenor M. Jones to Secretary of Commerce Herbert Hoover, August 4, 1923, August 25, 1924, Jones to Christian A. Herter, November 11, 1922, Leland Harrison to Harold Phelps Stokes, August 7, 1924, October 6, 1924, February 25, 1925, April 6, 1925, January 19, 27, 1926, Stokes to Harrison, August 28, 1924, October 9, 1924, April 8, 1925, October 16, 1925, January 21, 29, 1926, Harrison to Herter, October 11, 1922, August 28, 1923, J. Walter Drake to Harrison, August 30, 1923, Harrison to Richard S. Emmet, April 28, 1924, Emmet to Harrison, May 2, 1924, Herter to Harrison, October 13, 1922, Lawrence Richey to Harrison, August 11, 1924, Stokes to J. Butler Wright, October 16, 17, 1924, Wright to Stokes, October 16, 1924, Commerce Papers, Hoover Papers, Herbert Hoover Presidential Library.

49. George Nicolas Ifft to Secretary of State, March 31, 1919, File 125.312/2, Benjamin F. Chase to Secretary of State, File 125.952/3, RG 59, Department of State Central Files, National Archives; William H. Beck to Secretary of State, September 29, 1937, File 125, RG 84, Consular Post Records, Oslo, WNRC.

50. *Papers Relating to the Foreign Relations of the United States, 1928*, 3 vols. (Washington, D.C.: Government Printing Office, 1942–43), 3:593–662; Bryn to Secretary of State, June 1, 1922, Number 711.572/44, RG 59, Department of State Central Files, National Archives; telegrams from William R. Castle to American Legation, Oslo, April 7, 1932, Stimson to American legation, Oslo, September 13, 1932, File 710, RG 84, Diplomatic Post Records, Oslo, National Archives.

51. Swenson to Secretary of State, October 18, 1930, File 862, Bevan, "The Whaling Season 1932–1933," October 28, 1932, File 862.8, RG 84, Diplomatic Post Records, Oslo, National Archives; Thomas D. Davis, "Memorandum Suggesting Commodities of Trade Between the United States and Norway for Which More Lenient Tariff Treatment Is Desirable," August 25, 1934, File 611.5731/89, RG 59, Department of State Central Files, National Archives.

52. Aide-memoire from Royal Norwegian Legation, Washington, August 22, 1933, December 27, 1933, memo from Department of State, December 26, 1933, Pierrepont Moffat to Secretary of State, December 20, 1934, File 611.573/12, 17, 21, 58, RG 59, Department of State Central Files, National Archives; *Foreign Relations of the United States: Diplomatic Papers, 1933*, 5 vols. (Washington, D.C.: Government Printing Office, 1949–50), 2:624–29.

53. Moffat to Sayre, March 19, 1934, File 611.573/27, memorandum of conversation with Wilhelm T. von Munthe de Morgenstierne by F. B. S. [Sayre], June 21, 1934, Morgenstierne to Sayre, June 30, 1934, File 611.5731/78, 79, P. M. [Moffat], "Whale Oil," September 5, 1934, File 611.573 Whale Oil/5, RG 59, Department of State Central Files, National Archives.

54. Memorandum by Moffat, December 19, 1934, File 611.573/56, RG 59, Department of State Central Files, National Archives.

55. Moffat to Secretary of State, December 20, 1934, memorandum from Royal Norwegian Legation, December 21, 1934, File 611.573/58, 57, Benjamin Thaw, Jr., to Secretary of State, April 24, 1935, File 657.116/50, RG 59, Department of State Central Files, National Archives.

56. Memorandum of conversation between Dr. Halvdan Koht, Sayre, Morgenstierne, Hugh S. Cumming, and Mr. Ross, October 28, 1937, File 611.5731/172, RG 59, Department of State Central Files, National Archives; Cumming to Mrs. Harriman, November 3, 1937, Harriman Papers, Library of Congress.

57. Sayre to Biddle, March 6, 1936, File 611.573 Whale Oil/48, RG 59, Department of State Central Files, National Archives.

58. Hull to Roosevelt, May 9, 1935, File 611.573/73A, RG 59, Department of State Central Files, National Archives.

59. Wallace to Roosevelt, May 27, 1935, Roosevelt to Hull, May 31, 1935, File 611.573/76, RG 59, Department of State Central Files, National Archives.

60. Hull to Roosevelt, August 18, 1935, J.R.M. to Sayre, September 27, 1935, Biddle to Secretary of State, October 12, 29, 1935, File 611.573 Whale Oil/25, 30, 32, 34, RG 59, Department of State Central Files, National Archives.

61. Hull to Robert L. Doughton, January 20, 1936, May 11, 1936, Hull to Pat Harrison, May 11, 1936, H.M.C. to Mr. Hawkins, June 4 [1936], File 611.573 Whale Oil/39, 56, 57, 67, RG 59, Department of State Central Files, National Archives.

62. R. C. Hayes to William F. Allen, March 19, 1937, John Hilton to A. Harry Moore, March 24, 1937, J. M. Carpenter to Hull, June 17, 1937, telegram from F. M. Kelley to the President, June 21, 1937, Glen L. Ogle to John W. Boehne, Jr., June 26, 1937, B. H. Klivans to Claude Pepper, June 29, 1937, File 611.673 Whale Oil/79, 90, 125, 129, 140, 158, RG 59, Department of State Central Files, National Archives.

63. Memorandum of conversation between Hull and Bachke, March 30, 1933, telegram from Hull to American Legation, Oslo, July 19, 1934, File 611. 5731/60, 79A, RG 59, Department of State Central Files, National Archives.

64. Philip to Secretary of State, September 18, 1934, File 611.5731/91, RG 59, Department of State Central Files, National Archives.

65. Telegram from Bevan to Secretary of State, September 6, 1934, File 611.5731/88, RG 59, Department of State Central Files, National Archives.

66. Harriman to Secretary of State, October 26, 1938, Cumming to Mr. Culbertson and Mr. Moffat, January 18, 1939, Cumming to Sayre,

January 18, 1939, File 611.5731/199, 207, 208, RG 59, Department of State Central Files, National Archives.

67. Philip to Secretary of State, October 23, 1934, File 611.5731/102, RG 59, Department of State Central Files, National Archives.

68. The best scholarly books in English on Norway's peace policies between the wars are Nils Ørvik, *The Decline of Neutrality, 1914-1941: With Special Reference to the United States and the Northern Neutrals*, 2d ed. (London: Frank Cass, 1971), 119-94, and Linder, *The Reaction of Norway to American Foreign Policy, 1918-1939*. For United States policies see Wayne S. Cole, *Roosevelt and the Isolationists, 1932-45* (Lincoln, Nebr.: University of Nebraska Press, 1983).

69. Swenson to Secretary of State, April 7, 1922, February 11, 1924, File 500, Swenson to Secretary of State, November 18, 1925, File 800-China, RG 84, Diplomatic Post Records, Christiania (Oslo), National Archives.

70. Swenson to Secretary of State, August 28, 1928, February 15, 1929, File 710, RG 84, Diplomatic Post Records, Oslo, National Archives; *Foreign Relations of the United States, 1920*, 1:153-57, 161.

71. *Papers Relating to the Foreign Relations of the United States, 1929*, 3 vols. (Washington, D.C.: Government Printing Office, 1943-1944), 3:706-13.

72. Philip to Secretary of State, January 19, 1932, Hugh Gibson to Philip, April 20, 1932, File 500, Philip to Secretary of State, May 23, 1933, File 713, RG 84, Diplomatic Post Records, Oslo, National Archives; Robert H. Ferrell, *American Diplomacy in the Great Depression: Hoover-Stimson Foreign Policy, 1929-1933* (New Haven: Yale University Press, 1957), 194-214; Cole, *Roosevelt and the Isolationists*, 65-76.

73. See Gary B. Ostrower, *Collective Insecurity: The United States and the League of Nations During the Early Thirties* (Lewisburg, Pa.: Bucknell University Press, 1979), and Cole, *Roosevelt and the Isolationists*, 113-19.

74. Swenson to Secretary of State, August 3, 1926, June 25, 1928, May 14, 1929, March 19, 1930, May 10, 1930, File 500-League of Nations, RG 84, Diplomatic Post Records, Oslo, National Archives; Philip to Secretary of State, April 16, 1934, File 857.00 P.R./79, RG 59, Department of State Central Files, National Archives.

75. Swenson to Secretary of State, July 24, 1923, February 23, 1926, August 2, 1926, File 500-League of Nations, Swenson to Secretary of State, July 24, 1930, File 400-11th Assembly of League, RG 84, Diplomatic Post Records, Christiania (Oslo), National Archives; Biddle to Secretary of State, October 21, 1935, File 757.65/2, RG 59, Department of State Central Files, National Archives.

76. Swenson to Secretary of State, September 19, 1930, RG 84, Diplomatic Post Records, Oslo, National Archives.

77. Biddle to Secretary of State, October 21, 1935, January 30, 1936, telegram from Biddle to Secretary of State, October 26, 1935, File 500, RG 84, Diplomatic Post Records, Oslo, National Archives.

78. Biddle to Secretary of State, November 20, 1935, December 3, 1935, January 30, 1936, File 500, RG 84, Diplomatic Post Records, Oslo, WNRC.

79. Biddle to Secretary of State, February 15, March 6, 1936, Biddle to Secretary of State, May 28, 1936, File 500, RG 84, Diplomatic Post Records, Oslo, WNRC. See also Halvdan Koht, *Norway: Neutral and Invaded* (New York: Macmillan, 1941), 2–5.

80. Swenson to Secretary of State, November 9, 1922, Philip to Secretary of State, January 8, 1932, January 17, 1934, File 500, RG 84, Diplomatic Post Records, Christiania (Oslo), National Archives; Philip to Secretary of State, September 12, 1931, and enclosed report, Patterson to Secretary of State, April 1, 1938, File 857.00 P.R./17, 174, North Winship to Secretary of State, August 21, 1936, Rudolf E. Schoenfeld to Secretary of State, May 8, 1937, File 757D.00/17, 32, RG 59, Department of State Central Files, National Archives.

81. Philip to Secretary of State, December 27, 1930, November 1, 1932, File 631, RG 84, Diplomatic Post Records, Oslo, National Archives; Julius Wadsworth to Secretary of State, June 30, 1932, File 657.003/69, Adviser on International Economic Affairs, "Norway and the Oslo Agreements of 1937," September 16, 1937, File 611.5731/171 1/2, Harriman to Secretary of State, January 31, 1938, and enclosed report, File 857.00 P.R./170, RG 59, Department of State Central Files, National Archives.

82. Cole, *Roosevelt and the Isolationists*, 248, 297–302, 319.

83. The best scholarly history of American neutrality legislation in the 1930s is Robert A. Divine, *The Illusion of Neutrality* (Chicago: University of Chicago Press, 1962).

84. Patterson to Secretary of State, June 2, 1938, File 757.0011/1, RG 59, Department of State Central Files, National Archives.

85. Harriman to Secretary of State, May 20, 1939, File 757.62/13, Patterson to Secretary of State, April 27, 1938, File 757.00/11, RG 59, Department of State Central Files, National Archives; Koht, *Norway: Neutral and Invaded*, 5–7, 13–15.

86. Harriman to Secretary of State, September 1, 1938, File 800, RG 84, Diplomatic Post Records, Oslo, WNRC. See also Biddle to Secretary of State, June 14, 1937, File 857.00/301, RG 59, Department of State Central Files, National Archives; Greve, *Haakon VII of Norway*, 114–21.

87. Telegram from Harriman to Secretary of State, November 21, [1938], Harriman to Secretary of State, November 29, December 10, 1938, File 857.0011/23, 29, 30, RG 59, Department of State Central Files, National Archives; Greve, *Haakon VII of Norway*, 112–13.

88. Swenson to Secretary of State, July 24, 1924, October 6, 1924, March 23, 1929, File 857.0011/–, 1, 7, RG 59, Department of State Central Files, National Archives; Greve, *Haakon VII of Norway*, 104–10.

89. Roosevelt to Harriman, July 7, 1938, Harriman Papers; Harriman to Secretary of State, August 11, 1938, Roosevelt to Prince Olav, November 15, 1938, Olav to Roosevelt, December 19, 1938, File 033. 5711–Prince Olav/4, 9, 14, RG 59, Department of State Central Files, National Archives.

90. Harriman to Secretary of State, January 16, 1939, and attached report, File 857.00 P.R./193, Morgenstierne to Hull, April 10, 1939, Olav to Roosevelt, May 4, 1939, Harriman to Secretary of State, July 21, 1939, clippings from *Baltimore Sun*, April 30, 1939, *Washington Times-Herald*,

June 30, 1939, *Washington Post*, June 30, 1939, and *New York Times*, July 7, 1939, File 033.5711-Prince Olav/43, 57, 63, 74, 82, 106, RG 59, Department of State Central Files, National Archives; telegrams from Olav and Märtha to Roosevelt, July 6, 1939, Haakon R. to Roosevelt, July 6, 1939, President's Secretary's File, Norway 1935-1939 folder, Roosevelt Papers.

91. Harriman to Secretary of State, July 21, 1939, File 033. 5711-Prince Olav/106, RG 59, Department of State Central Files, National Archives.

CHAPTER 4

1. Good starting places for accounts in English of Norway during World War II written by Norwegian and Scandinavian scholars include Henrik S. Nissen, ed., *Scandinavia During the Second World War* (Minneapolis: University of Minnesota Press, Oslo: Universitetsforlaget, 1983), and Johs. Andenaes, Olav Riste, and Magne Skodvin, *Norway and the Second World War* (Oslo: Johan Grundt Tanum Forlag, 1974).

2. Benjamin Thaw, Jr., to Secretary of State, March 25, 1935, Florence J. Harriman to Secretary of State, September 11, 1939, File 857.00/278, 312, Thaw to Secretary of State, March 27, 1935, File 611.5731/118, Harriman to Secretary of State, January 22, 1940, File 857.032/52 RG 59, Department of State Central Files, National Archives. For the foreign minister's account see Halvdan Koht, *Norway: Neutral and Invaded* (New York: Macmillan, 1941), 16-44. For Koht's autobiography see Halvdan Koht, *Education of an Historian* (New York: Robert Speller, 1957). On neutrality policies in World War II see Nils Ørvik, *The Decline of Neutrality, 1914-1941: With Special Reference to the United States and the Northern Neutrals*, 2d ed. (London: Frank Cass, & Co., 1971), 195-246.

3. Wayne S. Cole, *Roosevelt and the Isolationists, 1932-45* (Lincoln, Nebr.: University of Nebraska Press, 1983), 297-306; Mark Lincoln Chadwin, *The Hawks of World War II* (Chapel Hill: University of North Carolina Press, 1968), 43-73.

4. Cole, *Roosevelt and the Isolationists*, 364-65, 426-31, 453-55, 479-81.

5. Harriman to Secretary of State, September 9, 1939, File 857.032/49, Harriman to Secretary of State, September 11, 1939, File 857.00/312, RG 59, Department of State Central Files, National Archives.

6. Cole, *Roosevelt and the Isolationists*, 320-30; Robert A. Divine, *The Illusion of Neutrality* (Chicago: University of Chicago Press, 1962), 286-335.

7. Telegram from Steinhardt to Secretary of State, October 24, 1939, telegram from Dunlap to Secretary of State, November 6, 1939, File 300.115(39) City of Flint/3, 52, 158, RG 59, Department of State Central Files, National Archives; Harriman to Emory S. Land, December 29, 1939, Harriman Papers. For a well-researched scholarly article on this episode see John Garry Clifford, "The Odyssey of City of Flint," *American Neptune*, April 1972, 100-16. Mrs. Harriman's account is in Florence Jaf-

fray Harriman, *Mission to the North* (Philadelphia: Lippincott, 1941), 229–45. Captain Gainard's account is in Joseph A. Gainard, *Yankee Skipper* (New York: Frederick A. Stokes, 1940).

8. Telegram from Harriman to Secretary of State, October 27, 1939, telegram from Dunlap to Secretary of State, November 6, 1939, 300.115(39) City of Flint/52, 158, RG 59, Department of State Central Files, National Archives.

9. Telegram from Hull to American Embassy, Moscow, October 24, 1939, telegram from Harriman to Secretary of State, October 26, 27, 1939, File 300.115(39) City of Flint/9, 20, 52, RG 59, Department of State Central Files, National Archives.

10. Supplementary affidavit by Joseph A. Gainard, November 9, 1939, File 711, RG 84, Consular Post Records, Bergen, WNRC; telegram from Steinhardt to Secretary of State, October 26, 27, 1939, File 300.115(39) City of Flint/13, 48, 49, RG 59, Department of State Central Files, National Archives.

11. Harriman to Secretary of State, November 8, 1939, Maurice P. Dunlap to Secretary of State, November 25, 1939, File 300.115(39) City of Flint/225, 268, RG 59, Department of State Central Files, National Archives.

12. Telegram from Hull to American Consul, Bergen, November 4, 1939, Dunlap to Secretary of State, November 16, 1939, December 23, 1939, File 711, RG 84, Consular Post Records, Bergen, WNRC; telegram from Kirk to Secretary of State, November 11, 1939, Dunlap to Secretary of State, November 30, 1939, File 300.115(39) City of Flint/192, 269, RG 59, Department of State Central Files, National Archives; telegram from Hull to Harriman, November 7, 1939, Harriman to Emory S. Land, December 29, 1939, Harriman Papers.

13. Dunlap to Harriman, January 6, 1940, Harriman Papers. For the foreign minister's account see Koht, *Norway: Neutral and Invaded*, 24–25.

14. Clifford, "Odyssey of City of Flint," *American Neptune*, 115–16.

15. Harriman to Secretary of State, September 23, October 4, December 6, 12, 1939, telegram from Harriman to Secretary of State, December 29, 1939, File 711, RG 84, Diplomatic Post Records, Oslo; Harriman to Secretary of State, December 16, 1939, File 857.00 P.R./214, RG 59, Department of State Central Files, National Archives. For the foreign minister's account see Koht, *Norway: Neutral and Invaded*, 25–30, 34–35.

16. Robert Dallek, *Franklin D. Roosevelt and American Foreign Policy, 1932-1945* (New York: Oxford University Press, 1979), 208–12.

17. Ibid.

18. Roosevelt to Crown Prince Olav, January 4, 1940, President's Secretary's File, Norway 1940 folder, Roosevelt Papers.

19. Hugh S. Cumming to Mrs. Harriman, February 3, 1940, Harriman Papers.

20. Mrs. Harriman to Roosevelt, February 27, 1940, Harriman Papers.

21. Mrs. Harriman to Dagfinn Paust, February 27, 1940, Harriman Papers.

22. Mrs. Harriman to Cumming, March 5, 1940, Harriman Papers.

23. Biddle to Secretary of State, January 4, 1937, and enclosed memoranda, File 857.20/22, RG 59, Department of State Central Files, National Archives. For the foreign minister's account see Koht, *Norway: Neutral and Invaded*, 8–10, 12–13.

24. Biddle to Roosevelt, April 23, 1936, President's Secretary's File, Norway 1935–1939 folder, Roosevelt Papers; Biddle to Secretary of State, November 9, 1935, Jefferson Patterson to Secretary of State, September 23, 25, 1936, telegram from Hull to American legation, Oslo, November 21, 1937, File 879.6, RG 84, Diplomatic Post Records, Oslo, WNRC; Biddle to Secretary of State, December 17, 1936, File 857.796/52, RG 59, Department of State Central Files, National Archives.

25. Harriman to Truman Smith, November 24, 1937, File 879.6, RG 84, Diplomatic Post Records, Oslo, WNRC; Harriman to Secretary of State, February 3, 1938, File 857.248/18, RG 59, Department of State Central Files, National Archives.

26. Patterson to Secretary of State, December 14, 1937, Harriman to Secretary of State, August 2, 1938, File 879.6, RG 84, Diplomatic Post Records, Oslo, WNRC; Harriman to Secretary of State, September 17, 1938, October 30, 1939, File 857.248/29, 56, RG 59, Department of State Central Files, National Archives.

27. Harriman to Secretary of State, March 14, 1939, File 857.20/48, RG 59, Department of State Central Files, National Archives.

28. Harriman to Secretary of State, August 16, 1939, and enclosed report, File 857.00 P.R./206, RG 59, Department of State Central Files, National Archives; Harriman to Roosevelt, December 5, 1939, Roosevelt to Harriman January 9, 1940, Harriman Papers.

29. Letter from Royal Norwegian Legation, Washington, January 13, 1940, Haakon R. to Roosevelt, January 15, 1940, letter from Department of State, January 29, 1940, Joseph C. Green to Eu, January 31, 1940, Roosevelt to King Haakon VII, February 15, 1940, J. S. Allard to Department of State, April 2, 1940, and enclosed contracts, Charles W. Yost to Curtiss-Wright Corporation, April 9, 1940, File 857.248/59, 61, 64, 71, 74, 75, 76, 77, 78, letter from Royal Norwegian Legation, Washington, February 14, 1940, File 857.01B11/32, RG 59, Department of State Central Files, National Archives; Harriman to George C. Marshall, January 13, 1940, Marshall to Harriman, February 13, 1940, Harriman Papers; Mr. Bell to Secretary of Treasury, February 12, 1940, H. E. Collins to Secretary of Treasury, February 20, 1940, Henry Morgenthau, Jr., Diaries, Franklin D. Roosevelt Library.

30. "Norway," by Major H. G. Schumann, August 16, 1943, RG 165, GS Regional File (Norway), WNRC. See also enclosure no. 1 to Cloyce K. Huston to Secretary of State, April 30, 1947, File 857.00/4-3047, RG 59, Department of State Central Files, National Archives.

31. Dunlap to Secretary of State, April 2, 1940, File 857.46462/1, RG 59, Department of State Central files, National Archives.

32. Harriman, *Mission to the North*, 247–49; Koht, *Norway: Neutral and Invaded*, 57–58.

33. Harriman, *Mission to the North*, 249–51; Winston S. Churchill, *The Gathering Storm* (Boston: Houghton Mifflin, 1948), 578–85.

34. Harriman, *Mission to the North*, 251–52.

35. Ibid., 253; telegram from Kirk to Secretary of State, April 11, 1940, File 124.576/34, telegram from Sterling to Secretary of State, April 25, 1940, File 125.0057/80, RG 59, Department of State Central Files, National Archives.

36. Telegram from Murphy to Secretary of State, April 9, 1940, File 757.62/36, telegram from Sterling to Secretary of State, April 19, 1939, File 857.01/14, RG 59, Department of State Central Files, National Archives; Raymond E. Cox to Secretary of State, April 19, 1940, RG 165, G2 Regional File (Norway), WNRC; Koht, *Norway: Neutral and Invaded*, 88–98; Carl J. Hambro, *I Saw It Happen in Norway* (New York: Appleton-Century, 1940), pp. 159-81.

37. Greve, *Haakon VII of Norway*, 132–35; Koht, *Norway:Neutral and Invaded*, 58–86; Hambro, *I Saw It Happen in Norway*, 12–46; Harriman, *Mission to the North*, 257–66.

38. Hambro, *I Saw It Happen in Norway*, 21, 27, 120–21; Harriman, *Mission to the North*, 280–81; Hans Christian Adamson and Per Klem, *Blood on the Midnight Sun* (New York: Norton, 1964), 17–109.

39. Greve, *Haakon VII of Norway*, 135–46; Koht, *Norway: Neutral and Invaded*, 86–87, 107–8; Harriman, *Mission to the North*, 257–89; Harriman to Roosevelt, April 30, 1940, President's Secretary's File, Norway 1940 folder, Roosevelt Papers.

40. Harriman to Roosevelt, April 30, 1940, President's Secretary's File, Norway 1940 folder, Roosevelt Papers; Harriman, *Mission to the North*, 260.

41. Nissen, ed., *Scandinavia During the Second World War*, 94–97; Greve, *Haakon VII of Norway*, 140–47; Koht, *Norway: Neutral and Invaded*, 117–28; Hambro, *I Saw It Happen in Norway*, 143–58.

42. Greve, *Haakon VII of Norway*, 148–66; Nissen, ed., *Scandinavia During the Second World War*, 115–19, 186–208, 245–58, 295–318; Koht, *Norway: Neutral and Invaded*, 186–203; Hambro, *I Saw It Happen in Norway*, 151–58, 182–202; Olav Riste and Berit Nokleby, *Norway, 1940–1945: The Resistance Movement*, 3d ed. (Oslo: Tanum-Norli, 1978); Tore Gjelsvik, *Norwegian Resistance, 1940–1945* (London: Hurst, 1977).

43. Among the many scholarly accounts on this subject see Cole, *Roosevelt and the Isolationists*, 363–500; Dallek, *Franklin D. Roosevelt and American Foreign Policy*, 218–313; William L. Langer and S. Everett Gleason, *The Undeclared War, 1940–1941* (New York: Harper & Brothers, 1953).

44. For example, see boxes 49 through 61, RG 84, Consular Post Records, Oslo, 1940. See also A. R. Preston to George Gundersen, April 29, 1940, File 310-G, Preston to Secretary of State, May 25, 1940, File 310, RG 84, Consular Post Records, Oslo, WNRC; Dunlap to Secretary of State, May 20, 1940, File 300, RG 84, Consular Post Records, Bergen, WNRC.

45. Telegram from Heath to Secretary of State, July 1, 12, 1940, telegram from Cox to Secretary of State, July 15, 1940, Cox to Secretary of State, July 15, 1940, File 124.57/40, 52, 54, 59, 60, RG 59, Department of State Central Files, National Archives.

46. Preston to Secretary of State, August 26, 1940, File 125.3111/57, Semi-Annual Report on Office Organization and Administration – January 1, 1941, American Consulate General, Oslo, Norway, from Preston, January 9, 1941, File 125.3116, Office Organization and Administration report from Dunlap, January 30, 1941, File 125.1936, Dunlap to Secretary of State, May 20, 1941, File 857.415/10, telegram from Morris to Secretary of State, June 19, 1941, File 125.0062/299, Dunlap to Secretary of State, July 4, 1941, File 125.1933/276, Preston to Secretary of State, November 10, 1941, File 123 P 922/394, RG 59, Department of State Central Files, National Archives.

47. Memorandum of conversation between Hull and Morgenstierne, April 12, 1940, File 857.01/6, RG 59, Department of State Central Files, National Archives.

48. Memoranda from Royal Norwegian Legation, Washington, D.C., June 5, August 9, 1940, File 857.01B11/34, 35, RG 59, Department of State Central Files, National Archives.

49. Harriman, *Mission to the North*, 311–17; Greve, *Haakon VII of Norway*, 155–56; telegram from Kennedy to Secretary of State for President, June 12, 1940, Sumner Welles to Roosevelt, July 10, 1940, telegram from Hull to American Legation, Stockholm, July 12, 1940, telegram from Welles to American Legation, Stockholm, for Mrs. Harriman, July 22, 1940, Breckinridge Long to George T. Summerlin, August 22, 1940, and enclosed item, telegram from Hull for President to American Embassy, London, for Crown Prince Olav, August 29, 1940, telegram from Welles to American Embassy, London, November 22, 1940, File 857.0011/40, 45, 51, 90A, 92A, 104A, RG 59, Department of State Central Files, National Archives; Olav to Roosevelt, June 22, 1940, President's Secretary's File, Norway 1940 folder, Roosevelt Papers.

50. Telegram from Welles to American Embassy, London, November 22, 1940, telegram from Johnson to Secretary of State, November 28, 1940, File 857.0011/104A, 106, RG 59, Department of State Central Files, National Archives; telegram from Johnson to Secretary of State, December 10, 1940, File 800.1, RG 84, Diplomatic Post Records, London, WNRC.

51. Telegrams from Welles to American Embassy, London, July 19, 29, 1940, telegram from Kennedy to Secretary of State, August 2, 1940, File 124.57/54A, 56A, 57, RG 59, Department of State Central Files, National Archives.

52. Hull to Biddle, February 24, 1941, Roosevelt to King Haakon VII, February 11, 1941, telegrams from Winant to Secretary of State, March 14, 20, 1941, File 123 Biddle, Anthony J. D./360, 339, 342, RG 59, Department of State Central Files, National Archives.

53. Telegram from Johnson to Secretary of State, December 25, 1940, File 857.48/18, RG 59, Department of State Central Files, National Archives.

54. Biddle to Roosevelt, September 2, 1941, File Nor 000–Haakon, King, RG 84, Diplomatic Post Records 1940/1941 (London Govt.), WNRC.

55. Morgenstierne to Hull, April 11, 1942, Edgar A. Innes to Mr.

NOTES TO PAGES 100–102

Clark, May 8, 1942, telegram from Winant to Secretary of State, December 18, 1943, memorandum from Department of State Division of Protocol, February 21, 1944, File 857.0011/126, 133, 140, 142, RG 59, Department of State Central Files, National Archives; "Descriptive Itinerary for Royal Norwegian Tour through United States and Canada, April–May 1942," President's Secretary's File, Norway 1942 folder, Roosevelt Papers.

56. Telegrams from Roosevelt to King Haakon VII, April 9, August 3, 1942, August 4, 1943, File 857.001H11/86A, 88C, 90, R. E. Schuermann to Secretary of State, June 23, 1942, Welles to Frank Knox, July 14, 1942, File 857.24/48, RG 59, Department of State Central Files, National Archives.

57. Press release from Stephen Early, September 16, 1942, File 857.30/7, RG 59, Department of State Central Files, National Archives.

58. Biddle to Secretary of State, March 23, 1942, E. W. Nash to Woodward and Summerlin, May 1, 1942, File 857.002/96, RG 59, Department of State Central Files, National Archives; Roosevelt to Watson, May 5, 1942, Stanley Woodward to Watson, May 6, 1942, Official File 123, Roosevelt Papers.

59. Telegram from Winant to Secretary of State, March 3, 1941, File 857.002/94, H. L. C. to Secretary of State, March 24, 1943, File 857.50/143 1/2, Lie to Hull, March 31, 1943, Hull to Lie, April 14, 1943, File 033.5711/66, RG 59, Department of State Central Files, National Archives.

60. Secret memorandum, October 20, 1943, File 857.44/1, RG 59, Department of State Central Files, National Archives; C. J. Hambro to Roosevelt, December 19, 1944, President's Personal File 5520, Roosevelt Papers.

61. Telegram from Hull to American Embassy, London, for Biddle, May 5, 1942, telegram from Winant to Secretary of State, from Biddle, May 6, 1942, Ray Atherton to Welles, May 8, 1942, File 124.57/69A, 70, 73, telegram from Hull to American Embassy, London, for Biddle, May 9, 1942, telegram from Winant to Secretary of State, from Biddle, May 12, 1942, File 123 Biddle, Anthony J. D./458, 452, RG 59, Department of State Central Files, National Archives.

62. Biddle to Roosevelt, January 20, 1944, Hull to Stimson, January 20, 1944, Roosevelt to Biddle, January 22, 1944, telegram from Winant to Secretary of State, January 23, 1944, File 123 Biddle, Anthony J. D./545, 547, 551, 552, RG 59, Department of State Central Files, National Archives.

63. Hull to Roosevelt, January 28, 1944, File 123 Biddle, Anthony J. D./553A, Hull to Osborne, October 17, 1944, 123 Osborne, Lithgow, RG 59, Department of State Central Files, National Archives; Roosevelt to Crown Prince Olav, September 15, 1944, President's Secretary's File, Norway 1943–45 folder, Roosevelt Papers; Richardson Dougall and Mary Patricia Chapman, *United States Chiefs of Mission, 1778–1973* (Washington, D.C.: Historical Office, Bureau of Public Affairs, Department of State, 1973), 115.

64. Warwick Perkins to Secretary of State, April 17, 1942, North Winship to Secretary of State, January 13, 1943, A. C. Frost to Secretary

of State, February 20, 1945, File 857.248/110, 115, 2-2045, RG 59, Department of State Central Files, National Archives; "The Royal Norwegian Armed Forces," attached to O. Munthe-Kaas to O. T. Jamerson, March 10, 1944, RG 165, G2 Regional File (Norway), WNRC.

65. Wesley Frank Craven and James Lea Cate, eds., *The Army Air Forces in World War II*, vol. 2, *Europe: Torch to Pointblank, August 1942 to December 1943* (Chicago: University of Chicago Press, 1949), 674–76.

66. George V. Strong to Dwight D. Eisenhower, September 8, 1942, Eisenhower to Strong, September 18, 1942, File 371.3 Norway, RG 319, Army Intelligence Project Decimal File 1941–1945, WNRC.

67. Among the many published accounts on this subject see Nissen, ed., *Scandinavia During the Second World War*, 253–54; Richard Petrow, *The Bitter Years: The Invasion and Occupation of Denmark and Norway, April 1940–May 1945* (New York: William Morrow, 1974), 138–58, 234–38; Adamson and Klem, *Blood on the Midnight Sun*, 112–84; and Thomas Gallagher, *Assault in Norway: Sabotaging the Nazi Nuclear Bomb* (New York: Harcourt Brace Jovanovich, 1975).

68. For Secretary of War Henry L. Stimson's explanation of this see Stimson to Secretary of State, January 11, 1944, RG 84, Diplomatic Post Records, Oslo, WNRC. See also telegram from Winant to Secretary of State, January 19, 1944, File Nor 711.2, Henry S. Villard to R. Gordon Arneson, January 28, 1949, RG 84, Diplomatic Post Records, Oslo, WNRC; telegram from Johnson to Secretary of State, July 24, 1944, File 857.6461/7-2444, RG 59, Department of State Central Files, National Archives; Petrow, *The Bitter Years*, 234–35; Adamson and Klem, *Blood on the Midnight Sun*, 174–78.

69. Petrow, *The Bitter Years*, 235–38; Adamson and Klem, *Blood on the Midnight Sun*, 178–84.

70. For a convenient compilation of many documents revealing those conflicts of interest see *Foreign Relations of the United States, Diplomatic Papers, 1942*, 3:78–99.

71. Morgenstierne to Hull, February 28, 1942, memorandum by H. Cumming, September 1, 1942, memorandum from Norwegian Embassy, Washington, D.C., September 22, 1942, File 857.85/347, 393, 9-2242, J. F. to Clarence Cannon, March 13, 1943, File 857.24/64, RG 59, Department of State Central Files, National Archives.

72. Charles Bunn to Eugene V. Rostow, July 10, 1942, Hull to Morgenstierne, July 11, 1942, Morgenstierne to Hull, July 11, 1942, and attached press release, File 857.24/52C, 53B, 54A, RG 59, Department of State Central Files, National Archives.

73. Memorandum by H. Cumming, September 1, 1942, File 857.85/393, J. F. to Clarence Cannon, March 13, 1943, File 857.24/64, RG 59, Department of State Central Files, National Archives; *Foreign Relations of the United States, 1942*, 3:81.

74. Memorandum from Norwegian Embassy, Washington, D.C., September 22, 1942, Roosevelt to Breckinridge Long, November 19, 1942, Morgenstierne to Hull, January 25, 1943, File 857.85/9-2242, 11-1942, 1-2543, telegram from Hull to American Embassy, London, for Biddle, October 26, 1942, File 857.852/39A, RG 59, Department of State Central

Files, National Archives; *Foreign Relations of the United States, 1942*, 3:90.

75. Morgenstierne to Hull, November 24, 1942, December 7, 1942, File 857.85/396, 402, RG 59, Department of State Central Files, National Archives; *Foreign Relations of the United States, 1942*, 3:91-97.

76. Memorandum from Norwegian Embassy, Washington, January 28, 1943, Memorandum of Conversation between Ambassador Morgenstierne and Mr. Long, May 20, 1943, File 857.85/1-2843, 414, RG 59, Department of State Central Files, National Archives.

77. Francis M. Shea to Secretary of State, March 20, 1945, memorandum by W. W. Bishop, May 23, 1945, File 411.57 Ships/3-245, 5-2345, RG 59, Department of State Central Files, National Archives; *Foreign Relations of the United States: Diplomatic Papers, 1945*, 5:108-9.

78. Memorandum of conversation between Hull and Morgenstierne, September 5, 1942, J. Galbe to Hull, October 30, 1942, memorandum from Norwegian Embassy, Washington, January 4, 1943, File 857.48/36, 34 1/3, 51, RG 59, Department of State Central Files, National Archives; American Friends of Norway folder, Harriman Papers.

79. Roosevelt to Under Secretary of State, November 16, 1942, Welles to Roosevelt, November 19, 1942, December 12, 1942, memorandum of conversation between Morgenstierne and Welles, November 23, 1942, memorandum of conversation between Noel Hall and Long, November 24, 1942, December 8, 15, 1942, memorandum of conversation between Morgenstierne, Dr. Evant, and Long, January 4, 1943, G. L. B. to Long, January 14, 1943, James W. Riddleberger to Secretary of State, August 19, 1943, File 857.48/43, 43 1/4, 43 3/4, 44, 46, 49, 51, 79, RG 59, Department of State Records, National Archives; Francis L. Loewenheim, Harold D. Langley, and Manfred Jonas, eds., *Roosevelt and Churchill: Their Secret Wartime Correspondence* (New York: Dutton, Saturday Review Press, 1975), 301, 304-5, 472.

80. Memorandum from Norwegian Embassy, Washington, March 16, 1944, Leo T. Crowley to Secretary of State, April 12, 1944, File 857.48/ 119, 123, RG 59, Department of State Central Files, National Archives.

81. Edward R. Stettinius, Jr., to Henry L. Stimson, December 22, 1944, April 2, 1945, Acheson to Roswell P. Barnes, February 16, 1945, James Clement Dunn to Secretary of State, March 5, 1945, and supplemental memorandum on relief shipments, Mr. Plitt to General Holmes and Dunn, March 6, 1945, memorandum of conversation between Joseph C. Grew and Morgenstierne, April 20, 1945, memorandum by Acting Chairman of State-War-Navy Coordinating Committee, April 25, 1945, File 857.48/12-244, 1-3045, 3-545, 3-645, 4-245, 4-2045, 4-2545, RG 59, Department of State Central Files, National Archives. See also *Foreign Relations of the United States, Diplomatic Papers, 1945*, 5:26-55.

82. C. Ulrick Bay to Secretary of State, August 22, 1949, and enclosed report by H. S. Villard, File 123 Villard, Henry S., RG 59, Department of State Central Files, National Archives.

83. Telegram from Hull to American Embassy, Moscow, March 15, 1944, telegram from Winant to Secretary of State, from Schoenfeld, April

28, 1944, telegram from Hamilton to Secretary of State, May 17, 1944, File 857.01/124A, 132, 141, RG 59, Department of State Central Files, National Archives.

84. Greve, *Haakon VII of Norway*, 170; Robert Murphy to H. Freeman Matthews, June 18, 1945, and enclosed SHAEF Mission (Norway) report no. 8, June 1, 1945, File 857.00/6-1845, RG 59, National Archives.

85. Telegram from Grew to American Embassy, London, May 9, 1945, File 124.6, RG 84, Diplomatic Post Records, Oslo, National Archives; Anders Andersen to Schweizerische Gesandtschaft in Deutschland, January 3, 1945, Lithgow Osborne to Secretary of State, May 23, 1945, and enclosed letter from Nielsen to Osborne, May 16, 1945, File 124.571/5-1745, 5-2345, RG 59, Department of State Central Files, National Archives.

86. Telegram from Winant to Secretary of State, May 25, 1945, File 124.6, RG 84, Diplomatic Post Records, Oslo, National Archives; C. Porter Kuykendall to Secretary of State, May 28, 1945, Osborne to Secretary of State, June 5, 1945, File 123 Osborne, Lithgow, RG 59, Department of State Central Files, National Archives.

87. Grew to Stimson, May 18, 1945, File 857.0011/5-1845, Osborne to Secretary of State, June 12, 1945, File 857.001H11/6-1245, RG 59, Department of State Central Files, National Archives; Greve, *Haakon VII of Norway*, 167–70.

88. Telegram from Osborne to Secretary of State, June 8, 1945, File 857.00/6-745, RG 59, Department of State Central Files, National Archives.

89. Telegrams from Osborne to Secretary of State, June 12, 15, 1945, File 857.01/6-1245, 6-1545, telegram from Osborne to Secretary of State, June 19, 1945, Osborne to Secretary of State, June 25, 26, 1945, File 857.00/6-1945, 6-2545, 6-2645, RG 59, Department of State Central Files, National Archives; Osborne to Secretary of State, December 1, 1945, File Number 800, RG 84, Diplomatic Post Records, Oslo, National Archives; Greve, *Haakon VII of Norway*, 171–75.

90. Telegram from Osborne to Secretary of State, June 21, 1945, Osborne to Secretary of State, June 25, 1945, File 857.00/6-2145, 6-2545, RG 59, Department of State Central Files, National Archives; Osborne to Secretary of State, December 1, 1945, File 800, RG 84, Diplomatic Post Records, Oslo, National Archives.

91. Telegram from Osborne to Secretary of State, June 23, 1945, File 857.01/6-2345, Osborne to Secretary of State, November 7, 1945, File 857.00/11-745, RG 59, Department of State Central Files, National Archives; American Embassy, Oslo, to Department of State, January 9, 1951, File 350.3, RG 84, Diplomatic Post Records, Oslo, National Archives.

92. Cable from Osborne to Secretary of State, June 17, 1945, RG 319, Records of Army Assistant Chief of Staff, G-2 (Intelligence), WNRC; telegram from Osborne to Secretary of State, October 23, 1945, File 711 Quisling, airgram from Bay to Secretary of State, September 10, 1948,

File 711.4, Marselis C. Parsons, Jr., to Department of State, January 9, 1951, File 321.6, RG 84, Diplomatic Post Records, Oslo, National Archives.

93. Telegram from Huston to Secretary of State, December 3, 1946, C. Ulrick Bay to Secretary of State, February 24, 1947, February 12, 1948, March 1, 1948, File 857.00/12-346, 2-2447, 2-1248, 3-148, RG 59, Department of State Central Files, National Archives; Gordon W. Prange, *At Dawn We Slept: The Untold Story of Pearl Harbor* (New York: McGraw-Hill, 1981), 582–738, 823–25.

94. Telegrams from Osborne to Secretary of State, July 17, October 11, 1945, Charles H. Wilson to American Embassy, Oslo, October 22, 1945, File 820, RG 84, Diplomatic Post Records, Oslo, National Archives; Osborne to Secretary of State, November 16, 1945, and attached summary report by Charles H. Wilson, October 20, 1945, File 857.00/11-1645, RG 59, Department of State Central Files, National Archives.

95. Telegram from Haakon R. to the President, October 19, 1945, File 820, RG 84, Diplomatic Post Records, Oslo, National Archives.

96. Osborne to Secretary of State, October 19, 1945, and enclosed translations, File 857.01/10-1945, RG 59, Department of State Central Files, National Archives.

97. Translation of article in *Verdens Gang*, September 8, 1945, enclosed with memorandum dictated by W. S. Greene, October 19, 1945, File 711.57/10-1945, RG 59, Department of State Central Files, National Archives. See also Osborne to Secretary of State, April 27, 1945, and enclosure, File 123 Osborne, Lithgow, RG 59, Department of State Central Files, National Archives.

98. Villard to Department of State, June 9, 1950, File 757.00(W)/6-950, USIE-OII-OEX report by Theodore B. Olson, July 6, 1950, 511.57/7-650, RG 59, Department of State Central Files, National Archives.

99. Ministère des Affaires Etrangeres to Embassy of the United States of America, July 13, 1951, File 321 Germany, RG 84, Diplomatic Post Records, Oslo, National Archives; John Gordon Mein to Department of State, July 20, 1951, File 757.00(W)/7-2051, memorandum from Norwegian Embassy, Washington, August 2, 1951, File 657.6229/8-251, RG 59, Department of State Central Files, National Archives.

100. Telegram from Snow to Department of State, April 1, 1952, File 320.1, RG 84, Diplomatic Post Records, Oslo, National Archives; Mein to Department of State, May 23, 1952, File 757.00(W)/5-2352, RG 59, Department of State Central Files, National Archives.

CHAPTER 5

1. For items describing the embassy staff at various times after the war see "1947 Foreign Service Personnel Estimates; Norway," enclosed with despatch from United States Embassy, Oslo, dictated by O. N. Nielsen, January 26, 1946, Nielsen to Secretary of State, April 2, 1946, C. Ulrick Bay to Secretary of State, August 28, September 6, 1946, "Organization and Administration of Oslo Embassy," enclosed with despatch from

United States Embassy, Oslo, dictated by L. L. Cowles, September 26, 1947, telegram from Marshall to American Embassy, Oslo, December 1, 1948, File 124.57/1-2646, 8-2846, 9-646, 9-2647, 12-148, Bay to Secretary of State, August 10, 1948, File 124.573/8-1048, Henry S. Villard to Secretary of State, June 3, 1949, File 124.575, RG 59, Department of State Central Files, National Archives; lists enclosed with memoranda dictated by R. Dunker, January 11, 1950, July 8, 1952, File 301–Diplomatic List, RG 84, Diplomatic Post Records, Oslo, National Archives.

2. Richardson Dougall and Mary Patricia Chapman, *United States Chiefs of Mission, 1778–1973* (Washington, D.C.: Historical Office, Bureau of Public Affairs Department of State, 1973), 115; telegram from Byrnes to American Embassy, Oslo, April 12, 1946, Thurman Hill to James F. Byrnes, June 19, 1946, 123 Bay, Charles Ulrick, file memorandum by H. Raynor, July 8, 1953, File 611.57/7-853, RG 59, Department of State Central Files, National Archives; Bay to Mr. Snow and Mr. Parsons, February 21, 1951, File 301–Protocol in Diplomatic Corps in Oslo, RG 84, Diplomatic Post Records, Oslo, National Archives; *Who's Who in America, 1958–1959*, 30:2687.

3. Clipping from *Minneapolis Sunday Tribune*, April 13, 1952, Morgenstierne Papers, Norwegian-American Historical Association Archives; interview with Per Aasen, counselor for press and cultural affairs, Norwegian Embassy, Washington, D.C., October 24, 1986.

4. Telegram from Winant to Secretary of State, March 3, 1941, File 857.002/94, memorandum, H. L. C., Department of State Division of European Affairs, to Secretary of State, March 24, 1943, File 857.50/143 1/2, telegram from Osborne to Secretary of State, February 2, 1946, File Number 857.021/2-246, A. J. Drexel Biddle, Jr., to Secretary of State, June 26, 1942, File 757.00/22, RG 59, Department of State Central Files, National Archives.

5. Telegrams from Osborne to Secretary of State, February 2, 4, 5, 1946, File 857.021/2-246, 2-446, 2-546, Osborne to Secretary of State, March 21, 1946, File 857.40632/3-2146, Cloyce K. Huston to Secretary of State, April 14, 1947, File 857.002/4-1447, John Gordon Mein to Department of State, September 25, 1952, John Foster Dulles to the President, March 3, 1953, and enclosed biographical sketch, File 757.13/9-2552, 2-2753, RG 59, Department of State Central Files, National Archives; enclosure to American Embassy, Oslo, to Secretary of State, January 9, 1951, File 350.3–Biographies of Norwegian Leaders, RG 84, Diplomatic Post Records, Oslo, National Archives.

6. Biddle to Secretary of State, June 26, 1942, Lithgow Osborne to Secretary of State, July 20, 1945, File 757.00/22, 7-2045, RG 59, Department of State Central Files, National Archives; Biddle to Secretary of State, February 10, 1942, File 711–Post War Settlement, RG 84, Diplomatic Post Records, Oslo (London Government), National Archives.

7. Biddle to Secretary of State, June 26, 1942, File 757.00/22, RG 59, Department of State Central Files. See also enclosure with Sumner Welles to Secretary of State, August 10, 1942, File 336 Norway, RG 319, Army Intelligence Project Decimal File 1941–1945, WNRS. The best scholarly study in English by a Norwegian historian on American relations with

Scandinavia in the cold war is Geir Lundestad, *America, Scandinavia, and the Cold War, 1945-1949* (New York: Columbia University Press, 1980). See also chapters by Olav Riste and Rolf Tamnes in Olav Riste, ed., *Western Security, The Formative Years: European and Atlantic Defence, 1947-1953* (New York: Columbia University Press; Oslo: Universitets-forlaget, 1985). For an excellent scholarly article on Norwegian historiography of the cold war see Helge Ø. Pharo, "The Cold War in Norwegian and International Historical Research," *Scandinavian Journal of History* 10 (1985): 163-89.

8. Biddle to Secretary of State, June 26, 1942, File 757.00/22, RG 59, Department of State Central Files, National Archives.

9. Among the scholarly books treating America's wartime planning for postwar peace see Wayne S. Cole, *Roosevelt and the Isolationists, 1932-45* (Lincoln, Nebr.: University of Nebraska Press, 1983), 514-28, and Robert A. Divine, *Second Chance: The Triumph of Internationalism in America During World War II* (New York: Atheneum, 1967), passim.

10. The best scholarly book in English on the Yalta conference is Diane Shaver Clemens, *Yalta* (New York: Oxford University Press, 1970). See also Robert Dallek, *Franklin D. Roosevelt and American Foreign Policy, 1932-1945* (New York: Oxford University Press, 1979), 503-28.

11. Divine, *Second Chance*, 279-315; telegram from Winant to Secretary of State, March 29, 1945, File NORWEG 37, 500, telegram from Osborne to London, November 15, 1945, File 711, RG 84, Diplomatic Post Records, Oslo, National Archives; memorandum dictated by W. S. Greene, January 15, 1946, and enclosed memorandum from United States Information Service, File 857.00/1-1546, RG 59, Department of State Central Files, National Archives.

12. Enclosure with Osborne to Secretary of State, October 18, 1945, File 857.002/10-1245, RG 59, Department of State Central Files, National Archives.

13. Among the better books by American scholars on the origins of the cold war are John Lewis Gaddis, *The United States and the Origins of the Cold War, 1941-1947* (New York: Columbia University Press, 1972), and Daniel Yergin, *Shattered Peace: The Origins of the Cold War and the National Security State* (Boston: Houghton Mifflin, 1977).

14. Telegram from Osborne to Secretary of State, February 14, 1946, File 857.021/2-1446, telegram from Osborne to Secretary of State, January 19, 1946, File 757.00/1-1946, RG 59, Department of State Central Files, National Archives.

15. Osborne to Secretary of State, December 1, 1945, File 857.00/12-145, RG 59, Department of State Central Files, National Archives.

16. C. Ulrick Bay to Secretary of State, October 2, 1946, File 757.00/10-246, RG 59, Department of State Central Files, National Archives.

17. For example, see Helge Ø. Pharo, "Bridgebuilding and Reconstruction: Norway Faces the Marshall Plan," *Scandinavian Journal of History* 1 (1976):125-26.

18. [A. E. Staley, Jr.], "Congressional Statement," [1949], RG 286, Records of Agency for International Development, Mission to Norway, Subject Files, 1948-52, WNRC.

19. Ibid.

20. Ibid. See also Harry Conover to Secretary of State, January 3, 1948, RG 286, Agency for International Development, Special Representative in Europe, Food and Agriculture Division, Country Subject Files 1948-49, WNRC; Bay to Secretary of State, April 2, 1948, Arne Skaug to Willard Thorp, October 27, 1948, and enclosed "Memorandum on a Norwegian Long Term Programme," File 840.50 Recovery/4-248, 10-2748, RG 59, Department of State Central Files, National Archives.

21. [Staley], "Congressional Statement," [1949]; telegram from Grew to American Embassy, Oslo, July 24, 1945, telegram from Osborne to Secretary of State, October 24, 1945, N. S. Ness to Bay, October 11, 1946, Charles F. Baldwin to Secretary of State, October 31, 1946, November 30, 1946, telegram from Acheson to American Embassy, Oslo, March 13, 1947, Bay to Secretary of State, June 19, 1947, File 857.51/7-2445, 10-2445, 10-1146, 10-3146, 11-3046, 3-1347, 6-1947, RG 59, Department of State Central Files, National Archives; *Foreign Relations of the United States, 1946*, 1:1435–36.

22. [Staley], "Congressional Statement," [1949], RG 286.

23. Baldwin to Bay, March 28, 1947, File 850, RG 84, Diplomatic Post Records, Oslo; Cloyce K. Huston to Secretary of State, November 18, 1947, File 857.6511/11-1847, Charles F. Baldwin to Secretary of State, January 15, 1948, File 857.5151/1-1548, Baldwin to Secretary of State, January 22, 1948, File 857.51/1-2248, RG 59, Department of State Central Files, National Archives.

24. *Foreign Relations of the United States, 1947*, 3:198–251.

25. Telegrams from Bay to Secretary of State, July 9, 12, 16, September 19, 1947, memorandum from American Embassy, Oslo, July 10, 1947, William K. Ailshie to Secretary of State, July 15, 1947, memorandum of conversation with Lange on Marshall Plan by Cloyce K. Huston, July 16, 1947, Bay to Secretary of State, September 11, 24, October 9, 13, 1947, April 7, 1948, File 840.50 Recovery/7-947, 7-1047, 7-1247, 7-1547, 7-1647, 7-2247, 9-1147, 9-1947, 9-2447, 10-947, 10-1347,4-748, RG 59, Department of State Central Files, National Archives; *Foreign Relations of the United States, 1947*, 3:438–39. For a thoughtful scholarly analysis of Norway's early reactions to the Marhsall Plan see Pharo, "Bridgebuilding and Reconstruction," 125–53.

26. Robert A. Lovett to Morgenstierne, April 22, 1948, File 840.50 Recovery/4-2248, RG 59, Department of State Central Files, National Archives; *Foreign Relations of the United States, 1948*, 3:408–9.

27. Telegram from Bay to Secretary of State, July 3, 1948, Bay to Secretary of State, July 6, 23, 1948, File 840.50 Recovery/7-348, 7-648, 7-2348, RG 59, Department of State Central Files, National Archives; *Foreign Relations of the United States, 1948*, 3:408–9, 463, 994.

28. Baldwin to Secretary of State, June 23, 1948, Bay to Secretary of State, September 7, 1948, File 840.50 Recovery/6-2348, 9-748, RG 59, Department of State Central Files, National Archives; press release from Economic Cooperation Administration, Office of Administrator, July 16, [1948], April 26, 1949, A. E. Staley, Jr., to Paul G. Hoffman, September 24, 1948, Staley to W. A. Harriman, March 8, 1949, Tor Torland to Alva

A. Swain, April 6, 1951, telegram from Bissell to all MSA Missions, January 14, 1952, RG 286, Agency for International Development, ECA, Office of Information, Country Subject Files, WNRC; telegram from Webb to Oslo, November 3, 1951, File 500–ECA–MSA, RG 84, Diplomatic Post Records, Oslo, National Archives.

29. Memorandum of conversation by C. K. Huston, May 20, 1948, Baldwin to Secretary of State, July 30, 1948, August 6, 1948, File 840.50 Recovery/5-2648, 7-3048, 8-648, RG 59, Department of State Central Files, National Archives; telegram from Baldwin to Department of State, June 11, 1948, RG 84, Diplomatic Post Records, Oslo, National Archives; Bay to Gross, September 2, 1949, W. A. H. to "Dear George," January 10, 1950, David Scott to Robert L. Cummings, January 30, 1950, RG 286, Records of Agency for International Development, Mission to Norway, Program Division, Subject Files, 1948–52, WNRC.

30. Harry Conover to Secretary of State, January 3, 1949, File 840.50 Recovery/1-349, RG 59, Department of State Central Files, National Archives.

31. Maurice P. Arth to Lincoln Gordon, April 14, 1950, telegram from Bissel to Oslo, May 6, 1950, telegram from Gross to Office for Special Representative in Europe, Paris, May 13, [1950], cablegram from Hoffman to American Embassy, Oslo, May 19, 1950, "ECA Mission to Norway Oslo, Norway July 14, 1950 Mission Comments on Norwegian Investment Program," RG 286, Agency for International Development Records, Special Representative in Paris, Administrative Services Division, Country Files, 1949–50, Norway, WNRC.

32. Hulley to Stevens, May 22, 1950, File 857.00/5-2250, RG 59, Department of State Central Files, National Archives.

33. Oslo to Secretary of State, July 2, 1948, File 840.50 Recovery/7-248, RG 59, Department of State Central Files, National Archives; Gross to Brofoss, June 8, 1951, April 2, 1952, translation of article from *Morgenposten*, December 22, 1951, RG 84, Diplomatic Post Records, Oslo, National Archives.

34. Tor Torland to Haakon Lie, August 25, 1953, RG 286, Agency for International Development Records, Mission to Norway, Program Division, Subject Files, 1948–53, WNRC.

35. "Norway: A Country Study," prepared by Information Division of MSA Special Mission to Norway, Oslo, January 1952, RG 286, Agency for International Development Records, Special Representative in Europe, Labor Information Division, Office of Director, Country Subject Files, 1948–51, WNRC; L. Corrin Strong to Department of State, November 6, December 11, 1953, File 757.00(W)/11-653, 12-1153, RG 59, National Archives.

36. Bay to Secretary of State, April 11, 1947, intelligence report by Kai E. Rasmussen, April 23, 1947, Huston to Secretary of State, May 20, 1947, File 800, RG 84, Diplomatic Post Records, Oslo, National Archives; Bay to Secretary of State, October 9, 1947, File 857.00/10-947, RG 59, Department of State Central Files, National Archives. For a scholarly analysis of the background and early phases of Norway's adherence to the North Atlantic Pact see Olav Riste, "Was 1949 a Turning Point? Norway

and the Western Powers, 1947–1950," in Riste, ed., *Western Security: The Formative Years*, 128–47.

37. Telegram from Huston to Department of State, October 25, [1947], File 711, RG 84, Diplomatic Post Records, Oslo, National Archives; telegram from Huston to Secretary of State, October 25, 1947, Huston to Secretary of State, October 28, 1947, and enclosed memorandum of conversation between Huston and Lange, October 24, 1947, File 857.00/10-2547, 10-2847, RG 59, Department of State Central Files, National Archives; *Foreign Relations of the United States, 1947*, 1:94–95.

38. Huston to Secretary of State, November 28, 1947, and enclosed memorandum from Theodore B. Olson to Huston, November 24, 1947, File 757.00/11-2847, RG 59, Department of State Central Files, National Archives.

39. Huston to Secretary of State, December 18, 1947, and enclosed memorandum of conversation with Lange, File 800, RG 84, Diplomatic Post Records, Oslo, National Archives.

40. "Survey of Soviet Interests and Activities in Norway," [by C. K. Huston], December 11, 1947, enclosed with Huston to Secretary of State, December 11, 1947, File 757.61/12-1147, RG 59, Department of State Central Files, National Archives.

41. Telegram from Warren to Secretary of State, March 5, 1948, telegram from Bay to Secretary of State, March 8, 1948, Department of State memorandum of conversation between Mr. Economou-Gouras and L. J. Cromie, April 1, 1948, File 757.61/3-548, 3-848, 4-148, telegram from Matthews to Secretary of State, March 12, 1948, File 757.6111/3-1248, RG 59, Department of State Central Files, National Archives. For an account of those developments and Norwegian responses to them, prepared by an able Norwegian historian, see Lundestad, *America, Scandinavia, and the Cold War, 1945–1949*, 176–82. For a contemporary summary of the developments see memorandum from Hickerson to Bohlen, February 21, 1949, File 840.20/2-2149, RG 59, Department of State Central Files, National Archives.

42. Telegram from Bay to Secretary of State, February 19, 1948, File 857.20/2-2948, RG 59, Department of State Central Files, National Archives; letter from A. C. Wedemeyer, March 11, 1948, RG 335, WNRC; *Foreign Relations of the United States, 1948*, 3:24–26.

43. Bay to Secretary of State, March 1, 1948, RG 319, Records of Army Assistant Chief of Staff, G-2 (Intelligence), WNRC.

44. Telegrams from Bay to Secretary of State, March 8, 11, 1948, telegram from Gallman to Secretary of State, March 10, 1948, File 757.61/3-848, 3-1048, 3-1148, RG 59, Department of State Central Files, National Archives; *Foreign Relations of the United States, 1948*, 3:44–45.

45. Telegram from Bay to Secretary of State, March 12, 1948, File 857.20/3-1248, aide-memoire from British Embassy, Washington, March 11, 1948, File 757.6111/3-1248, RG 59, Department of State Central Files, National Archives; *Foreign Relations of the United States, 1948*, 3:48–49.

46. Telegram from Bay to Secretary of State, March 11, 1948, File 757.61/3-1148, telegram from USMA, Oslo, to CSGID, State, Navy and

Air, March 17, 1948, File 857.20/3-1748, telegram, W. M. B to Secretary of State, March 18, 1948, File 857.30/3-1848, telegram from Bay to Secretary of State, April 8, 1948, File 857.032/4-848, RG 59, Department of State Central Files, National Archives.

47. Aide-memoire from British Embassy, Washington, March 11, 1948, File 757.6111/3-1248, RG 59, Department of State Central Files, National Archives; *Foreign Relations of the United States, 1948*, 3:46–48.

48. Memorandum from M. S. C. [Marshall S. Carter] to Secretary of State, March 12, 1948, and attached telegram Marshall to Forrestal, n.d., Carter to Lord Inverchapel, March 12, 1948, File 757.6111/3-1248, RG 59, Department of State Central Files, National Archives; *Foreign Relations of the United States, 1948*, 3:48.

49. Telegram, Marshall to American Embassy, Oslo, March 12, 1948, File 857.20/3-1248, RG 59, Department of State Central Files, National Archives; *Foreign Relations of the United States, 1948*, 3:51–52.

50. Harry S. Truman, *Memoirs*, vol. 2, *Years of Trial and Hope* (Garden City, N.Y.: Doubleday, 1956), 241–43. See also memorandum of conversation between Morgenstierne, Hickerson, and Hulley, March 17, 1948, File 840.20/3-1748, RG 59, Department of State Central Files, National Archives.

51. Aide-memoire from Norwegian Embassy, Washington, April 16, 1948, RG 335, WNRC; Robert A. Lovett to Forrestal, April 26, 1948, File 857.20/4-1648, RG 59, Department of State Central Files, National Archives.

52. Bay to Secretary of State, April 23, 1948, File 757.00/4-2348, RG 59, Department of State Central Files, National Archives; *Foreign Relations of the United States, 1948*, 3:44–45.

53. Department of State memorandum of conversation between William H. Draper, Bryn, Arne Gunneng, Colonel Eisley, and Benjamin M. Hulley, April 26, 1948, memorandum for files by C. E. Rogers, May 3, 1948, File 857.20/4-2648, 5-348, RG 59, Department of State Central Files, National Archives.

54. Forrestal to Marshall, June 14, 1948, Marshall to Forrestal, June 21, 1948, Marshall to American Embassy, Oslo, June 21, 1948, File 857.20/6-1448, 6-1448, 6-2148, RG 59, Department of State Central Files, National Archives.

55. Telegram from Marshall to American Embassy, Oslo, June 29, 1948, File Number 840.20/6-2948, RG 59, Department of State Central Files, National Archives.

56. Telegram from Bay to Secretary of State, July 7, 1948, telegram from Villard to Secretary of State, November 10, 1948, File 757D.00/7-748, 11-1048, telegram from Villard to Secretary of State, December 8, 1948, telegram from Bay to Secretary of State, January 12, 1949, File 840.20/12-848, 1-1249, telegram from Villard to Secretary of State, December 10, 1948, telegram from Bay to Secretary of State, January 12, 1949, File 857.00(W)/12-1048, 1-749, RG 59, Department of State Central Files, National Archives; reports by Col. Kai E. Rasmussen, Military Attaché, Norway, December 11 [1948], R-422-48, R-423-48, RG 84, Diplomatic Post Records, Oslo, National Archives; *Foreign Relations of the United States, 1948*, 3:160–63, 256–57.

57. Forrestal to Marshall, July 20, 1948, File 857.20/7-2048, RG 59, Department of State Central Files, National Archives.

58. Department of State memorandums of conversations by John D. Hickerson, August 27, 1948, November 23, 1948, File 857.24/8-2748, 11-2348, RG 59, Department of State Central Files, National Archives; *Foreign Relations of the United States, 1948*, 3:223–24.

59. "Report to the President by the National Security Council of the Position of the United States with Respect to Scandinavia," September 3, 1948, NSC 28/1, enclosed with Department of State to American Mission, Oslo, September 15, 1948, RG 84, Diplomatic Post Records, Oslo, National Archives; Hickerson to Walter Bedell Smith, September 17, 1948, File 711.57D/9-1748, RG 59, Department of State Central Files, National Archives. Conclusions of NSC 28/1 are printed in *Foreign Relations of the United States, 1948*, 3:232–34.

60. Department of State memorandum of conversation by John D. Hickerson, File 840.20/9-2348, RG 59, Department of State Central Files, National Archives.

61. Department of State memorandum of conversation by John D. Hickerson, December 23, 1948, File 840.20/12-2348, RG 59, Department of State Central Files, National Archives; *Foreign Relations of the United States, 1948*, 3:344–46, 348–51.

62. Airgram from Huston to Secretary of State, May 26, 1948, File 711.1, RG 84, Diplomatic Post Records, Oslo, National Archives.

63. Telegrams from Bay to Secretary of State, January 31, February 1, 1949, File 840.20/1-3149, 2-149, RG 59, Department of State Central Files, National Archives.

64. Memorandum of conversation between Lange, Morgenstierne, Torp, Acheson, Bohlen, and Hickerson, February 7, 1949, memorandum of conversation between Lange, Morgenstierne, Torp, Dag Bryn, Arne Gunneng, Silvert Nielsen, Hickerson, Theodore C. Achilles, and Benjamin M. Hullye, February 7, 1949, telegram from Bay to Secretary of State, February 7, 10, 1949, File 840.20/2-749, 2-1049, telegram from Bay to Secretary of State, February 7, 1949, File 757.6111/2-749, telegram from Bay to Secretary of State, February 11, 1949, File 857.00(W)/2-1149, RG 59, Department of State Central Files, National Archives; *Foreign Relations of the United States, 1949*, 4:91–93.

65. Charles E. Rogers to Hickerson, February 7, 1949, File 840.20/2-749, RG 59, Department of State Central Files, National Archives.

66. Memorandum of conversation between Lange, Morgenstierne, Torp, Bryn, Gunneng, Nielsen, Bohlen, Hickerson, Achilles, Hulley, and Walter S. Surrey, February 8, 1949, File 840.20/2-849, RG 59, Department of State Central Files, National Archives.

67. Department of State memorandum by DA [Dean Acheson], February 10, 1949, File 840.20/2-1049, RG 59, Department of State Central Files, National Archives.

68. Forrestal to Acheson, February 10, 1949, and enclosed memorandum for Secretary of Defense, "Anticipated Position of Scandinavia in Strategic Considerations," from Admiral Louis Denfield, for Joint Chiefs of Staff, February 10, 1949, Number 840.20/2-1049, RG 59, Department of State Central Files, National Archives.

69. Memorandum of conversation, "Final Visit of Norwegian Foreign Minister," February 11, 1949, File 840.20/2-1149, Morgenstierne to Osborne, March 18, 1949, enclosed with Hickerson to Bohlen and Gross, March 25, 1949, File 757D.00/3-2549, RG 59, Department of State Central Files, National Archives; *Foreign Relations of the United States, 1949*, 4:102–6.

70. Memorandum of conversation between Morgenstierne and Charles E. Rogers, February 19, 1949, memorandum of conversation between Nielsen and Rogers, February 23, 1949, File 757.61/2-1949, 2-2349, Bay to Secretary of State, February 17, 1949, telegram from Bay to Secretary of State, February 17, 1949, File 840.20/2-1749, RG 59, Department of State Central Files, National Archives.

71. Telegrams from Bay to Secretary of State, February 21, 1949, File 757.00/2-2149, telegram from Bay to Secretary of State, February 25, 1949, File 857.00(W)/2-2549, RG 59, Department of State Central Files, National Archives; memorandum from Director, Labor Division, ECA Mission to Norway, to Boris Shishkin, February 24, 1949, RG 286, AID Records, Country Files 1948-49, Norway, WNRC.

72. Telegram from Bay to Secretary of State, February 24, 1949, File 840.20/2-2449, RG 59, Department of State Central Files, National Archives.

73. Memorandums of conversations between Morgenstierne and Hickerson, March 3, 1949, telegram from Acheson to American Embassy, Oslo, March 4, 1949, Bay to Secretary of State, March 22, 1949, File 840.20/3-349, 3-449, 3-2249, RG 59, Department of State Central Files, National Archives.

74. Telegram from Bay to Secretary of State, March 3, 1949, File 757.6111/3-349, RG 59, Department of State Central Files, National Archives; *Foreign Relations of the United States, 1949*, 4:145–46.

75. Telegram from Bay to Secretary of State, March 30, 1949, Bay to Secretary of State, April 1, 1949, File 840.20/3-3049, 4-149, RG 59, Department of State Central Files, National Archives.

76. Dean Acheson, *Present at the Creation: My Years in the State Department* (New York: Norton, 1969), 278–86; *Foreign Relations of the United States, 1949*, 4:281–85. Volume 4 of *Foreign Relations* includes many relevant documents on the background of the North Atlantic Pact, 1–281.

77. North Atlantic Treaty Organization, *NATO Handbook* (Brussels: NATO Information Service, 1977), 9–12.

78. Telegram from Snow to Secretary of State, January 12, 1951, telegram from Gifford to Oslo, January 14, 1951, telegram from Snow to Department of State, January 14, 1951, memorandum from M. C. Parsons, Jr., to Snow, January 16, 1951, File 321 SHAPE, RG 84, Diplomatic Post Records, Oslo, National Archives; Marselis C. Parsons, Jr., to Department of State, January 19, 1951, File 757.00(W)/1-1951, telegram from Bruce, Paris, to Secretary of State, June 6, 1951, File 757.5/6-651, Bay to Department of State, September 17, 1951, File 757.5 MAP/9-1751, RG 59, Department of State Central Files, National Archives.

79. *Foreign Relations of the United States, 1949*, 1:398-99; Acheson, *Present at the Creation*, 307-13.

80. Telegram from Acheson to American Embassy, Oslo, January 25, 1950, telegram from Matthews to Secretary of State, February 21, 1950, Henry S. Villard to Department of State, February 23, 1950, telegram from Villard to Secretary of State, February 24, 1950, File 757.5 MAP/1-2550, 2-2150, 2-2350, 2-2450, RG 59, Department of State Central Files, National Archives; Royal Proclamation of Ratification of MDAA between Norway and United States, signed by Haakon R. and Lange, January 27, 1950, File 321 MDAP, RG 84, Diplomatic Post Records, Oslo, National Archives.

81. Telegram from Villard to Secretary of State, February 22, 1950, File 757.5 MAP/2-2250, RG 59, Department of State Central Files, National Archives.

82. Bay to Gen. Thomas T. Handy, August 25, 1950, NND 842482, RG 84, Diplomatic Post Records, Oslo, National Archives.

83. Villard to Lange, April 21, 1950, RG 84, Diplomatic Post Records, Oslo, National Archives; telegram from Villard to Secretary of State, April 21, 1950, William P. Snow to Department of State, August 29, 1950, File 757.5 MAP/4-2150, 8-2950, RG 59, Department of State Central Files, National Archives.

84. Telegram from Dulles to American Embassy, Oslo, June 19, 1953, telegram from Bay to Secretary of State, June 25, 1953, File 757.5-MSP/6-1953, 6-2553, RG 59, Department of State Central Files, National Archives. See also Rolf Tamnes, "Norway's Struggle for the Northern Flank, 1950-1951," in Riste, ed., *Western Security: The Formative Years*, 239-40.

85. James F. Hodgson to Department of State, February 20, 1950, March 2, 1950, File 757.5 MAP/2-2050, 3-250, RG 59, Department of State Central Files, National Archives.

86. Telegram from Villard to Secretary of State, April 20, 1950, File 757.5 MAP/4-2050, RG 59, Department of State Central Files, National Archives; Theodore B. Olson to M. A. P, May 3, 1950, File 321-MDAP, RG 84, Diplomatic Post Records, Oslo, National Archives; Department of State International Information and Educational Exchange Program country paper for Norway, July 1950, RG 286, Agency for International Development Records, Mission to Norway, Subject Files, 1948-52, WNRC.

87. Bay to Department of State, May 26, 1950, File 321-MDAP, RG 84, Diplomatic Post Records, Oslo, National Archives.

88. Mr. Mein to Ted Olson, July 19, 1950, File 321-MDAP, RG 84, Diplomatic Post Records, Oslo, National Archives.

89. "Preliminary Position Paper on Proposed Military Contribution of Norway," by E. P. D., August 16, 1950, RG 286, Agency for International Development Records, Country Subject Files of the Mutual Security Program, 1950-1951, WNRC; Memorandum of conversation, "Norwegian Defense Plans," by John H. Ohly, October 24, 1950, RG 84, Diplomatic Post Records, Oslo, National Archives.

90. MDAP general monthly report, June 1951, from Bay to Depart-

ment of State, July 16, 1951, File 757.5 MAP/7-1651, RG 59, Department of State Central Files, National Archives; *Foreign Relations of the United States, 1951,* 4:755.

91. Bay to Department of State, September 17, 1951, Number 757.5 MAP/9-1751, RG 59, Department of State Central Files, National Archives.

92. R. E. Jennings to Minister of Defense, May 7, 1951, File 321–MDAP, RG 84, Diplomatic Post Records, Oslo, National Archives.

93. Jennings to Director, JAMAG, July 20, 1951, RG 84, Diplomatic Post Records, Oslo, National Archives.

94. Telegram from Bay to London, July 25, 1951, File 321–MDAP, RG 84, Diplomatic Post Records, Oslo, National Archives.

95. Telegram from Gross to Department of State, July 25, 1951, RG 286, Records of AID, Mission to Norway, Subject Files 1948–55, WNRC.

96. Bay to Lange, August 6, 1951, RG 84, Diplomatic Post Records, Oslo, National Archives.

97. "Norway," ECC (51) D-18, prepared by ECC WG, October 26, 1951, attached to telegram from Spofford to Ambassador, Oslo, October 29, 1951, RG 84, Diplomatic Post Records, Oslo, National Archives. See also Tamnes, "Norway's Struggle for the Norther Flank, 1950–1952," in Riste, ed., *Western Security: The Formative Years,* 240; and letter from Helge Ø. Pharo to the author, February 5, 1987.

98. MCAP Monthly General Report, August, 1951, from William P. Snow to Department of State, September 18, 1951, File 757.5 MAP/9-1851, RG 59, Department of State Central Files, National Archives. See also *Foreign Relations of the United States, 1951,* 4:763, 763n.

99. Jennings to Administrative Officer, Chancery, March 31, 1952, File 124.1, RG 84, Diplomatic Post Records, Oslo, National Archives.

100. Jennings to the Ambassador, April 30, 1952, File 321–MAAG, RG 84, Diplomatic Post Records, Oslo, National Archives.

101. Translation of article, "Admiral Jennings on the Tasks of MAAG and the Norwegian Defense Tasks," in *Militaer Orientering,* May 24, 1952, enclosed with Jack M Fleischer to Department of State, May 11, 1952, File 757.5 MSP/5-1152, RG 59, Department of State Central Files, National Archives.

102. Telegrams from Bay to Secretary of State, November 14, 15, 19, 20, 1951, File 757.00/11-1451, 11-1551, 11-1951, 11-1951, Snow to Department of State, January 11, 1952, File 757.00(W)/1-1152, Perkins to Acting Secretary of State, August 18, 1952, File 757.11/8-1852, Acheson to Certain American Diplomatic Officers, September 3, 1952, telegram from Mein to Secretary of State, October 15, 1952, File 757.13/9-352, 10-1552, RG 59, Department of State Central Files, National Archives.

103. William P. Snow to Department of State, July 18, 1952, File 321–NATO, RG 84, Diplomatic Post Records, Oslo, National Archives.

104. Telegram from Mein to Department of State, December 12, 1952, File 321–MAAG, RG 84, Diplomatic Post Records, Oslo, National Archives.

105. Telegrams from Dulles to American Embassy, Oslo, April 20, May 11, 1954, File Number 757.5 MSP/4-2054, 4-2354, RG 59, Depart-

ment of State Central Files, National Archives.

106. L. Corrin Strong to Department of State, January 8, 1954, File 757.5 MSP/1-854, RG 59, Department of State Central Files, National Archives.

107. Department of State, *United States Relations with China, with Special Reference to the Period 1944–1949* (Washington, D.C.: Department of State Publication, 1949), iii–xvii.

108. *Foreign Relations of the United States, 1949*, 8:933–1051; Acheson, *Present at the Creation*, 340, 344; telegram from Acheson to Oslo, November 18, 1949, File 350.21, RG 84, Diplomatic Post Records, Oslo, National Archives.

109. Telegram from Bay to Department of State, December 28, 1949, File 360, Villard to Department of State, February 2, 1950, File 312, telegram from Bay to Department of State, June 28, 1950, File 321–Korea, RG 84, Diplomatic Post Records, Oslo, National Archives; telegram from Villard to Secretary of State, February 7, 1950, Elbert G. Mathews to Department of State, July 9, 1954, File 657.93/2-750, 7-954, RG 59, Department of State Central Files, National Archives; *Foreign Relations of the United States, 1949*, 2:215, 9:250–52, 259; *Foreign Relations of the United States, 1952–1954*, 3:627n, 689n, 781n.

110. *Foreign Relations of the United States, 1950*, 7:155–56; Acheson, *Present at the Creation*, 402–5.

111. *Foreign Relations of the United States, 1950*, 7:211; Acheson, *Present at the Creation*, 408–9.

112. Telephone message from Rogers to Villard, July 6, 1950, telegrams from Bay to Department of State, July 6, 7, 1950, Villard to Ambassador, July 7, 1950, File 321–Korea, RG 84, Diplomatic Post Records, Oslo; *Foreign Relations of the United States, 1950*, 7:328–29.

113. Telegrams from Bay to Department of State, June 27, 28, 1950, Department of State memorandum of conversation between Morgenstierne, Perkins, and Rogers, June 29, 1950, memorandum of conversation between Acheson, Morgenstierne, and Casper D. Greene, June 30, 1950, File 321–Korea, memorandum of conversation between Gerhardsen and Olson, September 7, 1950, File 350, RG 84, Diplomatic Post Records, Oslo; Henry S. Villard to Department of State, June 30, 1950, File 757.00(W)/6-3050, USIE-OII-OEX report by Theodore B. Olson, July 6, 1950, 511.57/7-650, RG 59, Department of State Central Files, National Archives.

114. Marselis C. Parsons, Jr., to Department of State, February 2, 1951, File 757.00(W)/2-251, RG 59, Department of State Central Files, National Archives; Snow to Ambassador, February 21, 1951, File 321–Korea (1951), RG 84, Diplomatic Post Records, Oslo.

115. Memorandum of conversation between Morgenstierne, Perkins, and Rogers, March 22, 1951, telegram from Snow to Department of State, April 12, 1951, File 321–Korea, RG 84, Diplomatic Post Records, Oslo; John Gordon Mein to Department of State, April 13, 1951, File 757.00(W)/4-1351, Mein to Department of State, April 18, 1951, File 957.61/4-1851, RG 59, Department of State Central Files, National Archives; *Foreign Relations of the United States, 1951*, 7:185n.

116. Parsons to Department of State, January 29, 1951, telegram from Bay to Department of State, March 5, 1951, File 321–Korea, RG 84, Diplomatic Post Records, Oslo, National Archives; telegram from Bay to Secretary of State, May 9, 1952, File 957.61/5-952, memorandums from Norwegian Embassy, Washington, February 1, 1954, March 4, 1954, File 957.53/2-154, 3-454, RG 59, Department of State Central Files, National Archives; *Foreign Relations of the United States, 1952–1954*, 15:761, 767, 840–52.

117. Mein to Department of State, July 27, 1951, File 757.00(W)/7-2751, RG 59, Department of State Central Files, National Archives.

118. Elbert G. Mathews to Department of State, July 9, 1954, Strong to Department of State, October 7, 1954, File 657.93/7-954, 10-754, Strong to Department of State, October 8, 1954, File 757.00(W)10-854, 12-1754, RG 59, Department of State Central Files, National Archives.

CHAPTER 6

1. Tim Greve, *Haakon VII of Norway: The Man and the Monarch* (New York: Hippocrene Books, 1983), 176–90; Maurice Michael, *Haakon, King of Norway* (New York: Macmillan, 1958), 190–205.

2. T. K. Derry, *A History of Modern Norway, 1814–1972* (Oxford: Oxford University Press, 1973), 408–24; enclosure to American Embassy, Oslo, to Department of State, January 9, 1951, File 350.3, RG 84, Diplomatic Post Records, Oslo, National Archives; John E. Gross to Bert M. Jewell and Robert Oliver, April 26, 1951, and enclosure, RG 286, Records of Agency for International Development, Mission to Norway, Subject Files, 1948–52, WNRC; John Gordon Mein to Department of State, September 25, 1952, File 757.13/9-2552, RG 59, Department of State Central Files, National Archives.

3. Telegram from Bay to Secretary of State, November 6, 1952, File 350, RG 84, Diplomatic Post Records, Oslo, National Archives; Mein to Department of State, November 7, 1952, File 757.00(W)/11-752, RG 59, Department of State Central Files, National Archives.

4. Marselis C. Parsons, Jr., to Department of State, January 12, 1951, File 757.00(W)/1-1251, RG 59, Department of State Central Files, National Archives; George W. Perkins to Bay, May 3, 1951, File 321, Mein to Department of State, November 7, 1952, File 350, RG 84, Diplomatic Post Records, Oslo, National Archives.

5. For a sympathetic scholarly analysis of Eisenhower's conduct of foreign affairs by a leading American diplomatic historian see Robert A. Divine, *Eisenhower and the Cold War* (New York: Oxford University Press, 1981).

6. Department of State, *Policy Statement: Norway*, September 15, 1950, 1–2, File 611.57/9-1550, RG 59, Department of State Central Files, National Archives. That document is also printed in *Foreign Relations of the United States, 1950*, 3:1530–39.

7. Department of State, *Policy Statement: Norway*, September 15, 1950, 1–9; *Foreign Relations of the United States, 1950*, 3:1530-39.

8. Bay to Department of State, July 31, 1953, File 611.57/7-3153, RG 59, Department of State Central Files, National Archives.

9. Ibid.

10. Mein to Department of State, November 2, 1951, Jerome T. Gaspard to Department of State, November 26, 1954, File 757.00(W)/11-2654, 11-251, RG 59, Department of State Central Files, National Archives; Mein to Department of State, November 5, 1951, File 321, RG 84, Diplomatic Post Records, Oslo, National Archives.

11. For a thoughtful analysis of more recent Norwegian foreign policies written by leading Norwegian scholars see Johan Jørgen Holst, ed., *Norwegian Foreign Policy in the 1980s* (Oslo: Norwegian University Press, 1985).

Bibliographical Note

This book is based largely on research in unpublished manuscripts and documents covering the years 1905–55 located in United States government depositories in the Washington, D.C., area. They were supplemented by research in a variety of private manuscript collections in scattered libraries and in published scholarly secondary accounts in Norway and in the United States. This note lists the principal depositories and the manuscript collections used in each.

Library of Congress, Washington, D.C.:
    Florence J. Harriman Papers.
Herbert Hoover Library, West Branch, Iowa:
    Herbert Hoover Papers.
Minnesota State Historical Society Library, St. Paul, Minnesota:
    Ole Nilsen, Jr., Papers.
    Jacob A. O. Preus Papers.
    Laurits S. Swenson Papers.
National Archives and Records Service, Washington, D.C.:
    Record Group 38. Naval Attaché Reports.
    Record Group 59. Department of State Central Files.
    Record Group 84. Diplomatic and Consular Post Records.
    Record Group 151. Commercial Attaché Reports.
    Record Group 165. Military Attaché Reports.
Norwegian-American Historical Association Archives, St. Olaf College, Northfield, Minnesota:
    Henry Bordewich Papers.
    Wilhelm T. M. Morgenstierne Papers.
Franklin D. Roosevelt Library, Hyde Park, New York:
    Harry L. Hopkins Papers.
    Henry Morgenthau, Jr., Diaries.
    Franklin D. Roosevelt Papers.
Washington National Records Center, Suitland, Maryland (WNRC):
    Record Group 84. Diplomatic and Consular Post Records.

Record Group 182. War Trade Board Records.
Record Group 286. Agency for International Development Records.
Record Group 319. Assistant Chief of Staff, G-2 (Intelligence) Records.
Record Group 335. Secretary of the Army Records.
State Historical Society of Wisconsin Library, Madison, Wisconsin:
Albert G. Schmedeman Papers.

Selected Bibliography
of English-Language Books and Articles

Adamson, Hans Christian and Per Klem. *Blood on the Midnight Sun*. New York: Norton, 1964.

Andenaes, Johs., Olav Riste, and Magne Skodvin, *Norway and the Second World War*. Oslo: Johan Grundt Tanum Forlag, 1974.

Andersen, Arlow W. *The Norwegian-Americans*. Boston: Twayne Publishers, 1975.

Bailey, Thomas A. *The Policy of the United States Toward the Neutrals, 1917–1918*. Baltimore: Johns Hopkins Press, 1942.

Beyer, Harald. *A History of Norwegian Literature*. New York: New York University Press for American-Scandinavian Foundation, 1956.

Blegen, Theodore C. *Norwegian Migration to America, 1825–1860*. Northfield, Minn.: Norwegian-American Historical Association, 1931.

_____. *Norwegian Migration to America: The American Transition*. Northfield, Minn.: Norwegian-American Historical Association, 1940.

Burgess, Philip M. *Elite Images and Foreign Policy Outcomes: A Study of Norway*. Columbus: Ohio State University Press, 1967.

Capps, Alan P. "Norway's Defense Industry." *Journal of Defense and Diplomacy* 4 (September 1986): 25–26.

Clemens, Diane Shaver. *Yalta*. New York: Oxford University Press, 1970.

Clifford, John Garry. "The Odyssey of *City of Flint*." *American Neptune* (April 1972): 100–116.

Cole, Wayne S. *Roosevelt and the Isolationists, 1932–45*. Lincoln, Nebr.: University of Nebraska Press, 1983.

Craven, Wesley Frank and James Lea Cate, eds. *The Army Air Forces in World War II*. Vol. 2, *Europe: Torch to Pointblank, August 1942 to December 1943*. Chicago: University of Chicago Press, 1949.

_____. *The Army Air Forces in World War II*. Vol. 3, *Europe: Argument to V-E Day, January 1944 to May 1945*. Chicago: University of Chicago Press, 1951.

Dallek, Robert. *Franklin D. Roosevelt and American Foreign Policy, 1932–1945*. New York: Oxford University Press, 1979.

Derry, T. K. *A History of Modern Norway, 1814–1972*. London: Oxford University Press, 1973.

Divine, Robert A. *Eisenhower and the Cold War*. New York: Oxford University Press, 1981.

_____. *The Illusion of Neutrality*. Chicago: University of Chicago Press, 1962.

_____. *The Reluctant Belligerent: American Entry into World War II*. 2d ed. New York: Wiley, 1979.

_____. *Second Chance: The Triumph of Internationalism in America During World War II*. New York: Atheneum, 1967.

Eckstein, Harry. *Division and Cohesion in Democracy: A Study of Norway*. Princeton: Princeton University Press, 1966.

Gallagher, Thomas, *Assault in Norway: Sabotaging the Nazi Nuclear Bomb*. New York: Harcourt Brace Jovanovich, 1975.

Gjelsvik, Tore. *Norwegian Resistance, 1940–1945*. London: C. Hurst, 1979.

Greve, Tim. *Haakon VII of Norway: The Man and the Monarch*. New York: Hippocrene Books, 1983.

Hambro, Carl J. *I Saw It Happen in Norway*. New York: Appleton-Century, 1940.

Harriman, Florence Jaffray. *Mission to the North*. Philadelphia: Lippincott, 1941.

Hauge, E. *Odds Against Norway*. London: Lindsay Drummond, 1941.

Holst, Johan Jørgen, ed. *Norwegian Foreign Policy in the 1980s*. Oslo: Norwegian University Press, 1985.

"Interview Gen. Sir Geoffrey Howlett, Commander in Chief Allied Forces Northern Europe." *Journal of Defense & Diplomacy* 4 (September 1986): 13–16.

Kaplan, Lawrence S. *A Community of Interests: NATO and the Military Assistance Program, 1948–1951*. Washington, D.C.: Office of the Secretary of Defense Historical Office, 1980.

"The Kingdom of Norway." *Journal of Defense & Diplomacy* 4 (September 1986): 28–37.

Koht, Halvdan. *Education of an Historian*. New York: Robert Speller, 1957.

_____. *Norway: Neutral and Invaded*. New York: Macmillan, 1941.

Langer, William L. and S. Everett Gleason. *The Challenge to Isolation, 1937–1940*. New York: Harper & Brothers, 1952.

_____. *The Undeclared War, 1940–1941*. New York: Harper & Brothers, 1953.

Leuchtenburg, William E. *Franklin D. Roosevelt and the New Deal, 1932–1940*. New York: Harper & Row, 1963.

_____. *The Perils of Prosperity, 1914-32*. Chicago: University of Chicago Press, 1958.

Lie, Trygve. *In the Cause of Peace: Seven Years with the United Nations*. New York: Macmillan, 1954.

Linder, Doris H. *The Reaction of Norway to American Foreign Policy, 1918-1939*. Ann Arbor, Mich.: University Microfilms International, 1961.

Link, Arthur S. *Woodrow Wilson: Revolution, War, and Peace*. Arlington Heights, Ill.: AHM Publishing, 1979.

Lovoll, Odd S. *The Promise of America: A History of the Norwegian-American People*. Minneapolis: University of Minnesota Press, 1984.

Lundestad, Geir. *America, Scandinavia, and the Cold War, 1945-1949*. New York: Columbia University Press, 1980.

_____. *East, West, North, South: Major Developments in International Politics, 1945-1986*. Oslo: Norwegian University Press, 1986.

_____. "Empire by Invitation: The United States and Western Europe." *Society for Historians of American Foreign Relations Newsletter* 15 (September 1984): 1-21.

Macintyre, Donald. *Narvik*. New York: Norton, 1959.

May, Ernest R. *The World War and American Isolation, 1914-1917*. Cambridge, Mass.: Harvard University Press, 1959.

Mead, W. R. *An Historical Geography of Scandinavia*. London: Academic Press, 1981.

Michael, Maurice. *Haakon, King of Norway*. New York: Macmillan, 1958.

Midgaard, John. *A Brief History of Norway*. 8th ed. Oslo: Tanum-Norli, 1982.

Nissen, Henrik S., ed. *Scandinavia During the Second World War*. Minneapolis: University of Minnesota Press; Oslo: Universitetsforlaget, 1983.

Norman, Erik-Wilhelm. "The Royal Norwegian Ministry of Foreign Affairs." *Norway*, 392-408.

Olsen, Oluf Reed. *Two Eggs on My Plate*. Chicago: Rand McNally, 1952.

Petrow. Richard. *The Bitter Years: The Invasion and Occupation of Denmark and Norway, April 1940-May 1945*. New York: Morrow, 1974.

Pharo, Helge Ø. "Bridgebuilding and Reconstruction: Norway Faces the Marshall Plan." *Scandinavian Journal of History* 1 (1976): 125-53.

_____. "The Cold War in Norwegian and International Historical Research." *Scandinavian Journal of History* 10 (1985): 163-89.

_____. "The Third Force, Atlanticism and Norwegian Attitudes Towards European Integration." EUI Working Papers no. 86/255. Florence, Italy: European University Institute, 1986.

Prange, Gordon W. *At Dawn We Slept: The Untold Story of Pearl Harbor*. New York: McGraw-Hill, 1981.

Riste, Olav, "Free Ports in North Norway: A Contribution to the Study of

FDR's Wartime Policy Towards the USSR." *Journal of Contemporary History* (1970).

_____. "The Genesis of North Atlantic Defence Co-operation: Norway's 'Atlantic Policy,' 1940–1945." *NATO Review* 29 (April 1981): 22–29.

_____. *The Neutral Ally: Norway's Relations with Belligerent Powers in the First World War.* Oslo: Universitetsforlaget, 1965.

Riste, Olav and Berit Nokleby. *Norway, 1940–45: The Resistance Movement.* 3d ed. Oslo: Tanum-Norli, 1978.

Riste, Olav, ed. *Western Security, The Formative Years: European and Atlantic Defence, 1947–1953.* New York: Columbia University Press; Oslo: Universitetsforlaget, 1985.

Schopfel, William H. "The MAB in Norway." *United States Naval Institute Proceedings* 112 (November 1986): 33–39.

Selbyg, Arne. *Norway Today: An Introduction to Modern Norwegian Society.* Oslo: Norwegian University Press, 1986.

Semmingsen, Ingrid. *Norway to America: A History of the Migration.* Minneapolis: University of Minnesota Press, 1978.

Singh, Elen C. *The Spitsbergen (Svalbard) Question: United States Foreign Policy, 1907–1935.* Oslo: Universitetsforlaget, 1980.

Skard, Sigmund. *The United States in Norwegian History.* Westport, Conn.: Greenwood Press, 1976.

Sloan, Stanley R. "NATO and Northern Europe: Perspectives on the Nordic Balance." *NATO Review* 29 (June 1981): 10–16.

Storing, James A. *Norwegian Democracy.* Boston: Houghton Mifflin, 1963.

Udgaard, Nils Morten. *Great Power Politics and Norwegian Foreign Policy.* Oslo: Universitetsforlaget. 1973.

U.S. Department of State. *Foreign Relations of the United States: Diplomatic Papers, 1905–1954.* Washington, D.C.: Government Printing Office, 1906–1984.

Vaerno, Grethe. "Norway and the Atlantic Alliance, 1948–1949." *NATO Review* 29 (June 1981): 16–20.

Wood, Robert S. "Maritime Strategy for War in the North: A Combined Arms Strategy Key to Forward Posture and Conventional Deterrence." *Journal of Defense and Diplomacy* 4 (September 1986): 17–20.

Wright, Robert. "Paradise Retained." *Wilson Quarterly* (Spring 1984): 115–29.

Ørvik, Nils. *The Decline of Neutrality, 1914–1941: With Special Reference to the United States and the Northern Neutrals.* 2d ed. London: Frank Cass, 1971.

Index